A PROCESSIVE WORLD VIEW
FOR
PRAGMATIC CHRISTIANS

A PROCESSIVE WORLD VIEW

FOR

PRAGMATIC CHRISTIANS

by

JOSEPH T. CULLITON, C.S.B., Ph.D.

PHILOSOPHICAL LIBRARY

New York

Printed in the United States of America

TO

Mary and Don Macaulay

TABLE OF CONTENTS

Acknowledgement is made to Harper and Row, Publishers, New York, for permission to quote from *Writings in Time of War* by Pierre Teilhard de Chardin, copyright © 1968 in the English translation by William Collins Sons & Co. Ltd., London, and Harper and Row, Publishers, Incorporated, New York.

I wish to acknowledge my deep indebtedness to Ewert H. Cousins, Robert O. Johann, Christopher F. Mooney, S. J., and Robert J. Roth, S. J. who introduced me to the thought of John Dewey and Pierre Teilhard de Chardin and from whom I gained many valuable insights. Without their instruction this book would never have been written. This is not to imply, however, that they are responsible for the interpretations or conclusions set forth in the book.

I wish to offer thanks to Philosophical Library Inc., New York, for their assistance in publishing the book and to Assumption University, Windsor, Ontario, Canada, for the financial support I received while working on this project.

My gratitude is also extended to Judith Knight who typed the manuscript and to Norah Badour and Geraldine Bryant for their secretarial assistance.

A PROCESSIVE WORLD VIEW
FOR
PRAGMATIC CHRISTIANS

INTRODUCTION

There are very few North American christians who have not been deeply influenced by the pragmatic policies, empirical method and naturalistic spirit which permeate the financial and even the very personal interactions of daily life on this continent. Most of us accept the general pragmatic criterion of determining the meaning and value of things in terms of their consequences even if we do so unreflectively. Science, or at least a very general empirical approach to life and its problems, has become so much a part of our nature that life would be unthinkable without it. We continually examine and develop both nature and ourselves on a scientific basis, and even in our specifically religious activity, humanistic and naturalistic ideals and concerns occupy more and more of our energy.

Neither humanistic nor naturalistic thought necessarily imply the rejection of a personal God; they do so only if meant to by a specific author or group of thinkers. Yet we are all aware of the increasing tendency for humanists and naturalists to exclude the existence of anything transcending sense experience. The writings of John Dewey undoubtedly compose a more complete exposition of American naturalistic philosophy than those of any of its other exponents. He refers to his position as "empirical naturalism," and in his thought naturalism has come to maturity not only in its thorough empiricism, but also in its rejection of a personal God and theistic religion.

Not only Dewey and the naturalistic *philosophers,* but also a number of American *theologians* have rejected a personal God and institutional religion. Yet in doing this they reject neither man's need for religious experience nor his need to aspire toward high spiritual values and attain intellectual and

1

moral growth through wholehearted commitment to the common effort of achieving self-realization for all men. For Dewey the most integral of all human experiences, namely, achieving self-realization for all men in community, is "experience that is religious." While maintaining the prime importance of such experience he rejects a transcendent God and theistic religion because for him they impose goals outside the natural process of the universe, divert man's attention from earthly pursuits and distract him from committing all his energy to natural, human values. Thus in his perspective a personal God and theistic religion prevent man from being truly human.

In order to emphasize terrestrial reality and the scientific basis on which nature must be examined and furthered, Dewey and other pragmatists and naturalists have found it necessary to reject the transcendent. Such an approach is not acceptable, however, to many christians who not only choose to judge by pragmatic standards but also cherish the same naturalistic values as Dewey. They regard his thought on religious experience to be an unacceptable reconstruction and "naturalization" of Christianity. Their aim is to mantain the authentic values of the naturalists in an integral view of reality which is open to the transcendent — they desire a theism which is thoroughly humanistic. These christians are searching for an over-all, comprehensive meaning in life in which natural, material pursuits are intimately related with religious aspirations and a personal relationship with a living God. The world views frequently presented to them by philosophers and theologians are inadequate in this regard; they are fragmented by seemingly rigid dichotomies such as those established and maintained between matter and spirit, body and soul, man and nature, natural and supernatural.

A man's spirituality flows in large part from his cosmic vision, and the style of spirituality that a dichotomized world view promotes tends to emphasize the otherworldly. The meaning of things is seen in terms of *either* the mundane *or* the spiritual, the latter of which is too often associated almost exclusively with the eschatological. Neither meanings of objects and events nor answers to problems are worked out in terms of long term consequences and pervasive and enduring aims, so that they are necessarily shallow and partial. Methods of approaching problems are limited and piecemeal because they are unrelated to each other and to one or other facet of man's existence. And too frequently when examining matters of faith christian scholars shy away from asking "what, *in the world,* does this mean?" so that they often fail to relate their faith as directly as possible to the meaning of earthly realities.

One outstanding christian who sought a more integral vision was Pierre Teilhard de Chardin, a French priest and paleontologist, whose numerous writings range from purely scientific articles through phenomenological-philosophical works to religious, ascetical and even mystical writings. He set out as a committed christian to provide a solution to one basic problem — the discontinuity he experienced between his passionate love for the world and his love of the christian God. The thrust of all his thought is toward achieving an over-all unity of vision concerning life for the christian. He saw that modern man's empirical vision of the universe has led him to develop a human religious ideal which stresses certain tendencies and expresses itself in terms which, at first, appear to differ radically from his christian religious ideal. Yet Teilhard insists that this dichotomy is unnecessary. He maintains that full commitment to human achievements and the development of one's personality are not only compatible with, but essential to Christianity. No person, therefore, needs to reject God in order to remain or become more authentically human. In fact, Teilhard claims that Christ is the fulfillment of the whole process of evolution; and ultimately, on the basis of revelation, he identifies the personal focus upon which the cosmic process converges with Christ. Thus Christ is seen not merely as a transcendent end, but also as an immanent force moving the whole of reality from within to achieve its fulfillment.

The extent to which Teilhard's thought has enabled christians who are pragmatic and empirically minded to develop an integral world view and style of spirituality is difficult to assess. Some estimate can be made in terms of the importance that has been attached to his writings. The fact remains, however, that Teilhard's works provide only a framework or skeleton which in many areas needs to be fleshed out if it is to be made really functional. At first sight it might appear as if there could be very little relationship between Teilhard's thought and that of John Dewey. We have already focused on the fact that their respective visions culminate in an acceptance or rejection of theistic religion and a transcendent God, a difference which bears directly on what each author proposes as the highest point of fulfillment for man and the universe.

Nevertheless, on further examination it is not difficult to see some obvious similarities between Dewey's process philosophy and Teilhard's evolutionary thought. In fact, both men emphasize the on-going, evolutionary quality of nature, and it is this evolutionary, historical perspective that enables these seemingly divergent thinkers to observe the unity in nature and overcome the dualisms scholars have unnecessarily established within it. Thus in attempting to set forth an integral cosmic vision for American christians the writings of John Dewey provide a rich source of fruitful insights which can complement the thought of Teilhard.

No one to date, however, has published an extensive, systematic study which brings together these two men's thought. There are, nevertheless, a few American authors whose writings reveal the influence of both Dewey and Teilhard. They include such persons as Eugene Fontinell, Robert O. Johann, Robert C. Pollock and Robert J. Roth. But then invariably we find that these men are working primarily within the Deweyan tradition and make only brief references to the thought of Teilhard. Johann has undoubtedly gone further than the others in assimilating ideas of Teilhard and incorporating them into his works, but these works are written primarily out of the context of Dewey's thought. Roth shows the similarity between the two men with regard to the importance of matter and a few other topics, and states specifically that he expects an article to be written showing the similarities between their thought;[1] yet he has not compared them in an extensive manner.

The world view set forth in this book is the result of an extensive comparative study of the works of Dewey and Teilhard done by the present author. Essentially it consists of the Teilhardian vision into which all the naturalistic values and many of the mature philosophical insights of Dewey have been incorporated. It is evident from the outset, therefore, that the resultant, third vision set forth here is deeply and extensively indebted for its content to the thought of these two men. It is a derived, yet a creative vision; one which is at one and the same time a synthesis and a development and updating of the thought of these authors.

The present study integrates an explicit faith in Christ as Saviour and Evolver with a communal commitment to fostering the evolutionary process. In its analysis of man's position in nature and his need to commit himself wholeheartedly to fostering evolution and achieving earthly fulfillment, this work enriches *christian thought* by showing how the naturalist's respect for matter and approach to personal self-realization are compatible with and necessary to christian salvation. Moreover, it includes many ideas which are of major importance for naturalists as well. In showing that a christian's faith in a personal God is compatible with a naturalist's respect for the material world and wholehearted commitment to progress, it shows the *naturalist* that his rejection of a personal God and theistic religion has set unnecessary limits to his cosmic vision.

In focussing immediately on the question of whether man achieves his highest fulfillment in relation to or apart from God, we have made a summary statement of the contribution of this work to both the naturalist and christian. The real scope and import of this world view cannot be grasped, however, by focussing on its religious element alone; these are seen best in the context of the whole. Therefore, to give the reader a quick overview of the vision which is to follow we shall sketch out its basic lines here in the introduction before proceeding to set it forth in detail.

This world view will be an evolutionary, processive or historical one because this perspective overcomes unnecessary dualisms, enables man to achieve unity of vision and reveals reality as it is. It will recognize that the study of reality is a study of the natural history of the world and that all things, including men, are their histories. It will regard nature as the whole process of becoming, so that its outlook will be future oriented, but will respect the past and present out of which the future is built. Causality will be considered in terms of the whole sequential order in reality showing the observable connections between things as well as their discontinuities.

This view will envisage *one* evolutionary process which will be prolonged and consummated through the working of grace in the building up of the Body of Christ. That is, it will see a continuity between the natural evolutionary process and the religious process which has its fulfillment beyond the natural. These will not be regarded as two separated processes occurring simultaneously.

Within the whole range of process philosophy there are many kinds of process proposed, each having its own underlying principle of movement which directs it and keeps it in progress. In each particular philosophy of process the principle of movement proposed has widespread consequences; for instance, it determines whether the process is unending or converging. The underlying principle of movement to be described here will be formulated in such a way as to incorporate Dewey's insights regarding interaction between organisms and their environments into the context of Teilhard's emphasis on the mutual interaction between the developing consciousness and increasing material complexity of organisms themselves.

There will be due recognition given to both the observable exterior and the interior of things. Interiority or spirit will be recognized at least to some degree in all reality. The twofold

6

interaction in nature referred to above, namely, that among the constituent elements within things and that between organisms and their environments, will emphasize achieving development through union. Every increase in real union will be regarded as an increase or development of spirit or interiority. This development is accomplished by what Teilhard describes as a process of centering or focussing things on themselves. The whole evolutionary process, therefore, will be one of spiritualization, one which has some inherent direction toward a special end.

The perennial problem regarding the relationship of spirit and matter will be approached in such a way as to overcome the dualism between them without denying the presence of a duality. Spirit-matter will be regarded as intimately related, but spirit will not be conceived as evolving from matter. The approach taken toward individual things and persons will strive to achieve a balance between conceiving of them as events and as beings. Thus it will be able to stress the fact that they are radically relational and processive while at the same time leaving ample room for acknowledging the continuity in things maintained by their interiority or spirit. The treatment of the appearance of life and man will recognize both continuity and discontinuity in the evolutionary process. Neither life nor man are accidental or secondary phenomena of nature's movement nor is man's capacity to think something injected, as it were, totally from outside nature. Yet neither life nor man are caused by the less complex material reality out of which they arose. Their uniqueness will be demonstrated in terms of transformations occurring at critical points or quantum jumps within the whole process.

The vision will include a theory of experience along the lines of that proposed by Dewey. Experience will be in and of nature, but it will not terminate there. Dewey's concept of experience is capable of being extended to recognize man's capacity to encounter the divine. Many of his specific insights such as the evolutionary function of experience, the instrumental role of intelligence within it and the denial of any inherent opposition between experience and reason will give back to experience the value and dignity it has lost within many schools of christian thought. Human observation and experience, and not abstract principles, will be recognized as the necessary starting point in initiating inquiries.

Man's responsibility to foster and direct the process of evolution by means of his various forms of experience will be of paramount importance in this vision because neither man nor the universe can come to its fulfillment apart from this activity. Man cannot realize himself apart from matter nor apart from his interaction with his environment and other persons. A truly incarnational approach to the world, to work and to matter will accept the fact that there are risks involved for the christian when he commits himself wholeheartedly to temporal progress, but it will also recognize this activity as a human co-operation in the creative activity of God.

Both genuine continuity and discontinuity exist between nature and its temporal development and grace or supernatural fulfillment in Christ. The work of developing oneself by striving co-operatively to achieve shared goals and by bringing the universe to its fulfillment is a necessary, but in itself, an insufficient condition of the *parousia*. This vision will reveal that there need be no real opposition between modern humanistic religious ideals and christian religious ideals. The christian must become fully human and authentically christian. Faith in the christian God and religion enhance man's commitment to science and evolutionary progress because they give them a new urgency and dimension. Man not only builds the earth, he assists in building up the Body of Christ at the same time through the working of grace in him. Science and technology, as instruments of evolution, must be given purpose and direction by man, and in such a context they can be used to promote the spiritualization process to its fullest dimension.

In a perspective in which all of nature is evolving and all of reality is to be transformed so as to enter in some way into the Body of Christ, all activity takes on deep, personal meaning. The christian can agree with the naturalist that man's fulfillment and the achievement of meaning in life depend on commitment to human affairs, but he can also add that the extended vision the christian message brings to man's efforts to achieve fulfillment and meaning enrich these beyond the limits proposed by naturalism.

A great deal of emphasis will be placed on the role of love in fostering evolution, an emphasis which will enable this view of reality to speak directly to modern man's very anxious search for fulfillment and meaning in a way the naturalistic vision proposed by Dewey does not do. The type of meaning sought today is not a purely intellectual explanation of reality and progress, but an extremely personal relevance which must include an emphasis on love. Many persons today are seeking to find meaning more in love than in material success, yet the christian religious vision based on love cannot exclude or be indifferent to earthly activity and success. It must balance and relate love and work and show the relevance of both for self-realization.

Our vision will emphasize the additive and reconstructive functions of knowing, its capacity to promote evolution, increase men's being and provide a liberal, fulfilling life for all. Since no dualism between the order of knowing and that of being will be recognized, experience will be respected more fully, and the extremes of subjectivity and objectivity in knowing and experience will be avoided in favour of a balanced, relational objectivity. The three traditional criteria for truth will be related in such a way that the criterion of coherence will predominate, but increasing emphasis will be placed on the pragmatic criterion and the correspondence involved in truth will be a dynamic, not a static correspondence.

Dewey's analysis of the dynamism within experience in terms of a balance between activity and passivity or suffering will be recognized as operative in all activity and growth. It will be shown that this is the same dynamism inherent in the redemptive act of Christ and in all redemptive activity performed by men. The balance between attachment and detachment found in both humanistic and christian thought will be an integral part of this world view, but the significance of detachment will be extended to encompass the radical detachment which is specifically christian.

The approach to morality set forth may be characterized as both reflective and dynamic. Some pragmatic and scientific criteria for determining the moral value of actions will be proposed, but the problem as to whether such criteria by themselves are ultimately adequate for a morality for christians will remain an open question. At any rate moving out beyond oneself and interacting and uniting with one's fellow men and God, sharing aims and striving for universal community will be the principal means of achieving personal growth. The primacy of love will be maintained. In fact, in its new on-going context love will be *the* motive force of the whole evolutionary process, and God in his person and love will be acknowledged not only as the source and immanent principle, but also as the attractive power or lure-from-beyond moving the whole evolutionary process to fulfillment in Himself. Man's responsibility to love and to forward evolution will be seen within this framework of God's activity.

Insights regarding what it means to be human will be incorporated within the vision. They will balance man's individuality and relationality and stress the significance of his interiority or spirit. In fact, affirming man's transcendence and immortality will be that which ultimately makes the universe open-ended for him. Dewey's esthetic theory, which logically is open to the christian supernatural in spite of his statements to the contrary, will find a place in the vision; and Teilhard's claim that man can encounter God in and through nature will provide a link between esthetic and mystical experience.

The modern humanistic religion of the world will not be regarded as a threat to God or as an overpowering temptation to men, but as a natural faith which can be incorporated within christian faith. As such it can enrich the latter and help men to see that salvation is no longer a matter involving merely the individual soul and God, but the whole person, the evolving universe and God. As a result christian faith will be humanized and made more acceptable to those who experience a passion for the earth while at the same time retaining its supernatural content.

The vision set forth here for christians will retain the reality traditionally referred to as the supernatural, but will avoid both extreme supernaturalism and a position in which the evolutionary process is regarded as having both a natural and supernatural term. Acknowledging *one* movement, *one* Center and *one* outcome will overcome a sharp dualism between the natural and supernatural. Thus some continuity can be maintained between the natural and the supernatural in which the whole of reality has been recast through the Incarnation. It will also regard the supernatural as a completely free gift of God. In this context the christian's responsibility to develop the earth can be highlighted.

A genuine balance concerning the transcendence and immanence of God and a fruitful combination of the mediator tradition and incarnational tradition in theology must find a place in this world view. The cosmic and christic are united to the Trinity in and through the mediating activity of the incarnate Christ. Emphasis on the development occurring in the entire Body of Christ (which includes the world) roots God in the natural and relates Him directly to the cosmic process. Not only man and the universe are in process; God too is being brought to completion in His own Incarnation with the co-operative effort of men who form His Body.

Acknowledging that the church is an observable community of *love* and *thought* in the world as well as being the religious community fructifying and celebrating men's efforts to develop universal community here and now, gives the church a dynamic mission to the whole of reality. A major deficiency in a purely naturalistic vision is its lack of a divine love concretely incarnated in a visible form, a love alone capable of enabling a person to love *all men*. A deeper sense of the christian community as a community of love and service on behalf of the world will take the emphasis off attaining individual salvation and lead men to recognize their solidarity in achieving it and accepting responsibility for the whole cosmic-christic process. The present is an era in which secular voices are emphasizing love and the church is asking for a new Pentecost, a new era of the Holy Spirit. This vision for christians will reveal the depths of God's love for men and the world. As any cosmic vision it will be limited and relative, but its relevance and significance will lie in its ability to relate the cosmic and christic and show that the former finds its ultimate meaning and purpose in the person of Christ whose love embraces all things.

To sum up the qualities of this vision arising out of the comparison of the thought of Dewey and Teilhard we may say that it is not *materialistic* but *spiritualistic* although it respects and develops the material. It balances tendencies which appear somewhat pantheistic with theism. The personal, transcendent God enters into nature without dissolving Himself in it in any way and can be encountered there. In fact, when nature has attained its fulfillment God will be all in everyone and everything. This vision is *deterministic* but yet *directed by God*. That is, all the internal laws of nature with their limitations and determinisms are operative, and yet God's attractive power is addressed to everything according to its capacity and moves each interiorly to freely orient itself toward Him. This vision not only balances the *immanent presence* of God with His *transcendence*, but reveals the necessity of transcendence for man if the universe is to remain open and not stifle him. Finally, it cherishes the *human* and *natural* and shows how they attain consummation in the christian *supernatural*. And all of this is accomplished through the mediating activity of the risen Christ with the co-operation of men.

1. Robert J. Roth, "The Importance of Matter," *America*, 109 (December 21, 1963), pp. 792-94; Robert J. Roth, "Humanism and Catholicism," *The Humanist*, (September-October, 1969), p. 29.

CHAPTER 1

THE EVOLUTIONARY OR PROCESSIVE PERSPECTIVE OF REALITY

I. *A Felt Need for Unification*

Probably the most advantageous point from which to begin to set forth the world view which follows is the need for an over-all unity of vision experienced by thousands of christians on this continent today. We need not go into an analysis of the factors which make this need more urgent today than in the past; certainly the rapid rate of change in all areas of life is paramount. Even where this need is not explicitly formulated and articulated as such, the christian's inability to see any complementary connections co-ordinating his commitment to God, the practice of his religion, his love of the earth and its attractive activities, his concern for peace, international trade and politics, success in his business and his desire for security in old age, create a tension and uncertainty in him which stifle his creative energies and dull his faith in God and the future of mankind.

For most persons this problem remains pervasive and ill defined; yet it is very specific. The christian needs to see at least the skeleton of a vision which can positively relate his faith in a transcendent, but immanent and personal God with a faith in mankind and the future of terrestrial activity. God and the earth are the two specific foci of his problem; he needs to achieve some unity between himself and nature and himself and God. Too many men are suffering from a view in which

God and the earth are at odds with one another or from a convenient vision in which they are merely superficially juxtaposed.

The plight of the christian is not lessened by the fact that so many of the traditional world views at his disposal propose dichotomies on the philosophical level between matter and spirit and subject and object, and, on the theological plane, sharp dualisms and dividing walls between body and spirit, the world and God, the sacred and secular. They do not situate man squarely within nature, but appear to propose an uneasy alliance between man and nature as if any organic connection between them would threaten man's transcendence. For many this perspective fails to ensure the integrity and unity of nature itself and does not allow man to be fully human. A genuine love and respect for matter and its development by man is also thwarted in such a view. In fact, in a perspective in which nature, man and God are not adequately related, many christians cannot see that their faith assists them to find any absolute principle of either success or unity for the contingent universe. Thus they find it difficult to see anything that can assure meaning to men and human activity; and they are right, at least to the extent that events obtain their meaning in relation to their ends or goals. If the success of the human adventure on earth is not directly bound up with the Incarnation and Christ, then its meaning is reduced to contingent, relative dimensions alone.

Vatican II was very much aware of this problem when it pointed out the inadequacy of limiting religion to acts of worship and moral obligations divorced from earthly affairs. It stated explicitly that the split between a person's religious faith and his daily life is one of the more serious errors of our age.[1] Somehow, the christian must be able to see that he can and must be fully human in order to be fully christian. He must be able to attain his own fulfillment in Christ by bringing the earth to its fulfillment. In brief, he must see the connection between his union with matter and his relationship to God through matter.[2] When a christian cannot see this possibility he will tend to liberate himself from the tension of trying to serve God and the world separately by rejecting a personal God because a commitment to God unrelated to his earthly activities divides his concerns and dissipates his energy. If man's relationship to God interferes with the integrity of earthly endeavours and hinders their present unification it is destructive of man himself. Certainly the message of Christianity is not that man has two possible independent goals either of which is adequate to merit his total commitment, namely, a natural fulfillment of himself and the universe or a supernatural or transcendent fulfillment in God. Since Christianity does not leave man free to choose between these goals as equally adequate ultimate ends for himself, and since it cannot leave him torn between them, it must show him how to relate and co-ordinate the two into one attainable, satisfying term of all his activity.

It is evident, therefore, that the basic issue with which the christian must come to grips is how to approach reality. Achieving a unified vision involves searching for the point of view which will enable him to see reality as it is. This, as we shall see, involves a work of reconstruction in both methods of observation and in accepted ideas and beliefs about reality. This reconstruction will extend beyond the realm of philosophy to what has been regarded as the traditional christian outlook toward terrestrial affairs, and will deeply effect the significance of all human activity in the world, the style of christian spirituality and even the study of Christology.

The problem of how to approach reality is one of how *to see* or *come to know* the truth of reality. We shall turn directly to the thought of Teilhard, and see that his analysis of the subjective-objective relationship in knowing enabled him to see quite clearly that reality is evolutionary or processive. The fact that he has been able to overcome a dualism between subject and object without denying the presence of a duality is of concern to our vision. Nevertheless, our primary concern is with establishing the processive or historical perspective as the true perspective for knowing reality because that is the way reality is.

II. *Seeing Reality as Processive or Historical*

In the preface to *Le Phénomène humain* Teilhard states that scientific investigation has established beyond doubt that there is *no fact which exists in isolation*. Every experience no matter how objective it may appear becomes enveloped in a series of assumptions as soon as the scientist attempts to formulate it. When the field of observation is limited, a subjective element in interpretation is present even though imperceptible; when the vision extends to the whole, this subjective element becomes more evident and of crucial importance.[3]

What is involved here is a denial that a fact exists automatically apart from a theory, a denial that the truth of a thing exists "objectively" outside of its relations to other things. Facts are not individual raw materials immediately observable, but through investigation of relations, facts are attained and formulated in proportions. This process necessarily involves an element of subjectivity. The larger the area of investigation the more room for subjective sensitivity in the formulation of judgments. Without saying so explicitly, Teilhard is denying a *pure objectivity* to knowledge or truth in the sense that things have one permanent essence grasped immediately apart from their alterable relations to other things. He is also implying that the truth of a proposition can be understood only in terms of the process of inquiry from which it developed. These points are implied in the statement on subjectivity made in the Preface to *Le Phénomène humain*, but they were not his main points of concern in that passage. Nevertheless, this approach to knowing and these implications are developed more explicitly elsewhere in his writings.

For a short time he accepted a dualism between the ontological order (the order of being or reality) and the order of knowledge. However, he appears to have reached a resolution to the epistemological problem fairly early in his career for in 1917 he wrote:

> This duality of the cognitive order and the real order has since seemed to me arbitrary and false. We have no serious reason for thinking that things are not made in the same pattern as that in which our experience unfolds them. On the contrary, that pattern may very well disclose to us the fundamental texture of Spirit.[4]

Teilhard shows great respect for the capacity of scientific inquiry to enable man to know reality as it is. Human experience unfolds reality as it is, that is, it unfolds it *scientifically or historically* as it is in process of developing. This approach to knowledge also reveals respect for human experience and indicates that all knowing must begin with phenomenological observation.

Because facts are not immediately observable and because there is always a subjective element in interpretation, Teilhard necessarily places a great deal of emphasis on seeing, perceiving, expending energy on the vast effort of visual focussing which will restore true perspectives.[5] Man must train himself to observe reality from the point of view from which it reveals itself. Only then can he grasp its objective truth. In "La Préhistoire et ses progrès" he gives a concrete illustration of the method of arriving at facts. Only after observing and plotting the observations on a graph so as to be able to see regularities and irregularities does he speak of discovering or establishing a particular fact.[6] It is evident that after observing, man must learn to relate his observations and formulate propositions in such a way as to approach reality from a perspective that enables him to grasp its true, natural meaning.

The visual focus which enables man to attain a *true perspec-*

tive of reality, namely, *that from which it can reveal itself*, is the *historical* or *evolutionary perspective*. Before man became really aware of the spatio-temporal context of reality, living things were regarded as fixed wholes set side by side by the *extrinsic operation* of intelligence. They were classified according to *logical* divisions which were thought to correspond to the creative idea of God. To know a thing scientifically today, however, is to place it in a physical system relating it to things which preceded it temporally and things to which it is spatially connected. To classify it one must find its *natural* place in the assembly of living forms considered as a whole in process of development. This involves reconstituting its organic history, explaining its biological surroundings and accounting for its geographical distribution.[7]

The natural perspective which enables man to grasp the truth of reality is that which recognizes that *time permeates the very essence of things*. However fixed their essences may appear, things are "termless and indefinite" in their preparation, maturation and completion. Without losing its individual value each element of the universe is co-extensive with the reality of the whole, that is, with history. This fundamental condition of all beings, namely, that they cannot be perceived except in connection with the whole past, expresses a law of man's perceptual experience. In the realms of both matter and life one cannot avoid acknowledging the fundamental unity of the universe and the interrelationship of the cosmic elements which allow a new being to enter man's experience only in the context of the entire past and present. Man cannot give up viewing things from the perspective of the unity of the universe and of the interrelationship among its elements because this perspective enables reality to grow clearer and more orderly as far as the eye can see.[8]

The historical perspective has begun to play a greater role in all the sciences, including metaphysics. In fact, Teilhard saw the beginnings of a single science of reality which he called the natural history of the world.[9] He felt that this science, relating the knowledge of the other disciplines, would be of inestimable value; yet it would not diminish the need for approaching reality from the perspectives of the sciences, philosophy and religion. He describes approaches to reality taken by various disciplines in terms of meridian lines which separate from one another at the equator but necessarily converge at the poles. Just as the meridian lines *converge but do not merge* so too the various disciplines meet at the pole where they approach the whole of reality but continue to the very end to investigate reality from different angles and on different planes.[10]

Before continuing to set forth a more detailed perspective of reality as processive or evolutionary we must take a few moments to examine in more detail Teilhard's thought on the way the various disciplines complement one another and yet retain their own identity and method. This question is of vital importance to the present work because it is a question of methodology and the methodology in this vision follows that in Teilhard's thought. Any vision arrived at by a method which has no inherent consistency or one which confuses the methods of various disciplines must be regarded as suspect and inadequate. As well, any method which arrives at its content according to the methods of various disciplines but then mingles ideas as if the presuppositions behind them were the same or as if the ideas all held the same kind or degree of certitude is also immediately suspect and to be rejected.

In spite of the fact that many critics of Teilhard have misunderstood his method and accused him of some or all of these inadequacies, he is not guilty of having committed them.[11] He uses the image of meridian lines to illustrate the distinction between concordism and coherence in thought. In a cosmic view in which the various approaches to reality are confused and over-simplified analogies are drawn between one plane of thought and another, the result is a generalized concordism, a distorted view of reality. This is like merging meridian lines at the equator instead of allowing them to converge naturally at the poles. Science and revelation are distinct; they must represent two different meridian lines, as it were, which must remain distinct, but which will ultimately converge or come together to complement one another.[12] In this way coherence of thought and an over-all vision which extends beyond the limits of any one discipline can be achieved. In fact, this is the way Teilhard developed his vision and the manner in which thought from various disciplines will be related in this present work.

Both the vision of Teilhard and this vision begin by observing man and the universe on the plane of appearances as a scientist observes reality. Every element of reality is treated as a phenomenon in the scientific sense; that is, as something to be observed from without. Thus in its beginning stages these views can be said to use a phenomenological approach. Nevertheless, neither Teilhard nor the present author will be restricted to externals alone, because as Teilhard put it, the external, observable effects of an object reveal its within, its interiority or spirit. Thus a phenomenological method which fails to observe and take account of the interiority of reality as made evident through its external manifestations is inadequate.[13]

An adequate phenomenology must not only take into account the visible effects of the interiority of things, it must also observe that things are in process. Phenomenology, therefore, concerns the study of processes. Aware of this fact, Teilhard set out on the experiential level to establish an experimental chain of succession in nature, that is, a chain of antecedences and consequences. But to observe and establish an experimental process in the universe (or to discover an experimental law of recurrence expressing the successive appearance in time of its various elements) is *not*, according to Teilhard, to give a *philosophical explanation* of the universe. He referred to his approach as "physics" in the Greek sense of a generalized physics, and more frequently as hyperphysics.[14] His distinction between his method of phenomenology and philosophy is an essential one. One must recognize, however, that in spite of certain statements to the contrary, Teilhard uses his method of observing and establishing an experimental process in the universe as far as it can go, and then, on the basis of the evidence accrued by this method, continues by way of philosophical reflection. He was aware that his attempted synthesis would appear to be a philosophical work due to the fact that philosophy is directed toward a study of the whole. He never defined philosophy, but he did characterize its method as reflective as opposed to the observational method of phenomenology. In fact his hyperphysics is philosophical reflection; and, if I am not mistaken, when used by the Greeks the term also referred to reflective, philosophical thought. A large portion of both Teilhard's world view and this view will be philosophical.

One of the essential dimensions of any phenomenon is that it not only makes itself perceptible to observation as in process, but makes itself perceptible as an element in a universal process of cosmic development or evolution. In this way Teilhard's phenomenology differed from that of Husserl and Merleau Ponty, whom he criticized for having ignored this dimension of reality.[15] Once again, therefore, both Teilhard's method and that found in the vision being presented will differ from that of classical phenomenology which has developed from the thought of Husserl. This does not mean, however, that the approach used here lacks internal consistency. In fact it enables the scholar to observe and relate phenomena in a manner other methods do not.

Teilhard sought a global view in order to develop as synthetic a cosmic vision as possible. His phenomenology was directed toward the *whole of reality* which is *one organic movement* or evolution so that it is similar to a natural history of the world. Precisely because he overstepped the methods of the particular sciences in his phenomenology by attempting to observe the whole process of evolution, he says that his phenomenology approached a natural history of the universe much more than a metaphysics.[16] There is no doubt that his perspective and that of this work see things in terms of their natural history; whether these views contain a considerable amount of metaphysical reflection may be open to question. I maintain that they do. It is not, however, a static metaphysics; but to that point we shall have to return later. For the moment it is sufficient to note that in taking an historical approach to reality this work is in line with virtually all contemporary thought. Today, all positive knowledge of things, whether they be organisms, ideas, religions or institutions, is identified with the study of their development.

Before going on to further analyze reality as processive we can sum up what has been said regarding methodology. Teilhard started by observing and developed his own method of phenomenology, one which recognized the interiority of things and observed that things are in process themselves within a larger world process. On this latter point his thought is in total accord with that of empirically minded American thinkers who regard science as being concerned with connections in process and maintain that any attempt to classify reality must reveal the course it has pursued in developing itself. Teilhard's observations led him to philosophical reflection concerning the whole of the cosmic process. He developed this thought as far as he could philosophically, that is, to the point of recognition of a personal goal which is both immanent and transcendent, a goal in which the whole process will find its fulfillment. At that point he could go no further philosophically so that he discontinued his philosophical reflection and turned to revelation. He did not mix the data of philosophical reflection and that of revelation, but he showed that it was possible to identify the ultimate personal goal of the evolutionary process arrived at philosophically with the Christ of revelation. In this way he extended his vision to encompass revealed knowledge, and showed how phenomenological, philosophical and revelational knowledge complement one another.

In examining Teilhard's thought on epistemology and methodology we have seen that the way he approached reality enabled him to recognize that it is processive or evolutionary.

And then it was the evolutionary perspective which enabled him to overcome many of the dichotomies so common to many approaches to reality. So too in the thought of Dewey and other empirical thinkers it is an evolutionary perspective which enables them to achieve a high degree of real unity in their thought. Thus along with these men, the present work maintains that the historical or evolutionary perspective is that which enables men to grasp the true view of reality. Evolution is not a possible hypothesis which if accepted may shed some light on reality as it is; it is a fact of existence.[17]

The law of evolution is the general law of life and growth. It may also be regarded as a generalization of the scientific method insofar as that method recognizes and follows the history by which phenomena develop. Process is universal; the whole of reality is one organic movement the study of which is a study of the natural history of the world. An evolutionary perspective has not only enabled men to see the fundamental unity of the whole universe and the organic interrelation of its elements, it can also enable the christian to bring God and the world together in one organically-related whole.

There are many consequences of recognizing reality as processive. In some philosophies "the fixed," "final" and "the permanent essence" are regarded as superior, while change and origin are signs of inferior being. In an evolutionary or process philosophy the dualism between inferior and superior realms of being according to which some things were regarded as immutable and independent of time and space is abolished. All reality is both spatially and temporally conditioned; these are fundamental conditions of its existence. Things can neither exist nor be known apart from their connection with the entire past. Time permeates to the very essence of things; it is not an accidental attribute. Thus a thing *is* its history. Things are always incomplete and in process, and man must assist in bringing them to completion.[18] One must certainly distinguish and analyze the origin, developments and transitions which take place during the course of an object's history, but one must not attempt to establish clear cut lines of demarcation between the appearance and subsequent development of things and events in the universe. Even the traditional concepts of God's instantaneous creation and subsequent preservation of reality must undergo reconstruction in this processive context. Creation is seen to be a continuous activity of God accomplished through transformation, a process by which God makes things develop themselves — creation through transformation, *not* creation *and* transformation.

When all things are recognized as spatially and temporally conditioned the relativity of reality and of all knowledge of it must be recognized. When the processive quality of reality is admitted a new method of thinking is introduced which transforms the logic of knowledge and thus influences all the sciences including the study of morality and religion. More emphasis can be placed on the *present meanings* and *uses* of things, and it becomes more imperative that philosophical investigations begin from observation and analysis of concrete human experience.

Where these methods make insight into specific conditions of value and specific consequences of ideas more readily available, philosophy becomes a method of locating and interpreting the serious conflicts in life and a method of projecting ways to deal with human problems. It becomes criticism of life, and must submit itself to the test of the practical consequences of its ideals. In a relational context such as the one being described here (one could say the context of relativity, but this term has many pejorative connotations) standards arise out of the very difficult task of investigating the actual connections of things in space-time.[19]

It is evident by now that in this processive world view the type of unity striven after, whether in the realm of ideas, things or events, is not a static harmony. Unity is unification, a process by which the degree of on-going harmonious relations or interactions among things is continually deepened and extended by the activity of men. This process of unification, as we shall see later in much greater detail, involves the interaction of man with his environing conditions. Through the various modes of human experience both man and the universe evolve and are brought to their full realization. Nevertheless, at one and the same time, this whole process of evolution is in a real sense transformed by the love energy which motivates and impels it so that the whole of reality is attaining synthesis or unification in the person of Christ.

Another consequence of an evolutionary world view is the rejection of a *static* metaphysics. Such a world view does not approach reality primarily from the point of view of the essences of things nor does it attempt to establish or define causal or ontological relations which make things to be what they are. The present author is very aware that not all classical metaphysics, which studies being as such, is static; nor does he deny the validity of such an approach to metaphysics. In fact, there is a considerable amount of traditional metaphysical reflection in this world view. It is complemented, however, by a descriptive approach to metaphysics, one which is concerned with the functional relations of things which also make them what they are and at the same time enable men to know them.

An evolutionary perspective moves the emphasis away from regarding an individual existent reality as a cause having a one to one relationship to a succeeding reality called its effect. In this context a cause is regarded as a condition of appearance in a process. Any adequate analysis of causality must examine the successive stages of the phenomenon from its appearance to its culmination and control this examination by discovering the conditions under which the various stages appeared. Causality, therefore, is treated in terms of the whole sequential order showing the observable connections among things.

Concern with origins is directed toward locating objective conditions under which specific facts appear and in relation to which they have meaning. It is also concerned with assuring that higher forms are not reduced to lower ones. The evolutionary process is neither reductionistic nor deterministic in that it neither limits the possibility of more complex forms succeeding the less complex nor attempts to imply that the whole reality of the more complex has been caused by the preceding, less developed being.

The study of causality is a study of the unfolding of the existence of phenomena themselves, a study which enables man to know things by their natural histories. In pursuing such an approach both the real values and the qualities of things are discovered because in nature there is an inseparable connection between the qualities of things and their circumstances. A quality of an object is the response it makes to specific conditions, and its meaning is the contribution it affords to the movement of the whole process in which it is involved.[20]

The above analysis of the type of metaphysics found in our evolutionary world view is incomplete; additional pertinent metaphysical problems will be discussed later. At this point it is sufficient to stress the basic point of contrast between the descriptive metaphysics being proposed and classical metaphysics. Whereas in the latter approach process and relations are of secondary importance, being regarded as accidental to being rather than of its essence, in the present approach process and relations are primary and central.

In this brief chapter we have posed the problem at hand in terms of the twentieth century American christian's vital need for unification and set forth basic principles of methodology which enable us to propose that the most accurate perspective of reality is the evolutionary one. We have also offered a few fundamental observations regarding reality as processive. In the following chapter we must focus specifically on the evolutionary process. If observation leads men to see that reality is, in fact, historical and evolutionary, then man must also be able to observe some underlying evolutionary principle or law by which reality evolves. If this were not possible we would have to admit that man cannot know reality and analyze it in depth. The underlying law of evolution proposed in this work will be substantially that proposed by Teilhard de Chardin as the present author regards Teilhard's thought in this area to be exceptionally perceptive. We shall attempt to develop Teilhard's thought somewhat by showing how the underlying law by which John Dewey sees evolution progressing is not only compatible with Teilhard's thought, but enriches it. Thus Teilhard's thought will be fleshed out somewhat and its real significance further clarified.

FOOTNOTES

1. Walter M. Abbott, ed., "The Church Today," *The Documents of Vatican II* (New York: Herder and Herder, 1966), no. 43, pp. 242-43.

2. For Teilhard's analysis of this matter see: "La Vie cosmique," *Écrits du temps de la guerre* (Paris: Bernard Grasset, 1965), pp. 7-8 [Eng. trans. p. 17], hereafter cited *ÉTG*; "Mon Univers," *ÉTG*, pp. 269-79; "Le Coeur de la matière," (unpublished mimeographed manuscript, pp. 23, 25); *Lettres de voyage* (*1923-1939*) (Paris: Bernard Grasset, 1956), Letter of January 21, 1936, p.197 [Eng. trans. pp. 218-19], hereafter cited *LV*. For a detailed treatment of the anxiety or grave personal difficulty experienced by Teilhard on account of these dualisms, as well as the strength of christian faith which he brought to this experience, see: Christopher F. Mooney, "Anxiety and Faith in Teilhard de Chardin," *Thought*, 39 (1964), pp. 510-30.

3. Pierre Teilhard de Chardin, *Le Phénomène humain* (Paris: Éditions du Seuil, 1955), Avertissement, p. 22 [Eng. trans. p. 30], hereafter cited *PH*.

4. "L'Union créatrice," *ÉTG*, p. 184 [Eng. trans. p. 162].

5. Pierre Teilhard de Chardin, "Les Hommes fossiles," *L'Apparition de l'homme* (Paris: Éditions du Seuil, 1956), p. 49 [Eng. trans. p. 31], hereafter cited *AppH*; Pierre Teilhard de Chardin, "Les Fondements et le fond de l'idée d'évolution," *La Vision du passé* (Paris: Éditions du Seuil, 1957), pp. 182-83 [Eng. trans. p. 130], hereafter cited *VP*; *PH*, Prologue, pp. 25-29 [Eng. trans. pp. 31-35].

6. "La Préhistoire et ses progrès," *AppH*, p. 25 [Eng. trans. p. 13].

7. "L'Histoire naturelle du monde," *VP*, pp. 146-47 [Eng. trans. pp. 103-05].

8. "Les Fondements et le fond de l'idée d'évolution," *VP*, pp. 181-83 [Eng. trans. pp. 129-30]; "L'Histoire naturelle du monde," *VP*, p. 147 [Eng. trans. p. 104].

9. "Les Fondements et le fond de l'idée d'évolution," *VP*, pp. 179-80 [Eng. trans. p. 128].

10. *PH*, Avertissement, p. 22 [Eng. trans. p. 30].

11. Throughout his works on Teilhard, Henri de Lubac explains and defends Teilhard's methodology. For a very enlightening but brief analysis of Teilhard's method see: Bruno de Solages, *Teilhard de Chardin* (Paris: Edouard Privat, 1967), pp. 60-78.

12. Pierre Teilhard de Chardin, "La Pensée du Père Teilhard de Chardin par lui-même, pour un article qui devait lui être consacré," *Les Études philosophiques*, 10 (1955), p. 581; Pierre Teilhard de Chardin, "Barrière de la mort et co-réflexion," *L'Activation de l'énergie* (Paris:

Éditions du Seuil, 1963), pp. 426-29 [Eng. trans. pp. 403-06], hereafter cited *AÉ*.

13. *PH*, pp. 54-55 [Eng. trans. p. 58].

14. Pierre Teilhard de Chardin, *La Place de l'homme dans la nature* (Paris: Éditions du Seuil, 1956), Avertissement, pp. 17-18 [Eng. trans. p. 13], hereafter cited *PHN*; *PH*, Avertissement, pp. 21-22 [Eng. trans. pp. 29-30]; *PH*, p. 54 [Eng. trans. p. 58]; Pierre Teilhard de Chardin, "L'Esprit nouveau," *L'Avenir de l'homme* (Paris: Éditions du Seuil, 1959), p. 109 [Eng. trans. p. 82], hereafter cited *AH;* "Évolution de l'idée d'évolution," *VP*, pp. 347-48 [Eng. trans. p. 245]; "La Centrologie," *AÉ*, pp. 105-06 [Eng. trans. p. 99]; "La Pensée du Père Teilhard de Chardin par lui-même, pour un article qui devait lui être consacré," *Les Études Philosophiques*, 10 (1955), pp. 580-81.

15. Letter of Teilhard to M. Claude Cuénot, April 11, 1953, cited by Bruno de Solages, *Teilhard de Chardin*, pp. 61-62.

16. *PH*, p. 41 [Eng. trans. p. 46]; "L'Histoire naturelle du monde," *VP*, pp. 146, 157 [Eng. trans. pp. 104, 113]; "Les Fondements et le fond de l'idée d'évolution," *VP*, pp. 179-82 [Eng. trans. pp. 127-29]; Letter of Teilhard to Auguste Valensin, October 13, 1933, cited by Bruno de Solages, *Teilhard de Chardin*, n. 31, p. 70.

17. Teilhard distinguishes three degrees or meanings of evolution each with varying degrees of certitude. The fundamental element of evolution affirming that all objects and events in the universe have antecedents which condition their appearance and make them links in an unending chain is the most general meaning or degree of evolution, a meaning which is *always certain and applicable*. On a second level he points to two currents in cosmic matter which can be distinguished empirically: 1) entropy (a current leading to the diffusion of energy) and, 2) the current which leads to greater complexity and increased consciousness (that which constitutes the phenomenon of life). Science is definitely assured of the existence of these currents although it is *not certain* as to their relative importance, their complementary character or their final conditions of equilibrium. This meaning or degree of evolution is certain as to the existence of the currents. Only on a third level concerning the current of life do we reach the unsubstantiated level of hypothesis concerning evolution. For the six hundred million years scientists are able to follow this current it has *certainly* never ceased globally to rise toward increased *complexity* and consciousness. Yet the scientist can only form hypotheses as to: 1) whether it is still rising; 2) if rising, whether in a divergent or convergent manner, and 3) in what direction its course is thrust. Pierre Teilhard de Chardin, "Sur les Degrés de certitude scientifique de l'idée d'évolution," *Science et Christ* (Paris: Éditions du Seuil, 1965), pp. 245-47 [Eng. trans. pp. 192-94], hereafter cited *SC*.

18. John Dewey, "The Influence of Darwin on Philosophy," *The Influence of Darwin on Philosophy* (Bloomington: Indiana University Press, 1965), pp. 1-2; John Dewey, *Reconstruction in Philosophy*, enlarged edition with a new introduction by the author (Boston: Beacon Press, 1962), pp. xiii-xl.

19. John Dewey, *Problems of Men* (New York: Greenwood Press, 1968), pp. 12-13; "The Influence of Darwin on Philosophy," *The Influence of Darwin on Philosophy*, pp. 9-19.

20. Much of what has been said here regarding metaphysics comes from the thought of John Dewey. See: John Dewey, *Essays in Experimental Logic*, Dover edition (Chicago: University of Chicago Press, 1916), pp. 93-94; *Experience and Nature* (New York: Dover Publications Inc., 1958), pp. 99-100, 109; " 'Consciousness' and Experience," *The Influence of Darwin on Philosophy*, pp. 261-63; "Soul and Body," *Philosophy, Psychology and Social Practice*, ed. by Joseph Ratner (New York: Capricorn Books, 1965), p. 64; John Dewey and Arthur Bentley, *Knowing and the Known* (Boston: Beacon Press, 1960), pp. 321, 325.

For Teilhard's thought on metaphysics see: "La Centrologie," *AÉ*, pp. 105-06 [Eng. trans. p. 99]; "L'Étoffe de l'univers," *AÉ*, p. 397 [Eng. trans. p. 375]; "L'Esprit nouveau," *AH*, p. 109 [Eng. trans. p. 82]; *PH*, Avertissement, p. 21 [Eng. trans. p. 29]; *PH*, p. 54 [Eng. trans. p. 58]; Letter of Teilhard to Henri de Lubac, April 29, 1934, quoted in: " 'Ascent' and 'Descent' in the Work of Teilhard de Chardin," *Pierre Teilhard de Chardin Maurice Blondel Correspondence*, with notes and commentary by Henri de Lubac, trans. by William Whitman (New York: Herder and Herder, 1967), n. 18, p. 163, hereafter cited *Correspondence*.

CHAPTER 2

FUNDAMENTAL EVOLUTIONARY
PRINCIPLES

I. *The Laws of Complexity - Consciousness and Transformism*

Teilhard expressed his fundamental intuition into the underlying principle which causes reality to be evolutionary by what he called the law of complexity-consciousness. This law, which is at the basis of all his processive thought, describes the correlation between a being's material complexity and its degree of psychic development. It is also, therefore, a description of the relationship between matter and spirit in all reality. We shall set forth Teilhard's most mature insights regarding this law insofar as these are necessary to clarify its function as the motor force of evolution and to show how the specific relation between matter and spirit and between the two energies of the universe enable him to maintain an intimate balance between the material and spiritual while removing any opposition or radical independence between them. He maintains a duality between spirit-matter while avoiding a dualism.

All matter, that is, all reality has a "within" and a "without," a "psychic" and a "physical" aspect which are co-extensive with each other. The "within" of things is equated with consciousness and spontaneity, and consciousness is understood as an analogous term, which,

> . . . is taken in its widest sense to indicate every kind of psychism, from the most rudimentary forms of in-

terior perception imaginable to the human phenomenon
of reflective thought.[1]

The psychic in reality is seen as having a primordial origin
so that it is not conceived of as originating with the first appearance of life. There is no dualism similar to that found in
static concepts of matter since matter and consciousness are
never established in separate realms of being.

In further analyzing the psychic and material or the "within"
and "without" of things Teilhard sees an interdependence of
energy between them. He postulates two different energies, one
of which is axial, growing and irreversible. This energy he
calls radial; it draws the elements or units of reality forward
towards ever greater material complexity and centricity because
it is an internal dynamism within them. The other energy is
called tangential (from tangent) because it, being constant,
tangential and reversible, causes elements of reality to unite
with other elements which have the same complexity and centricity. Whereas in time radial energy promotes further development or evolution of the element involved, tangential
energy facilitates reproduction on the same level or order.
These energies are bound to one another in arrangement but
neither compose one another nor are they directly transform-
able into one another since they operate on two different levels.[2]
Once again in this conception of the energy of the universe a
duality is recognized but a dualism is denied.

Radial energy is primary, the source of consistency in reality.
It increases with the arrangement of the elements or units of
reality into a unity, and yet these elements only arrange themselves when prompted by the radial energy.[3] The measure of
the relationship between radial and tangential energy is the law
of complexity-consciousness, a law which functions analogously
on all levels of reality. It is also the key to understanding
evolution so that we must examine it and eventually see how
it applies, as a law of recurrence, to the natural, historical development of the world.

When matter is left to itself over a long period of time it arranges itself in groupings of ever greater material complexity and at the same time in ever higher degrees of consciousness. There is, therefore, a double and combined movement of physical unification or development and psychic interiorization or centration which not only continues but accelerates to its utmost extent.[4]

The complexity referred to is not achieved by any form of unification, but refers to a combination or grouping which knits together *a fixed number of elements upon themselves within a closed whole of determined radius.* What is of significance in facilitating an increase in the material complexity of a thing is not only the number of elements or groups of elements involved, but also the number, variety and proximity of the links between these elements at a minimum volume. This type of combination produces a unit which is structurally completed around itself, one which starts from a particular class, but is indefinitely extensible from within. In brief, the complexification spoken of here involves increasingly complicated organization and the movement from subatomic units to atoms, to inorganic and finally to organic and living units.[5]

To describe the universal tendency toward this particular arrangement which constantly results in a centering or convergence on itself Teilhard uses the metaphors "organic coiling in on itself" or "folding in on itself." He then shows that the process or movement whereby the cosmic stuff coils more and more on itself leading to ever greater complexity is accompanied by, and in fact measured by, a correlative increase in psychic tension or interiorization. On the phenomenal plane each unit of reality is similar to an ellipse having two foci — one of material complexity and the other of psychic centering. These are experimentally bound up with each other so that the degree of centricity or concentration of a consciousness varies in direct proportion to the complexity of the material compound which is its foundation. Consciousness and material complexity are, in fact, two connected parts of the one phenomenon. The law of complexity-consciousness not only points out the intimate connection between the degree of material complexity of a thing and its level of consciousness, but also implies a psychically convergent structure for the whole cosmic process,[6] a point which is of great significance in our over-all world view because the converging structure of the process necessarily implies points of transformation. Thus the law of complexity-consciousness requires the complementary law of transformism, a law which, in its broadest scope, is as universal as evolution itself and one which permeates and colours man's whole view of reality.

Teilhard does not identify transformism with any of the particular mechanistic or materialistic transformist theories. Independent of and underlying these specific theories there is a transformist conception of the world which culminates in a vision of an organic universe the, parts of which are physically linked together in their appearance and destiny. Transformism is not a simple hypothesis but a realization that the history of life can be plotted just as the history of matter and of civilizations can be plotted. It is a general method of research and the extension of a form of historical science to the biological sciences as well as to other human sciences.[7]

Teilhard defines transformism as

> . . . the particular expression, applied to the case of life, of the law which conditions our whole knowledge of the sensible universe: the law that we can understand nothing, in the domain of matter, except as part of a sequence or collection.[8]

For him it is inseparable from and even equivalent to evolution in its most fundamental tenets. Like evolutionary theory, the law of transformism is not an hypothesis, but a dimension of the universe which effects all its elements and relations. As such evolution and transformations are reality; they are conditions which all hypotheses must fulfill if they are to be tenable.

Opponents of transformism have accused it of destroying faith in God and in the human spirit and of leading to materialism. Yet Teilhard says:

> Transformism does not necessarily open the road to an invasion of spirit by matter; it testifies, rather on the side of an essential triumph of spirit. Evolution is as capable as the theory of fixed species, if not more so, of investing the universe with that greatness, depth and unity which are the natural climate of Christian faith.[9]

He is able to maintain what he calls "cosmic embryogenesis" (each new being has antecedents which condition its appearance) and at the same time insist that new beings have an historic birth because the law of complexity-consciousness not only allows for but demands "critical points" in the process of evolution. At such thresholds a transformation or change in nature suddenly occurs so that something totally new is produced and yet a continuity with the earlier stage is also maintained. Such a transformation may be described as follows:

> In every domain, when anything exceeds a certain measurement, it suddenly changes its aspect, condition or nature. The curve doubles back, the surface contracts to a point, the solid disintegrates, the liquid boils, the germ cell divides, intuition suddenly bursts on the piled up facts. . . . Critical points have been reached, rungs on the ladder, involving a change of state — jumps of all sorts *in the course* of development. Henceforth this is the *only* way in which science can speak of a 'first instant'.[10]

This brief analysis of transformism leaves a number of questions to be answered especially since we have not yet approached the problem of whether it is reconciliable with a christian concept of divine creation. Nevertheless, it has enabled us to get some insight into how there can be continuity in evolution, and yet allowance made for discontinuity at moments when entirely new plateaus or levels of being appear. We shall see the working out of these joint laws of complexity-consciousness and transformism when we examine the appearance of life and of man. For the moment we have exposed the basic principles and laid a sufficient foundation to enable us to analyze in more detail the relationship between matter and spirit.

II. *The Interaction Between the Material and Psychic Faces of Reality*

When we examine the meaning of the terms matter, spirit, body and mind and the relationship between matter and spirit and body and mind in an evolutionary context we find that the traditional dualistic approach to these concepts is inappropriate. The way in which Teilhard has described these concepts and re-examined their relationship to one another in time and space is significant for the world view we are proposing. He has not set out to define or analyze the metaphysical structure of matter or spirit, but analyzes them more in terms of their observable functions and relations and the effects produced by these relations. Nevertheless, his analysis is an examination of the internal functioning of existences. In this he achieves a balance not found in the thought of John Dewey, who in reaction to dualistic approaches, has reduced matter and spirit or mind to functional characters of natural events and in so doing has denied that they are existences or elements of existing things. The more balanced view achieved by Teilhard and reflected in this work is of major significance in determining the direction and goal of the evolutionary process.

Traditional approaches frequently posited a fundamental dissimilarity between matter and spirit, regarded them as substances of different natures or as two different species of being. In the discussion which follows we shall see that they are not two separate things, that they do not exist in opposition to one another, that they cannot be established in separate realms of beings, and that one cannot be regarded as the cause of the other.

Matter and spirit present themselves as related variables; that is, as the two conditions or faces of the one cosmic stuff. The material and spiritual aspects of the real are related to one another in a complementary way as the two terms *a quo* and *ad quem of one movement*. From a phenomenological perspective even in the most elementary pre-living corpuscles some sort of "consciousness" or "psychism" is present, and at the other pole of reality no spirit can exist structurally without an associated multiple. At the lower zones of the stuff of the universe there are large numbers of fragmentary centers and a high degree of physical determinism at which stage the "psychism" or form unifying these centers is almost imperceptible.[11] As one moves beyond these lower zones, the stuff of the universe coils in upon itself or centers itself in such a way as to effect more complex material groupings and a deeper, more centered, more interiorized consciousness, the degree of interiorization, centration or spiritualization of each thing being in direct proportion to its degree of material organization or complexification.

It is evident, therefore, that the phenomenologist can observe and outline *one* curve or axis of matter-spirit. And, in fact, this axis reveals that in the universe there is *only spirit* in different states or degrees of organization or plurality. There is not matter and spirit, but matter becoming spirit; the stuff of the universe is spirit-matter. Pure spirituality is as inconceivable as pure materiality. Every spirit derives its reality and its nature from some particular type of universal synthesis so that spirit is always the crown and the expression of a *genesis* and cannot be separated from that process. It is not formed gradually by a simple effect of polarization and summation. Throughout the process of complexification new centers arise and unifying transformations occur.[12] In other words, the law of complexity-

consciousness involves reaching critical points at which qualitative transformations or quantum jumps occur.

We indicated earlier that the concept of unity in an evolutionary perspective really meant unification; now we can see that
the name for spirit is spiritualization. This approach to spirit
emphasizes the totality of the process of transformation that is
taking place in time and space and rejects any notion of spirit
as static or isolated. The phenomenon of spirit reveals a movement from the inanimate toward the conscious and self-conscious; spirit or spiritualization is a cosmic change of state.
In this perspective matter can be spoken of as the matrix of
spirit and spirit as the superior state of matter. Spirit is the
structured term of a defined operation.[13]

To help visualize this structure Teilhard compares the structure of things and of the universe as a whole to that of a cone
having an apex or center of convergence and a base or zone
of indefinite divergence. If one follows the axis of the cone
toward the apex one reaches a point of union; movement in
the opposite direction leads toward more and more disunited
elements. In his later, more mature thought he saw that the
consistency of reality comes from spirit, not matter, and recognized that this ennobles matter rather than degrades it. If
spirit supports matter in the ascent toward consciousness, matter enables spirit to subsist because it provides it with a point
on which to act and provides it with nourishment. Spirit holds
reality together, and its sublimity is linked with the organic
multiplicity which it embraces. The purity of the spiritual apex
of any being is always in proportion to the material breadth
of its base.[14]

Thus far we have seen what Teilhard regarded to be a basic
fact well established by experience, namely, that the higher
the level of consciousness attained in all living beings known
by man, the more closely this consciousness is associated with
a complex organism. Nevertheless, he does not terminate his
inquiry into the relationship between the unity of the multiple within a being and its degree of consciousness on the

experiential level, but moves from a level characterized primarily by observation to a more reflective or philosophical level and develops his original phenomenological principle of "spiritualization by union" into a philosophy of creative union, a reflective explanation of how union causes an increase of being in the thing united. He uses this basic principle as a point from which to view all reality. At times he tended to express his thought in metaphysical terms and insisted that the union in question was an ontological union, and yet he also made the following statement:

> Creative union is not exactly a metaphysical doctrine. It is rather a sort of empirical and pragmatic explanation of the universe, conceived in my mind from the need to reconcile in a solidly coherent system scientific views on evolution (accepted as, in their essence, definitively established) with the innate urge that has impelled me to look for the Divine not in a cleavage with the physical world, but through matter, and, in some sort of way in union with matter.[15]

Teilhard's concept of creative union was certainly practical insofar as it enabled him to examine the distinction between the animal and human spirits and the relationship between the one and the multiple in a concrete manner. In animals with large brains the numerous elements which constitute psychism are loosely combined and the animal spirit or soul is unstable. It is weak and disappears with the animal because as a principle of union it is not sufficiently centered or knit together. In man, the spirit or principle of union has centered on itself (concentrated on one point); thus the human spirit can survive the death of the body. In such a state it survives as an incomplete principle or unitive force separated from the united whole. Even under these circumstances, however, the human soul retains its solidarity with the multiple which genetically and potentially never ceases to persist in it.[16]

39

The being which is more perfect and more conscious is so because in it more elements are more completely united. Animation is proportionate to union. Nevertheless, consciousness is not merely the result of material elements brought into mutual harmony. The growth in being represents something completely new, a recasting and formation of a new substance formed by a new principle of union. Creation occurs by an act of uniting. The emphasis is not on the *multiple,* but on the *union.* Quality is born of quantity, but is higher than it. It is not the multiple that makes a reality more conscious or spiritual, but rather the union that reduces the multiple to one whole. In speaking of the principle of any union Teilhard maintains that to be more is to unite more, and he frequently re-affirms that the one is not composed of the multiple, but that the one appears in its wake and dominates it because the essential act of the One (or of Spirit) is to unite. He recognizes very concretely the activity of unitive principles, but also acknowledges that in either case, whether receiving or communicating increased union, the creative influence of God, who creates by uniting, is present. He also makes it clear that "to be" ought not to be regarded as interiorly definable by "to unite," but that the notions of being and union be regarded as a natural couple of which the two terms are inseparable and simultaneously variable in the same sense. Their relationship varies, therefore, from the natural couples spirit-matter or unity-plurality in which the associated terms vary inversely.[17] Once again we can see that in this analysis of "coupled entities" in metaphysics the concern is with overcoming dualisms while at the same time recognizing the distinct identity of the elements; matter and spirit do not exist in mutual opposition to each other nor can they be fused.

The significance of the matter-spirit relationship proposed above and its consequences for understanding human action and determining moral values can be seen from a brief exposition of what Teilhard called the matter-spirit slope. The concept of such a slope is perfectly consistent with not only the fundamental evolutionary law of complexity-consciousness, but also with the detailed metaphysical analysis of spirit-matter. Matter is a slope on which all men are situated at a specific point determined by time, place and personal vocation. Man, of course, must climb toward fuller spirit; but matter is not an obstacle which hinders him; it provides footholds, nourishment, intermediaries to be used as well as that which can be purified and made part of him. From this point of view matter is divided into two zones; that which has already been traversed and to which man must not return and that which is still open to his renewed efforts and progress. The border between these two zones is relative and shifting. Every man must pass through the lower levels on the slope; nothing can attain spirit except by moving along a determined road through matter. No position on the slope is purely material, not even the zone described as "carnal." The roots of spirit extend down to the very depths of the slope. Man's relation to the material world is always relative; what can be misleading for one man (a descent toward the carnal) may be spiritual and elevating for someone who is less spiritually developed.[18]

Man is embedded necessarily in the material universe through which he deliberately evolves toward ever greater consciousness or spirit. When he turns to matter in the "material" sense he is turning toward dispersion and disunity and away from greater psychic concentration. Although we have not progressed far enough in our vision to set forth a foundation for morality, it is evident from the above that in this view of reality the moral is connected with the process of spiritualization. It is also evident that in this context it is inadequate to label a particular physical action and to say that it is always gravely reprehensible or highly virtuous from a moral point of view. Such an oversimplified ethical stance ignores the differences in the degree of spiritualization of different persons and the differences within an individual person at various stages of his development. It also fails to relate moral culpability and the degree of one's personal development at any one stage of his life.

Reflection on the matter-spirit slope leads one, therefore, to see the inadequacy of attempting to establish universal categories classifying acts as always sinful or virtuous when considering physical acts alone apart from the circumstances and persons performing them. Without going further afield by discussing other ethical consequences of the matter-spirit slope, we can see the merit in the way Teilhard describes the *correlation* between a being's complexity and its degree of consciousness, that is, between its matter and spirit. His analysis is not reduced to merely pointing out what each designates or their mere functions. He goes beyond that level of precision and examines and correlates their activity in such a way as to qualify the evolutionary process as a whole and to imply many far-reaching consequences for human life and behaviour. That is, he goes much beyond merely indicating the functional type of order given to natural events by spirit and matter, the point at which many scholars terminate their discussion of this topic.

From what we have seen above it is accurate to say that Teilhard de-objectifies matter and spirit in the sense of denying them separate existences. He does this in such a way, however, that he is still able to conceive of them in ontological terms. He does not deny the existence of spirit-matter nor become involved in a reductionistic approach as does John Dewey who rejects any internal, vital, principle in things known as spirit and defines matter as a character of natural events. Teilhard also succeeds in making spirit-matter relational and processive; they are neither isolated from each other nor do they exist independently of the evolutionary process. At this point we conclude our analysis of the interaction between the material and psychic faces of reality, and find ourselves at a good point from which to begin to discuss the inanimate and animate within nature, namely, the balance between emphasis on things as existences and as events.

III. *The Non-Living and Living Within Nature*
A. *Things as Beings and as Events*

Before attempting to analyze life and the appearance of both life and man in an evolutionary world view it is necessary to say a few words about things as beings and as events. This is a point at which there is need of further development in Teilhard's thought. His strength is in his precise analysis of things as beings with an interiority or animate principle. Although it is quite compatible with his entire approach to reality as evolutionary, Teilhard does not emphasize things as events. He recognizes that a thing is its history, which in effect is to say that it is an event; but a more explicit emphasis on existences as events would create a better balance between things as beings and as events and overcome any connotation that the word "being" implies something static. In brief, it would make it more clear that one does not have to shy away from recognizing the metaphysical in order to acknowledge the processive. A being is an event.

The modified thought of John Dewey on this topic will flesh out Teilhard's thought and enrich the vision we are presenting. Although our object is not to contrast the men's thought, preceding for a short time in such a way as to enable the reader to observe the differences in their positions will help him to recognize the force of not only Teilhard's thought, but of the combined views being presented.

In order to get away from describing reality in terms of independent substances which are complete in themselves and not radically dependent upon their relations with other things, Dewey rarely puts emphasis on an individual existence apart from its interaction and relations with other individuals and its environing conditions. Nor does he discuss the interaction within the individual existence nor the organization of its elements with any frequency. The emphasis is always on a field of interaction and on events and functions rather than on existences. For him substance expresses function not being

43

or principle of being; and structure is a character of events not something belonging to an individual existence, something intrinsic or *per se*. This amounts to an outright rejection of "substance" in the traditional philosophical sense. Nature does not consist of substances but of *events*. A mountain is not a permanent or unchanging thing but an event or history which has a birth, growth and decay. Nature is characterized by histories not by beings which exist independently of the evolutionary process. Certainly Dewey does not deny the existence of beings with such things as physical limits which mark them off from other beings, but this is not the basis of individuality. He constantly reacts against a conception which establishes a being in existence *first* and then conceives it as entering into relation with other beings. Beings are primarily in process and relational, where relation denotes

> . . . something direct and active, something dynamic and energetic. It fixes attention upon the way things bear upon one another, their clashes and unitings, the way they fulfill and frustrate, promote and retard, excite and inhibit one another.[19]

It must not be thought that relations are things in an ontological sense according to Dewey; they are not. But then they will not be regarded as ontological in the world view being presented, although it will be emphasized that modifications in relations among beings effect ontological change in those beings. This, however, is a small point. The point of major concern here is that Dewey does not have to reject the concept of substance nor take all the emphasis off things as beings in order to maintain that all things are events and that they are radically relational and processive. Teilhard also reacts against a conception which establishes a being in existence first and then conceives it as entering into relations with other things. And the present author will emphasize defining creation in terms of God bringing things into relation with Himself and other things in order to safeguard the same point.

Beings do not come into existence, grow and decay apart from the evolutionary process, and Dewey's almost total de-emphasis on beings as existences weakens the degree of precision with which he was able to pinpoint the direction of the evolutionary process. On the other hand, the insufficient emphasis on beings as events in Teilhard's thought enables his readers to conceive of interaction in his process as occurring only within beings. There is not sufficient explanation of the fact that the law of complexity-consciousness necessarily implies a great deal of interaction between the being and its environment. Balancing being and event can overcome this shortcoming.

A further word about the role of interaction in Teilhard's thought will be of assistance if presented now before ideas on life are set forth. All interaction to be found in evolution must occur in accord with and in terms of the law of complexity-consciousness. According to it, as we have already seen, the being which is more fully evolved is more conscious, and is so because in it more elements are more completely united. Material complexity is in proportion to interior centering, but the multiple does not make the being more conscious or spiritual. It is the *union* which reduces the multiple to a whole and thus effects a change or evolution. Animation is in proportion to union, and every growth in being is a recasting; a new principle of union forms a new substance. To be more is to unite more and to be more fully united.

At this point the emphasis on union or centering in Teilhard's thought is on the union of the elements *composing beings themselves*. In the process just described above, recognizing both radial and tangential energy and acknowledging the former as primary and the source of consistency ensures interaction. Tangential energy is brought forth through the interaction of various centers of consciousness. An increase in energy is always associated with increased arrangement, and therefore with interaction. Uniting is a specific form of interaction.

In analyzing socialization in terms of complexity-consciousness the interacting foci became the consciousnesses of all men and the material complexity of their social, industrial and cultural milieu. All beings are, in fact, centers of interaction, the scope of their respective fields of interaction being in proportion to the degree of internal centering or stability of their centers. In brief, the whole law of complexity-consciousness by which evolution progresses is entirely based on interaction and the more complex organization and centering which accompany it.

There is no doubt, therefore, that there is a great deal of emphasis on interaction *within beings* and also *among men* in society once evolution has reached the stage of occurring through socialization. The problem with Teilhard's thought in this area is that he does not explicitly show that throughout the entire process the law of complexity-consciousness necessarily implies an immense amount of interaction between beings and their environments. The proportionate increases in consciousness and material complexity of beings does not occur in a vacuum, but is absolutely dependent upon their interaction with their environing conditions. Thus *external relations and interactions* of all beings, and especially of men, with their environment should be stressed more in Teilhard's thought. If this were done it would reduce the danger of his process and even his entire world view appearing to be overly anthropocentric. Many scholars have criticized Teilhard for centering all things on man and for not stressing the fact that man's evolution occurs only in proportion as he develops the universe along with himself. In fact, man is not the center of the universe but the leading shoot of the cosmic process and the responsible agent of evolution. The consequences of these points regarding the over-all relevance of this vision for today and what it can say to man regarding his responsibilities in the area of ecology will be pointed out later. At present it is sufficient to warn the reader in advance of all the forms of interaction taking place in the description of the appearance of life which is to follow.

B. *The Appearance of Life*

The appearance of life and man are two major critical points in the evolutionary process. A brief examination of the former will be helpful in the subsequent examination of man and his place in evolution because man, the highest form of life in the world, cannot be situated in the universe accurately until an adequate perspective regarding life is attained. Teilhard rejects the thought of those scholars who, while affirming that they are seeking for a coherent view of the whole universe, maintain that life is an epiphenomenon of matter. In reality, there is no opposition between physics (the study of matter) and biology (the study of life); they complement one another. The biological must be naturally incorporated in the physical if coherence in the universe is to be had. Thus he recognizes in life an expression of one of the most fundamental and significant movements in the world. "Life, . . . , appears experimentally to science as a *material effect of complexity.*"[20] In other words, it represents a directed combination of properties which appeared and continued to develop in function of the physico-chemical complexity arising from the material organization of groupings of molecules.[21]

The appearance of life is accounted for by Teilhard in terms of the relation of the "within" and "without" of things and the universal law of complexity-consciousness. The question at issue in its appearance is how to regard the change or jump from the pre-consciousness of pre-life to the consciousness of the first living creature. In principle such a jump between two forms of consciousness is conceivable because there are many ways in which something can have a "within." An irregular closed surface can become centered; a circle can become a sphere. The thing may undergo a re-arrangement of its parts or acquire a new dimension so that its "within" varies to the point where it suddenly rises to a new level. This critical change in the arrangement of the elements automatically induces a change of nature in the state of consciousness of the particles involved. In accord with these principles Teilhard says that at the appearance of life there was an external realization of a new type of corpuscular grouping which allowed for a superior organization of an unlimited number of substances and at the same time an internal beginning of a new type of conscious activity and determination. This is what is original in the metamorphosis from molecule to cell, or from pre-life to life.[22]

It is the same insistence on coherence and on continuity which led Teilhard to develop the concept of a biosphere and to deny that it is restricted to the peripheral surface of the earth to which life is confined. For him the biosphere is the whole skin of organic substance which envelops the earth, a structural layer of the earth. When regarded in this manner the concept of biosphere enables us to see the bond which unites biology, physics and astronomy in one cosmic dynamism.[23] This one cosmic dynamism, which is that of life, manifests itself as a universal current opposed to the current of entropy.[24] Precisely because it opposes entropy the current of life advances in what would appear to be the direction of the improbable, that is, in an ascent toward increased consciousness, greater freedom, inventiveness, thought and more complex organic constructions.[25]

Many scholars have criticized Teilhard's vision for being unrealistically idealistic. And there is no doubt that the reality the physicists call entropy as well as the forces causing deterioration and regression introduced into the world through man's failure to commit himself to the pursuit of growth must be given serious consideration and combatted if evolution is to continue. We shall not attempt to discuss human failure at this point, but one can certainly defend Teilhard's handling

of the reality of entropy. In fact, his analysis of the evolutionary process enables him to cope with it more effectively than
does the thought of other process thinkers. The recognition
of both tangential energy which moves elements to unite with
others on the same level and radial energy which is the driving
or attractive force moving units forward toward greater complexity and centricity provides a very firm foundation on which
to establish a movement counteracting entropy. This vision is
able to consider entropy in its full seriousness and to describe
the evolutionary movement (complexity-consciousness) which
counteracts it effectively because it recognizes an *internal
dynamism in things.*

The current of life in this vision is, therefore, equivalent
to the current of spirit. If we concentrate on the current of
spirit as opposed to that of entropy (on the "within" and not
the "without" of things) it is possible to see that on the level
of living beings evolution has a *set direction.* Among all the
different modes of life it is the *differentiation of nervous tissue*
or the development of brain which is outstanding. The brain
is constantly perfecting itself with time so that a given quality
of brain is linked with a given phase of duration. The degree
of cerebralization is not only the sign but also the measure
of consciousness; looked at from this perspective an order is
given to the whole process of evolution among living things.
Furthermore, as evolution moves toward increased life and
spirit, chance, which appeared to govern the formation of the
complexes on the level of pre-life, plays a lesser and lesser
role so that after the appearance of reflection with the coming
of man it is the psychic which predominates in the individual.[26]

It may be that some readers may find the analysis of the
move from the inanimate to the animate described above to
be extraordinary and untenable. No full scale defense of it
will be made at this time, but by way of both comparison and
contrast it is enlightening to see how Dewey analyzes this
movement.[27] He does not accept that matter, life and mind
represent kinds or levels of beings or existence; the non-living,

living and human represent fields of interaction or fields of related events. These three plateaus of such fields are interpreted in terms of natural events and specific functions or interactions. He states that life appeared at a point in the development of natural affairs when fields of interaction which had not been linked together became interrelated but does not indicate specifically or in depth why or how this came about. Nevertheless, new properties appeared, new ways of acting occurred and new energies were released. The new and more complex field of activities designated as life is characterized specifically by new organization and all it implies. The appearance of life does not merely entail the addition of the psychic to the physico-chemical. The major difference is effected by *the way* the energies are interconnected and operate. Thus the living being, because it has *entirely new properties,* is able to achieve a *new kind of interaction and support* from its environment.

The three plateaus of interacting events are distinguished, therefore, by way of different degrees of *increasing complexity* and *intimacy of interaction* among the elements or natural events involved. The similarity here with the law of complexity-consciousness is striking; and it is also worth noting that both authors place great emphasis not only on the continuity between the non-living and living, but also on the discontinuity. Something entirely new appears — according to Dewey new energies and new interactions, according to Teilhard, a transformation. He sees a change of nature in the state of consciousness of the particles involved; this entails both a superior grouping of an unlimited number of elements and an internal beginning of a new type of conscious activity and determination.

Although we may not agree with Dewey that "life is a character of events in a peculiar condition of organization,"[28] we can agree that *as an empirical affair* living is not restricted within the physical limits of the organism. It involves connection and interaction between what is within and outside

50

of the organism in space and time.[29] In one sense, "life" and "history" ultimately have the same fullness of meaning; and "life" may denote a function or comprehensive activity including both organism and environment. This can be analyzed into external conditions and internal structures, but the integral reality includes both. When used in an even broader sense to denote the whole range of human experience, "life" includes such things as customs, institutions, beliefs and occupations.[30]

As long as an organism endures it attempts to use the surrounding energies as means of furthering its own life; the return it gets for this activity is growth. Life, therefore, is a process of self-renewal through action on the environment. This process cannot be kept up indefinitely, and life (as a physical thing) must end; the continuity of the life process is not dependent on the continued existence of any one individual. Not only individuals, but even whole species die out; nevertheless the life process continues in more and more complex forms. New species appear. There is a continual re-adaptation of the environment to the needs of living organisms and so continuity of life is maintained.[31]

In the light of our earlier statement regarding the interaction between a being and its environment which is implied in Teilhard's law of complexity-consciousness the compatibility of this empirical analysis of living and growth within our present vision is evident. It not only has the advantage of showing man how dependent he is on his environment, it also highlights man's responsibility for acting on or interacting with his environing conditions in such a way as to not merely consume, but also develop them. The very clear statement of life's radical dependence on such interaction makes this a moral imperative.

Having set forth the basic laws promoting the whole evolutionary process, discussed the spirit-matter relationship and analyzed the non-living and living, we are in a position to approach the next major critical point of transformation in the evolutionary process, the appearance of man. We wish to develop this in somewhat more detail and to demonstrate that man is within nature. At the same time we also want to show that the evolutionary principles being set forth here are compatible with a christian concept of creation by God. Thus we shall devote a separate chapter to these matters.

FOOTNOTES

1. *PH*, n. 1, p. 53 [Eng. trans. n. 1, p. 57].
2. *PH*, p. 62 [Eng. trans. p. 64]; "L'Activation de l'énergie humaine," *AÉ*, p. 416 [Eng. trans. p. 393].
3. "Les Singularités de l'espèce humaine, . . . ," *AppH*, p. 363, n. 1, p. 363 [Eng. trans. p. 265, n. 1, p. 265].
4. "La Structure phylètique du groupe humain," *AppH*, p. 195 [Eng. trans. p. 139].
5. *PHN*, pp. 28-30 [Eng. trans. pp. 19-21]; "La Place de l'homme dans l'univers: Réflexions sur la complexité," *VP*, pp. 312-13 [Eng. trans. p. 222]. In "Agitation ou genèse?," *AH*, n. 1, pp. 279-80 [Eng. trans. p. 217), Teilhard distinguishes, in a somewhat similar manner, between a "coiling" or "in-folding" of mass which does not organize it and a real coiling of complexity.
6. *PH*, pp. 54-58 [Eng. trans. pp. 58-62]; *PH*, Résumé, pp. 334-35 [Eng. trans. pp. 301-03]; "L'Atomisme de l'esprit," *AÉ*, pp. 36-39 [Eng. trans. pp. 30-32]; *PHN*, pp. 68-69 [Eng. trans. pp. 47-48].
7. *PH*, pp. 241-43 [Eng. trans. p. 218-19]; "Comment se pose aujourd'hui la question du transformisme," *VP*, p. 39 [Eng. trans. p. 25]; "Les Fondements et le fond de l'idée d'évolution," *VP*, p. 191 [Eng. trans. p. 137]; "Que fait-il penser du transformisme?," *VP*, pp. 214-15 [Eng. trans. p. 152]. See also: "L'Histoire naturelle du monde," *VP*, pp. 146-48 [Eng. trans. pp. 103-05].
8. "Comment se pose aujourd'hui la question du transformisme," *VP*, p. 39 [Eng. trans. p. 25].
9. "Que fait-il penser du transformisme?," *VP*, p. 223 [Eng. trans. p. 159]. See also: "Les Fondements et le fond de l'idée d'évolution," *VP*, pp. 186-96 [Eng. trans. pp. 133-41], where Teilhard shows that transformism can lead man to a higher spirituality and morality.
10. *PH*, p. 78 [Eng. trans. p. 78].
11. "Le Coeur de la matière," August 15, 1950 (unpublished mimeographed manuscript, p. 9); "La Centrologie," *AÉ*, p. 131-32 [Eng. trans. pp. 124-25].
12. "La Centrologie," *AÉ*, p. 132 [Eng. trans. p. 125]; "Mon Univers," *SC*, pp. 77-81 [Eng. trans. pp 49-53]; Pierre Teilhard de Chardin, "Esquisse d'un univers personnel," *L'Énergie humaine* (Paris: Éditions du Seuil, 1962), pp. 73-75 [Eng. trans. pp. 57-59], hereafter cited *ÉH*.
13. "Le Phénomène spirituel," *ÉH*, pp. 121-23 [Eng. trans. pp. 96-98]; "Le Coeur de la matière," (unpublished mimeographed manuscript, p. 17).
14. "La Vie cosmique," *ÉTG*, pp. 10-13 [Eng. trans. pp. 19-20]; "Science et Christ ou analyse et synthèse," *SC*, pp. 55-57 [Eng. trans.

pp. 29-31]; "Mon Univers," SC, pp. 77-79 [Eng. trans. pp. 49-51].

15. "Mon Univers," SC, p. 72 [Eng. trans. p. 44].

16. "L'Union créatrice," ÉTG, pp. 178-79 [Eng. trans. pp. 156-57].

17. "L'Union créatrice," ÉTG, pp. 177-78, 188 [Eng. trans. pp. 155-56, 166]; "Mon Univers," SC, pp. 73-74 [Eng. trans. p. 45]; Pierre Teilhard de Chardin, "Comment je vois," August 26, 1948 (unpublished mimeographed manuscript, pp. 23-24).

18. Pierre Teilhard de Chardin, Le Milieu divin: Essai de vie interieure (Paris: Éditions du Seuil, 1957), pp. 124-26 [Eng. trans. pp. 107-08]; "Mon Univers," SC, p. 105 [Eng. trans. pp. 76-77]. For a further examination of Teilhard's treatment of matter see: "Les Noms de la matière," ÉTG, especially pp. 423-30.

19. John Dewey, Art as Experience (New York: G. P. Putnam's Sons, 1958), p. 134.

20. PHN, p. 28 [Eng. trans. p. 19].

21. "Comment je vois," (unpublished mimeographed manuscript, p. 2).

22. PH, pp. 90-92 [Eng. trans. pp. 88-90].

23. PH, p. 57 [Eng. trans. p. 40].

24. "Entropy, as is known, is the name that physics gives to that apparently inevitable fall by which collections of corpuscles (the scene of all physico-chemical phenomena) slide, by virtue of statistical laws of probability, towards an intermediate state of diffuse agitation, a state in which all exchange of useful energy ceases on our scale of experience. Everything around us seems to be descending towards this death of matter; everything except life." "Les Mouvements de la vie," VP, p. 209 [Eng. trans. p. 149].

25. LV, Letter of January 19, 1929, p. 118 [Eng. trans. p. 151]; "Les Mouvements de la vie," VP, pp. 209-10 [Eng. trans. pp. 149-50]; "Le Phénomène humain," SC, pp. 125-26 [Eng. trans. pp. 94-95].

26. PH, pp. 154-59 [Eng. trans. pp. 142-46]; PHN, pp. 155-56 [Eng. trans. p. 108]. See also: "L'Union créatrice," ÉTG, pp. 176-77 [Eng. trans. pp. 154-55].

27. For an analysis of Dewey's most enlightening texts on this subject see: Experience and Nature, pp. 8-9, 253-63, 271-73, 284-86; Democracy and Education (New York: The Free Press, 1966), pp. 1-2.

28. Experience and Nature, p. 258.

29. Experience and Nature, p. 282.

30. Experience and Nature, pp. 8-9; Democracy and Education, p. 2.

31. Democracy and Education, pp. 1-2.

CHAPTER 3

MAN IN THE EVOLUTIONARY PROCESS

I. *The Appearance of Man*

The study of the appearance of man and of his development is a study to be made within, and as an application of, a study of life. The appearance of man is not of partial or local significance; man descended from the *total* effort or current of life and is the point on which cosmic energy coiled in on itself and converged, the most advanced point on the principal axis of evolution.[1] Because Teilhard regards life as an ascent toward ever greater consciousness, he can see that life could not continue uniting indefinitely on the level of animal psychism without being compelled to reach a critical point where it had to transform itself in depth in order to remain itself. The jump from the level of instinct to that of reflection or thought is not merely a matter of a change of degree of consciousness, but a change of state brought about by the organic laws of the whole evolutionary movement of life.[2]

Once again we see the importance of Teilhard's notion that as the material complexity and consciousness of a thing interact with each other the process involves a coiling in, a centering, and not a dispersion or fragmentation. Thus once again the converging nature of the whole process leads to a critical point which, within the over-all continuity, effects a new beginning. The law of transformism stresses that the universe is one organic whole of which the parts are physically linked both in appearance and destiny, and when applied specifically to the appearance of man, affirms that all the stages of evolution prior to him imply the appearance of thought. Life in man is a renewal or modification of life prior to his existence, but not an entirely new life. Cosmic embryogenesis, which affirms that a new being has antecedents which condition its appearance, can be applied to man and yet he can be given an historical birth.

Teilhard describes the transformation which occurred at the appearance of man by using analogies taken from the physical state of bodies and the development of geometrical figures. As he says, he uses these remote comparisons to help us imagine the mechanism involved at this critical threshold of reflection.[3] When the anthropoid had been brought to boiling point mentally, some more heat was applied; or, using the analogy of the cone, when the anthropoid had almost reached the summit a final effort along the axis occurred. In either case this addition was sufficient to upset the whole inner equilibrium. What had previously been a centered surface became a center. Because of a small "tangential" increase the "radial" was turned back on itself and this coiling resulted in an infinite leap forward. The external remained almost unchanged but an internal revolution occurred in the level of consciousness of life on earth — the level of reflection was attained for the first time.[4]

By means of these analogies Teilhard is not only able to stress the discontinuity, but also the continuity in hominization; discontinuity does not mean a break in the evolutionary movement. The renewal of life which occurred at the appearance of man does not mean there is an *entirely* new life in him. Man is an hereditary organism who carries in himself many qualities and capacities which were developed throughout the whole earlier course of evolution, capacities which he has inherited as a primate. Yet even when looking at man as a zoological group it is necessary to recognize

that these inclinations and capacities have undergone a transformation or metamorphosis as they crossed the threshold of
reflection. Speaking of each of these capacities on entering man
Teilhard says:

> Beyond this point it is enriched by new possibilities,
> new colours, new fertility. It is the same thing, if you
> like, but it is something quite different also — a figure
> that has become transformed by a change of space
> and dimension, discontinuity superimposed upon con-
> tinuity, mutation upon evolution.[5]

The transfiguration of the vital capacities which man inherited
shows us that when an organism begins to grow in one of
its accessory parts it is thrown out of equilibrium and becomes
deformed. To maintain its beauty or integrity it must be
modified simultaneously throughout along the direction of one
of its principal axes. Reflection reshapes but conserves all the
lines of the phylum in which it develops. As man continues
to evolve all the capacities and inclinations inherited by him
continue to be enriched beyond the original level attained at
hominization. Teilhard also refers to the progressive elabora-
tion of these capacities as hominization so that we see two
distinct meanings for the term. It not only applies to the individual instantaneous jump from instinct to thought, but also
to the progressive phyletic spiritualization in human civilization of all the forces which compose the animal world.[6]
This second meaning of hominization will be examined later;
at the moment it is necessary to delve more deeply into the
transition from instinct to thought. Before attaining the threshold of reflection the individual living being was not wholly
centered; rather it was spread out and divided over a varied
circle of perceptions and activities. It was not completely individualized. At the first moment of reflection the individual
was constituted as a center in the form of a point at which
all its perceptions and experiences converged to form one

unity which was conscious of its own organization. Stated otherwise, reflection is the power a consciousness has acquired to turn in upon itself, to take control or possession of itself as an object with its own consistence and value. The being who has attained the power of reflection not only knows but knows himself and knows that he knows. Consciousness has coiled back upon itself to become thought and there are many consequences of this; the appearance of reflection introduced into the world for the first time the ability to carry out abstraction, reasoned choice, invention, logic, calculation of space and time and the capacity to experience feelings of anxiety and love. Furthermore because man's intelligence is able to universalize and foresee, the species man tends to become co-extensive with the earth, that is, to planetize itself.[7]

In the above we see a successful effort to achieve a balance recognizing what is unique in man while at the same time stressing his continuity with nature. The difference between man and animals has been safeguarded by recognizing that when there was a modification in the nervous system of the more advanced mammals, causing growth in the direction of reflection, this also effected a loss of equilibrium in them so that a more radical modification of their whole being along the direction of this axis of growth occurred. There is, therefore, a *qualitative* change at that critical point of transformation. At the threshold of reflection there was a re-shaping, but also a conservation of all the lines of the phylum from which reflection had sprung. These capacities were retained and continued to develop in man. Discontinuity occurred, but within an over-all context of continuity, so that a sudden jump or rupture between the organic and the intellectual was avoided. The mental, therefore, is not regarded as a mysterious intrusion in nature nor as an epiphenomenon of it.

Intimately related to the power of reflection is the capacity of the whole human species to overcome the tendency of the lower forms of animal life to spread out and *sub-divide* into sub-species. Mankind *remains one* and as such is able to spread over the whole universe (planetize itself) while at the same time retaining various racial and cultural groupings which complement one another. In Teilhard's thought mankind can do this because it is able to coil in on itself or center itself on itself in a more total manner than any lower species. We have already seen that throughout the entire process critical points of transformation are reached because all the stuff of the universe coils in upon itself. With the appearance of reflection (man) the perfection of this process of coiling in is achieved; and since in this perfect form it is intimately connected with the power of reflection (it is possible only because man not only knows himself, but knows that he knows), Teilhard refers to this phenomenon as reflexion.[8] He also shows that the rise to the level of reflection introduced a new layer above the biosphere, a new continuous layer of thought surrounding the universe which he named the noosphere.

If we take a moment now to review the connections between the concept of reflexion and the laws of cerebralization and complexity-consciousness, we shall see that there are significant consequences resulting from these intimate connections. The distinction between the psychism or spirit of the animal and man was made on the basis of their respective degrees of cerebralization. The animal has a large brain with many loosely combined elements so that its psychic organization is weak and unstable. Because its psychic interior is not wholly centered it is not completely individualized. At the moment of reflection the individual person is constituted as a center who is conscious of his own organization; man is *wholly centered or completely individualized.* His principle of union has centered on itself, and this is accompanied by a simplification or unification of the elements which compose his brain.

The concept of the psychic interior centering on itself at the threshold of reflection not only justifies but demands the presence of an interior principle of union or spirit in man. Man's spirit has something in common with the animal's vital principle, but yet is distinct and vastly superior to it; man's spirit enables him to transcend sense experience. John Dewey and many other naturalists have denied that man possesses a spirit or soul in the traditional sense of a principle which transcends the material. For Dewey a subsistent, ontological spirit must be an independently existing reality which necessarily implies a separation of man from nature and his fellow man. Thus it degrades individuality by separating man from nature and from things experienced so that his relationship to them is either mechanical or miraculous.

We reject the naturalist's position and maintain along with Teilhard that without in any way downgrading the continuity of man with nature (a value which the naturalists foster and cherish) it is essential that we recognize in man the existence of a spirit or principle of unity and activity arising within the evolutionary process. In fact, instead of degrading individuality, the complete centering of the vital principle on itself at the appearance of reflection causes the complete individualizing of man and lays a foundation on which one can develop a complete theory of the person. Throughout his philosophy Dewey shied away from examining the interior of things and placed almost exclusive emphasis on their relations or interaction with other things. And as Robert J. Roth pointed out this became a weakness on the level of the human person. Interaction itself became objectified and regarded as outside the persons interacting, and there was a fear in Dewey of entering the self due to the danger of becoming subjective.[9] In the more balanced view we are presenting we have recognized a twofold interaction, or more precisely, a combined interaction which occurs not only within the organism itself but also between it and its environment. We have also acknowledged that for mankind to be whole it must not only appear as part of the cosmic current of life (that is, within nature), but he must also possess an inner spirit which enables him to transcend sense experience.

There are other consequences of the intimate connection

between the laws of cerebralization and complexity-consciousness and the concept of reflexion. The formulation of the law of cerebralization and its relation to the law of complexity-consciousness adds weight to Teilhard's observation that on the empirical level the theory of evolution shows that the more spiritual succeeds the less spiritual. Thus it also adds weight to the affirmation that the current of life or of evolution is a current with a direction, a current of increasing spiritualization. And finally, as we shall see later, the relation of the law of cerebralization to that of complexity-consciousness and to the process of reflexion enables Teilhard to recognize socialization as an organic process which is really an extension of the process of individual cerebralization.

In the above analysis we have obtained considerable insight into the appearance of man from a phenomenological-philosophical perspective, but we have insisted that we are setting forth a vision of reality for North American christians. There is no doubt, therefore, that something must be said to indicate that such a perspective is compatible with the judaeo-christian conception of creation by God *ex nihilo*. Therefore, before continuing further to discuss man's intimate connection with nature we shall discuss the problem of creation.

II. *An Evolutionary Perspective of Creation*

It is quite beyond the scope of this work to do a detailed exegesis of the two accounts of creation found in Genesis 1-2. To do so would be merely to duplicate part of a vast body of literature which has had wide circulation for a number of years. Thus we shall merely make a summary statement of the position found acceptable by virtually all serious scripture scholars to-day of both Jewish and christian persuasion. None but a few strict fundamentalists will find it problematic or opposed to faith. In fact, one does not have to look far to find official statements acknowledging its compatibility with strict orthodoxy made by the authoritative teaching bodies of most christian denominations which have such organs.

The creation narratives fall under the literary genre of reconstructed myth or religious pre-history. The sacred authors were not scientific experts but knew only the popular cosmology and science of their day. They knew nothing of a concept of evolution, and if asked about it would probably, on the basis of personal opinion, have denied its validity. The point at issue is that they had neither revealed knowledge nor expert scientific knowledge of the *details of how God created* either the universe or man. The two narratives are obviously written from within different literary traditions and stress different points; nevertheless, the purpose of both accounts is to teach the faith of the Hebrew people in the fact that in the beginning God created everything from nothing and that his creation is good.

The author of the second narrative describes God in very anthropocentric terms. He is a potter molding man of clay. A brief analysis of the brilliant literary image of Eve being cast from the rib of Adam reveals that its purpose is to teach the equality of the sexes, the dignity of woman. The image culminates in the teaching that man must leave his parents and cling to his wife with whom he is one flesh. Undoubtedly the text must be understood in the context of the Hebrew's encounter with the Canaanite fertility cults. At any rate there is absolutely no basis on which to maintain that the *details* of this creative act are a matter of revealed faith. The details of the act of creation are beyond the teaching purpose of the sacred authors. There is no way, therefore, that we can turn to the texts of Genesis 1-2 to either condemn or support a theory of evolution. The Bible says nothing on that topic.

The christian theologian starts from the belief that God's original act of creation (the details of which he does not know) was an act of creating *ex nihilo*. He can examine the various theories of evolution to see if they are compatible with his belief in such an act by God. But he cannot automatically exclude the possibility of evolution on the grounds of its incompatibility with the judaeo-christian faith as presented in Genesis 1-2. He is confronted with the constant challenge to gain deeper insight into his faith, interpret the scriptures and relate the knowledge of faith with secular insights into reality.

It is not an over-simplification to state that the traditional concept of creation was that of an all powerful God who through an instantaneous action brought beings into existence in a mature state. Although it was presupposed that God in some way planned for a compatible relationship among newly created beings, other creatures and the environment, there was no explicit reference to the relational aspect of all reality in the teaching on creation itself. There was emphasis on neither the dependence of creatures on each other in their respective processes of development nor explicit reference to preparing matter for the vital principles of beings (other than slight reference to God preparing matter to receive a human soul). The divine activity was conceived as occurring in two stages; after the instantaneous act of creating came the prolonged act of preserving or conserving beings in existence.

Even apart from the type of processive world view being presented here the inadequacies of the traditional view of creation are becoming more and more evident. And since christians have begun to experience reality as processive and to achieve a richer appreciation of the dignity of matter and its intimate connection with spirit such an approach to creation has become inadequate to the point of being untenable.

Throughout his works Teilhard presents an evolutionary approach to creation which overcomes the weaknesses of the traditional view while at the same time being compatible with traditional doctrine. After recognizing an initial act by which God created matter in its most dispersed state *ex nihilo*, creation ought not to be conceived as an instantaneous act performed by God alone, but as a process or controlled movement of synthesis involving the intimately coordinated effort of both God and created beings acting as secondary causes. Creation covers the entire process of cosmogenesis and takes the form of a creative transition or transformation from a state of initial dispersion to one of ultimate unity and harmony. Teilhard argues that because pure act and non-being are diametrically opposed in the same way as perfected unity and the pure multiple, God (because of His perfections) cannot communicate Himself immediately to creatures but must make them capable of receiving Him. If He is going to give Himself to the plural or to that which is dispersed He must unify it to His own measure. Thus the building up of the *pleroma,* that is, the fullness of the Body of Christ (which includes all of creation, and not just mankind), must occur and be apparent to men by a progressive advance from the fragmented toward the unified — from the dominantly material to the spiritual.[10]

The present author would support this argument by defining creation in terms of the gift by which God brings things into relationship with Himself and the other beings He has created. A creature does not merely exist; it exists in relation to its creator and other creatures as is implied by the words creator and creature themselves. Once the creative activity is seen as a personal act of giving, the laws of personal relationships must be operative in creation even when it is a matter of God giving to the inanimate and to sub-human beings. God can only give to any object to the extent that He prepares it to receive that gift of Himself. If matter is to be prepared to receive animation by a plant, animal or human principle of activity it must be developed or unified so as to be able to receive this gift, and it is most fitting that this preparation take place in time and in relation to specific environing conditions. Thus the concept of creation as an on-going process appears at least initially to be an appropriate one, but let us examine it in more detail.

In creationist language the law of transformism implies that God, as the primal cause, acts directly on the natures of things so that it is less a matter of God making things as it is His making them make themselves. Great emphasis is placed on the traditional role of secondary causes as well as on the divine activity. Teilhard insists that the notion of creative transformation or creation through transformation is more adequate than the Scholastics' notions of creation *and* transformation. When creation is seen from within it has the form of a transformation, and God's creative activity is not restricted to an initial act but is co-extensive throughout the whole duration of the universe. There are not two acts or moments of action, one in which God creates and one in which the secondary causes develop. These actions are fused into one creative action which continuously raises things toward fuller being on the basis of their earlier development and by means of their continued secondary activity. Creation does not involve periodic, instantaneous intrusions of divine activity into the natural; God's activity is co-extensive with the whole in such a way that, seen from within, it takes the form of a process of transformation.[11]

Teilhard illustrates the compatibility of transformism and creation by God in the appearance of man. In a special, free act God decided man was to be the crown of the world. This act of God influenced and pre-organized the entire course of the evolutionary process before man so that, because of this act or choice of God, man appears to be the accomplishment naturally expected by the development of life. All the stages of evolution imply from the beginning the appearance of thought on earth. In such a process each human spirit, whether that of the first man or of his descendents, has been specially and uniquely willed by God and caused to be born by an action geared from the beginning to foster the evolutionary process of the universe.[12]

In the approach being presented here there are beginnings or critical points in the process of evolution, and certainly the appearance of the human spirit is one of these. This approach is not materialistic in the sense that the spiritual is regarded as being educed from the material — the lesser from the greater. On the perceptible level these critical points are not always evident and affirmed by scientists. The creation of the human soul occurs in a manner that is so continuous with the biological development that scientific observation cannot point to any break in that chain of development at the moment of its creation. This does not mean that on the level of phenomenology the universe is given divine attributes. In fact, one is forced to recognize that on this level the further back one looks the further matter is dispersed and the less capable one becomes of observing beginnings. The limits of the phenomenological perspective make it possible for man to see only matter and not God or His activity.[13] Nevertheless, because His activity is not perceptible does not mean that it is not present.

In the over-all process of creation we have seen three specific activities: one in which God creates *ex nihilo,* one in which the potentiality of an existing being is developed through transformations, and a third in which an existing being is used and built up into an entirely new being. All three acts are acts of creation, and the divine activity is operative in all of them, that is, God is active throughout the entire operation of the law of complexity-consciousness.

In an article entitled "Teilhard de Chardin and the Body-Soul Relation,"[14] Joseph Donceel relates Teilhard's thought with that of Karl Rahner on this topic, and in fact, rounds out the thought of the former with that of the latter. The human soul is produced in a manner similar to the appearance of all other new beings in the world in spite of the fact that it is not merely accidentally but essentially different from any other soul or principle of life on earth. God wills and directly creates each human spirit insofar as the act of begetting a child is an act in which the parents transcend themselves. They produce an effect which is beyond their capacity and possible only because the power of God is present rendering their self-transcendence possible. The divine power is immanent in their human causality in act without belonging to the constitutive factors of their essence.[15] In other words, there is one act which phenomenologically appears to be an exclusively human act, and yet the divine and human causality are so intimately connected that the divine causality enables the parents to produce an effect which transcends their human power. This divine causality is operative *in the action* of the parents and effects a result more proportionate with divine power than human power, yet the divine power does not become part of the being of the parents. The parents are not divinized through their procreative activity any more than are the lower levels of being given divine attributes to perform their evolutionary activity.

It is evident from the above that it is possible to reconcile the christian concept of creation with an evolutionary view of even the appearance of man. From the opposite point of view, however, the question arises as to whether the very process of evolution itself is destroyed in any way by the recognition of a Being who transcends it but also acts immanently within it making it evolve itself according to its own natural laws. We can give an immediate positive answer to this question *only if* we define the process within strictly naturalistic limits. But certainly the thought presented here indicates that another concept of evolution, or more specifically, another kind of process in which inherent natural laws are operative and yet the whole operation is dependent upon a transcendent, but also immanent divine activity, is also functional. In fact, this latter type of process appears to achieve more balance and to recognize and maintain the radical difference between the non-living and living, the animal and human within the continuity of the one cosmic current of life more clearly than it can be achieved in a rigidly naturalistic approach to evolution.

Having completed our analysis of the problem of creation we shall continue to discuss man's place in nature. The discussion which follows will undoubtedly tie together many of the main lines of thought in these first three chapters as well as present some more specific ideas on this topic.

III. *Man's Place in Nature*

Because only one vast phenomenon of cosmic evolution can be seen across man's whole range of experience, man himself must see himself experientially as part of this one organic movement. The universe and everything in it is in process so that man's place in nature is not a static position. The present author agrees with Teilhard that what is vital for modern American man is not so much the metaphysical question of knowing "what man is" as the question of gaining empirical evidence as to 1) the movement of man in nature in the past and at present, and 2) being able to determine whether there is something ultra-human, in the framework of time, lying ahead of the human.[16]

Teilhard necessarily objects to the separation of the sciences of man and those of nature. To study man apart from nature is to fall into the error of regarding both life and thought as epiphenomena of matter and to mistake man for the center of the universe rather than for the leading arrow pointing the way to the final unification of the world in terms of life. To study nature apart from man is to fail to see the organic unity, historically and structurally, of the whole process of cosmic evolution and to overlook the pre-eminent significance of man in nature. Once humanity is regarded as an extension of animal life and the highest form that consciousness has attained on earth, a study of humanity sheds much light on the methods and laws of evolution. What is required, therefore, is neither 1) a philosophy of man and sciences of man, and 2) a philosophy of nature and many sciences of nature, but rather 1) a philosophy of man in nature, and 2) sciences which constitute man an organic and pre-eminent part of nature.[17] Teilhard is so insistent on this that he even refers to mankind as "hominized" nature, and states that 'nature' is equivalent to 'becoming.' Everything is the sum of its past; not even the human soul is comprehensible except through its history.[18]

Man is part of one vast *organic* movement and as such is

subject to biological determinisms and limitations. In one of his earlier essays Teilhard presents in a very concrete way the depths of this organic union between man and nature. He describes in a very dramatic but specific way the radiations and influences which penetrate man and limit and mold his activity because he is a part of the one evolutionary current which formed him, a current which he must freely foster.

Man recognizes his solidarity with the one immense process of becoming. Innumerable radiations and influences which penetrate him from outside not only influence him but make him what he is. He can feel the turmoil of the generally well-organized matter beneath his own person and experience its tendency to move toward disorganization. Man realizes that his soul can discipline and complete the activities of this same matter so that a vital force, an aptitude to evolve, results; but even this is never solely his own. In him it is concentrated, yet behind him there is the labour of the infinite succession of beings whose efforts have brought the human phylum to its present stage of perfection. He realizes that ultimately his life is not his own. His dependence on the whole of nature is evident even in what is most spiritual in him. His freedom is a reality, but a reality which represents an imperceptible point among the indeterminate mass of laws and relationships over which he has no absolute control. In him is a law of his own evolution which cannot be suppressed but continues throughout all the stages of his development. This personal driving force is prior to and higher than free will; it is the heritage life has embedded in man's character, in the rhythm of his thoughts and the surge of his passions. It is the evidence in him of the one all-pervading vital current which forms him and of his subjection to the great task of cosmic development which he must forward. Man's contact with nature is so fundamental that it is the cosmos itself which is emerging and being brought to perfection in man as man continues to evolve.[19]

The above exposition is a very clear illustration that man

is both a being-within-nature and a being-in-relation. And, although Teilhard frequently appears to regard nature as a sort of foundation or basis on which man acts, it is evident that he does equate it with the whole process of becoming. Thus man's place is within nature, not vis-à-vis it. Nature is the whole cosmic process and all it entails; that is, the whole continuous process of interaction between man and his environment including the entire past and everything in the future that man can realistically project. Nature is characterized by histories, processes of growth culminating in critical points at which the various levels of beings succeed one another, the earlier ones enabling the later ones to come into existence.

Some of the specific details of John Dewey's thought complete that of Teilhard on this point. He emphasizes the fact that at every new level the vital organization composing the new reality must be an organization of antecedent realities or the living organism would have no natural connections. It would be out of place in its environment and unable to obtain from it even such fundamental necessities as material for nutrition and self-defense. If life and mind had no instrumental dependence on the material, they would have no mechanism and such things as education and deliberate modification and prevention of occurrences would be impossible. Dewey also maintains that *all* man's habits, institutions and ideals are within nature, an integral part of it. He shows that in such a universe human effort can find in nature an ally in the struggle to attain authentic human ideals and goals, whereas a universe conceived by dualistic philosophies cannot provide such an advantage.[20]

In the vision being presented there is no opposition to Dewey's emphasis on the integration and dependence of all human experience on the terrestrial so long as this is not implied to arbitrarily restrict all man's experience to the sensible. The present vision places great stress on the fact that man is a being-within-nature and a being-in-relation. In such a view man, knowledge and the control of change all become part of nature, and nature itself is seen to be an extensive, *human* affair. As well, man's constant relation to and interaction with other persons and the whole of nature and its evolution makes him to be what he is, retains him in his being as man and enables him to evolve and in evolving to cause the whole cosmos to emerge and attain its perfection.

In this perspective it is impossible to situate man complacently at the center of nature as if he were free to use or abuse it at his pleasure. As the leading shoot of the evolutionary process he is at the frontiers of progress, frontiers which he must create for better or for worse. All process is not necessarily progress. When man realizes in a very concrete way that his own progress or self-realization is attained *only* through interaction with his environment in such a way that both he and it attain fulfillment simultaneously, he will come to see that actions which produce benefits for himself at the expense of the environment are not progress, but regression. By the very laws of life and evolution themselves such benefits are necessarily short-lived and their accompanying long-term consequences are disastrous.

It is at least mildly humorous to hear some scholars comment that the needs of Americans have moved beyond the insights of the American naturalistic philosophers. I grant that most scholars working in that tradition today are not surpassing the thought of Dewey, but if we had seriously examined Dewey's writing on man's constitution within nature and the way in which he must respect and interact with it, we might well have avoided the abuses of the past decade and averted the crises we are facing today. In a similar manner it is tragic to hear scholars comment that Teilhard's thought is too idealistic, that he did not foresee that man would abuse nature and use up his resources, and that his whole vision puts too much emphasis on man, placing him in a complacent, self-centered position at the heart of reality which he can dominate as he pleases. None of these accusations are founded.

Both authors present man as the moral agent whose primary

responsibility is to foster the evolution of the whole universe. They emphasize long-term, expansive goals, and present visions which are social and contain many political and economic ramifications. In fact, both men explicitly condemn the economic greed and laissez-faire capitalism which have created our problems regarding resources and ecology. We shall return to this aspect of their thought in subsequent chapters. The major point at issue here, and one which provides an excellent concluding statement for this chapter on man in the evolutionary process, is the fact that Dewey, Teilhard and the present author are presenting a view of nature and of man within it which *by its very structure* forces man to recognize himself as an integral part of the whole current of life, a current on which he depends, but also one which he must direct responsibly if it is to achieve any sort of fulfillment.

FOOTNOTES

1. *PH*, pp. 199-200, 209 [Eng. trans. pp. 181, 189]; "L'Esprit de la terre," *ÉH*, pp. 29-30 [Eng. trans. p. 23]; *PHN*, p. 49 [Eng. trans. pp. 35-36]; "Évolution de l'idée d'évolution," *VP*, pp. 348-49 [Eng. trans. p. 246].

2. *PH*, p. 182 [Eng. trans. p. 166]; "L'Hominisation," *VP*, p. 104 [Eng. trans. p. 73].

3. "When water is heated to boiling point under normal pressure, and one goes on heating it, the first thing that follows — without change of temperature — is a tumultuous expansion of freed and vaporised molecules. Or, taking a series of sections from the base towards the summit of a cone, their area decreases constantly; then suddenly, with another infinitesimal displacement, the surface vanishes leaving us with a *point*. Thus by these remote comparisons we are able to imagine the mechanism involved in the critical threshold of reflection." *PH*, p. 185 [Eng. trans. p. 168].

4. *PH*, pp. 185-86 [Eng. trans. pp. 168-69]. Teilhard insists in a footnote that his explanation is restricted to the phenomenological level (the experimental relations between consciousness and complexity) and says nothing as to metaphysical causes. He also affirms that on a different plane of thought the possibility of a creative operation by the christian God is not excluded. We shall examine this point in more detail.

5. *PH*, p. 198 [Eng. trans. p. 180].

6. *PH*, pp. 198-99 [Eng. trans. p. 180]. For further insight into the discontinuity and continuity in hominization in the first sense, see: "L'Hominisation," *VP*, pp. 93-96 [Eng. trans. pp. 64-66]; "Le Phénomène humain," *VP*, pp. 233-34 [Eng. trans. pp. 166-67]; "L'Esprit de la terre," *ÉH*, pp. 34-35 [Eng. trans. p. 28]; "Les Singularités de l'espèce humaine, . . . ," *AppH*, pp. 298-321 [Eng. trans. pp. 21-30].

7. *PH*, pp. 180-82 [Eng. trans. pp. 164-66]; "Les Singularités de l'espèce humaine, . . . ," *AppH*, pp. 313-15 [Eng. trans. pp. 224-25]; "Le Phénomène humain," *VP*, pp. 227-28 [Eng. trans. p. 161]; "Du Préhumain à l'ultra-humain," *AH*, pp. 381-82 [Eng. trans. p. 293].

8. See the translator's note, *The Future of Man*, trans. by Norman Denny (New York: Harper and Row, 1964), p. 9.

9. Robert J. Roth, *American Religious Philosophy* (New York: Harcourt, Brace and World Inc., 1967), p. 181.

10. Pierre Teilhard de Chardin, "Christologie et Évolution," *Comment je crois* (Paris: Éditions du Seuil, 1969), pp. 101-02, hereafter cited *CJC*. [Eng. trans. entitled *Christianity and Evolution*, trans. by René Hague (New York: Harcourt Brace Jovanovich, Inc., 1971), pp. 82-83].

11. "Comment se pose aujourd'hui la question du transformisme," *VP*, pp. 39-40 [Eng. trans. p. 25]; "Les Hommes fossiles," *AppH*, pp. 49-50 [Eng. trans. p. 32]; "Sur la Notion de transformation créatrice," *CJC*, pp. 29-31, especially p. 31 [Eng. trans. pp. 21-23].

12. "Les Fondements et le fond de l'idée d'évolution," *VP*, pp. 189-90 [Eng. trans. pp. 135-36].

13. "Les Fondements et le fond de l'idée d'évolution," *VP*, p. 184 [Eng. trans. pp. 131-32].

14. Joseph Donceel, "Teilhard de Chardin and the Body-Soul Relation," *Thought*, 40 (1965), pp. 383-89.

15. Karl Rahner, *Hominization: The Evolutionary Origin of Man as a Theological Problem*, trans. by W. J. O'Hara (New York: Herder and Herder, 1965), pp. 98-101, especially p. 99.

16. "Un Problème majeur pour l'anthropologie," *AÉ*, p. 327 [Eng. trans. p. 313].

17. *PH*, pp. 245, 248-49 [Eng. trans. pp. 221-22, 224]; *PHN*, Advertissement, pp. 17-18 [Eng. trans. p. 13]; "Le Phénomène humain," *SC*. pp. 117-18, 121 [Eng. trans. pp. 86-87, 90]; "L'Hominisation," *VP*, pp. 96-98 [Eng. trans. pp. 66-68]; "Le Phénomène humain," *VP*, pp. 227-29 [Eng. trans. pp. 161-62]; "L'Esprit de la terre," *ÉH*, pp. 26-28 [Eng. trans. pp. 20-22].

18. "Le Phénomène humain," *SC*, p. 125 [Eng. trans. p. 94]; "Note sur le progrès," *AH*, p. 25 [Eng. trans. pp. 12-13].

19. "La Vie cosmique," *ÉTG*, pp. 15-17 [Eng. trans. pp. 25-27]. This particular passage has been chosen to illustrate the intensity of man's relationship with nature because it is so concrete and dramatic. The passages contain the inaccurate scientific notion of the "ether" which permeates all reality, but the use of this erroneous concept does not influence or detract from Teilhard's basic thought. Man is treated phenomenologically, not metaphysically, and there is no attempt on Teilhard's part to deny or destroy free will; free will is respected (and examined elsewhere) by Teilhard. It is the underlying vital impulses which in one sense limit the exercise of free will, but which are on the other hand, the foundation without which free will could not function which are under discussion here. Even man's most spiritual activities, knowing and willing, are intimately bound up with the organic process of cosmic evolution.

20. *Experience and Nature*, pp. 263, 284, 286; John Dewey, *Individualism, Old and New* (New York: Capricorn Books, 1962), p. 153.

CHAPTER 4

EVOLUTION THROUGH SOCIALIZATION, SCIENCE AND TECHNOLOGY

I. *Socialization Prolongs the Main Axis of Evolution*

It has already been demonstrated that nature involves processes of evolution or growth through or by which the non-living, living and human succeed each other, the earlier enabling the later to come into existence. On the human plane appetite is perceived in its meanings and its consequences are experimented with and seen to be either inconsistent or capable of serially ordered achievement. The intimate, organic connection between the physical and mental must not be lost sight of; activities which have arisen on the lower levels of beings are conditions which must exist before mind and mental activity are possible. If mind (and its activity) did not develop as an extension of the patterns of organic behaviour, it would not be pertinent to nature and nature would not be a suitable setting for its inventions and plans nor the subject matter of its knowledge.[1]

The nervous system and other organic structures, which existed prior to and independently of thought, were modified, yet remained "physical," when thinking began. Thought always remains closely connected with the physical, because every meaning has its basis in a definite biological act. Man combines meanings, however, so they can enter into new interactions and bring about new consequences. By mental re-enactment means-consequences can be tried out without effecting physical results. Man can establish a specific purpose for an activity, project an end-in-view and foresee its consequences. Since he can also foresee its undesirable consequences he can alter the end before acting overtly. Thus thought, being capable of producing desired consequences, is really a function added to the biological, but one which indicates that a critical point of evolution has been reached. A qualitative difference exists between the activity of animals and men.[2]

Interaction and connections in nature are not to be found everywhere, yet there are no isolated occurrences in nature. The biological, mental and social are organically connected and the social has an integral and necessary place within the evolutionary process. Mind involves association, communication and participation. Language is not an epiphenomenon of nature, but is an extension as it were of a less complex activity on the animal level. Animals use signaling acts to co-ordinate their activity and to perform mutual action. This function, on the human level, is speech. With the development of recorded speech the possibility of integrating the consequences of the experience of different forms of life into present human behaviour is indefinitely expanded so that

> . . . in principle the cycle of objective integration within the bahavior of a particular organism is completed. Not merely its own distant world of space-time is involved in its conduct but the world of its fellows.[3]

Language is an instrument of social cooperation and mutual participation, which once again emphasizes the intimate connection between the mental and social. Man's capacity to develop and respond to meanings elevates him to the realm of the ideal and spiritual. Social participation through language is the natural link which abolishes the dualistic tendency to divide the objects of experience into a physical and an ideal world.[4] The social incorporates the physical into wider systems of interaction thereby enabling it to take on new properties. The social does not merely "lie on top" of the physical; strictly organic properties are transformed when incorporated into human associations. Thus the social is not a category of experience alien to the physical; in fact, since biological evolution appears to have discontinued evolution progresses through the development of civilization, that is, through socialization.

The intimate connection between the biological, mental and social and the fact that the social prolongs the evolutionary process can be clearly demonstrated in terms of the law of complexity-consciousness which we have proposed as the underlying law of evolution. Teilhard referred to the entire cosmic process as cosmogenesis and showed that it developed in phases, geogenesis, biogenesis and noogenesis, each of which succeeded the former and formed a new layer encompassing the surface of the earth. These layers, however, are not piled on top of one another. Each appeared at a point where the previous sphere had developed by coiling in on itself or centering itself completely so that any further increase in complexity demanded a transformation which effected the appearance of a new reality. Just as the appearance of life (biogenesis) introduced the biosphere which incorporated within itself the inanimate, so too the appearance of man (called noogenesis after the Greek term *nous* or mind) effected a new integration of both the inanimate and biological which were organically integrated within both the human and human activity.

We have already examined the observable, universal tendency in all matter to move toward units of ever increasing complexity, a movement when can be referred to as the cosmic process of corpusculation. We have also observed that throughout the sub-human forms of life there is an inclination and capacity not only to ramify or spread out, but also to draw together and co-ordinate themselves. This same process is continued on a new level among men. The process of civilization or socialization is neither para-biological nor artificial but natural and organic. It is the process which generates organization among men, and as such is simply zoological "specialization" extended to man.

The psychic influence, which played only a very minor role on the lower levels from the point of view of their classification in different species predominates on the human level. The numerous collective human units which have developed throughout history due to culture and race are *natural* groups no longer ordered primarily in terms of physiology and morphology, but rather on the level of reflection and freedom.[5] These natural groups do not tend to separate themselves completely; there is a tendency in man (not found in the lower animals) to form one vast group of all the smaller family groups. The whole human phylum unites to form one great corpuscle of planetary extension.

There is ample evidence to indicate that biological evolution has undoubtedly reached its upper limit in man. It is even possible that the individual human brain has achieved its maximum physico-chemical complexity. Through reflexion upon itself in man life in a sense has become stabilized; yet the social phenomenon represents a *continued working of the same forces of complexity-consciousness* which moved life to the level of reflection. In civilization we see 1) a *material element*, an irreversible technical-economic-cultural arrangement of ever increasing complexity, and 2) a correlative *psychic element*, an increasing intensification of thought. Men develop material arrangements which generate psychic growth, and the development of more complex psyches in turn generates further arrangement. In socialization we find not merely individual reflection nor simply the reflexion of an individual on himself but an advance in reflection and co-reflection or the birth of collective reflexion. As a whole phylum, through socialization, humanity is synthesizing itself organico-psychically on itself. This co-reflexion involves a centration of the whole noosphere on itself and represents the principal axis of evolution today.[6]

In order to represent and express the *historical development* of the noosphere or, in other words, the planetary convolution of mankind upon itself, Teilhard uses the image of a wave penetrating the inside of a sphere at its south pole and spreading in the direction of the north pole. As the wave moves outward and upward it passes through two principal phases. The movement from the south pole to the equator represents a phase of expansion; that from the equator to the north pole a phase of contraction or compression. Similarly, from its origin up to the present time mankind gathered itself together and centered its organization upon itself but under circumstances of very little pressure because it could expand with ease geographically. Recently, due to geographical expansion and increased population, mankind has crossed the equator as it were, and the thinking mass is forced on a global scale to fold back upon itself, to become planetized. Socialization of expansion has become socialization of compression, and further advances by the thinking layer can occur only by contraction and concentration on itself.[7]

Teilhard suggests that perhaps the most universal law explaining the continued development of the human sphere is the law indicating that when living matter is compressed (within limits) it organizes itself. The more mankind is compressed on itself due to increased numbers, the more it is forced to find new ways to arrange its elements in order to conserve energy and space. At first the subsequent tension and the new arrangement appear to be mechanical and imposed; however, these take the form of a rise in interiority and liberty within the more harmoniously interrelated whole. According to the law of complexity-consciousness an improved social arrangement will be accompanied by an increase in consciousness. At the same time this increase in mental interiority and inventive power increases the radius of action and the power of mutual penetration of each of the persons involved. The direct effect of this is further compression (or super-compression) upon itself of the noosphere, which, in turn, effects further organization (or super-organization). The cycle continues following an organically linked chain which builds up its own intensity. Thus through the combined influence of the shape of the earth and the self-attraction of reflective beings mankind moves irreversibly in a continually accelerating vortex of self-totalization.[8]

It is essential to note that the inherent dynamism which propels the evolutionary process in an irreversible direction is not a deterministic one which is bound to reach its term in the centering of mankind upon itself simply because of the shape of the earth, that is, without the free, responsible co-operation of mankind. The mere fact that the earth is a sphere of limited proportions, which means that men cannot continue indefinitely to move to new geographical colonies or retreat from the cities to the suburbs, does not in and by itself mean that men will unite with one another so as to develop the type of social organization which will further evolution. Teilhard's image of the wave penetrating the inside of a sphere is merely a convenient means of illustrating the historical facts that the socialization of mankind has passed through a phase of expansion, and that men are being forced to live in closer association with one another. Today the races are dispersed (we live in a diaspora) and the earth appears to us as a "global village" due to increased population and rapid means of travel and communication. These are realities which must be taken into account in any analysis of the evolutionary process.

We have seen a tendency within all of matter to unite and form units of ever-increasing complexity, but we have pointed out that not every combination of material elements produces a type of complexity which effects an evolutionary, forward thrust. Evolution prior to the appearance of man was not one tidy forward stream; nor is all process after the appearance of man authentic progress. The tendency of material to unite is carried forward into man as a *natural* inclination, but *because* it is *natural* to man to unite, genuine human union must be both reflective and freely chosen. It is love which causes men to unite in a personal, center-to-center fashion. On the human level the energy which effects union is love, and men can combine or unite in many ways which are impersonal and even destructive. Such union does not foster evolution nor bring about the super-organization of mankind socially.

We have seen that socialization prolongs the evolutionary process. Let us now, in one brief paragraph, jump ahead of ourselves to see the broad lines indicating where the process of socialization can and will lead mankind, before we examine the roles of science and technology within the process.

Using the law of complexity-consciousness and observing what has happened in the past and what is happening at present Teilhard extrapolated and projected that if socialization continued it must culminate in a super-humanity, a super-unity of mankind totalized on itself. He insisted that the super-humanity to be attained is neither a speculative nor utopian ideal, but the higher biological state mankind must attain if it continues the process of evolution to its term. He also maintained that accepting this super-humanity as the most consistent outcome of extrapolating the curve of anthropogenesis is the only logical stance in the light of present phenomenological evidence. This super-humanity is not merely a collectivized humanity nor a multi-centered humanity, but a humanity totalized under one supreme Center.

In the above analysis of socialization we have seen that Teilhard has applied or extended the law of complexity-consciousness beyond the individual. The same forces which developed life to the level of individual reflection are still at work in civilization, the material focus of technical-economic-cultural arrangement developing in complexity proportionately with the increased intensification of both individual and corporate thought. We can see, therefore, that both science and technology play central roles in the cosmic evolutionary process; thus their functions must be examined. Since evolution occurs through the process of socialization men are at the rudder of the whole evolutionary process. In order to examine this process further we shall expand the notion that man is responsible for evolution and then discuss the relationship between

81

increased social organization and the release of free human energy. This discussion will show how these processes involve technology, invention, research and education.

II. *Man is Responsible for Evolution*

The realization that thought must not be regarded as an epiphenomenon, but like matter, as a reality of cosmic and evolutionary nature, has many consequences. Cosmogenesis penetrates and is prolonged in human consciousness. Once incorporated into the organic movement of space-time, thought takes the ascendancy in the process. It does not merely participate in evolution; evolution is identifiable with the process toward thought, and man's psychic activity both expresses and measures the process of evolution since the time of his appearance. Teilhard quotes Julian Huxley's expression that man is evolution having become conscious of itself. Cosmogenesis having reached the level of mind is confronted with noogenesis.[9]

The inner movement of the world is no longer carried along or determined by the activity of beings who work unconsciously for the general progress of life. Neither man nor nature have absolutely fixed, pre-ordained goals toward which they evolve and realize themselves. Within limits both can be directed toward a number of ends. Man must deliberate and choose the ends toward which nature will be directed and the means and avenues by which he will develop his own potential and then he must commit himself to achieving these goals. He is not the center of the universe but the leading shoot consciously promoting and directing the whole evolutionary process. Through his various modes of experience man directs events to fulfillments or consummations whereas without human thought many events in nature would result in mere closures or stoppages. Man makes himself at the same time as he is making the world and in doing both he remains faithful to his own nature. He can choose to interact with nature so as to bring it and himself to fulfillment or he can isolate himself from the interacting processes of nature. Man is the free, responsible agent of evolution fostering it in all that he becomes and does.

To the extent that the human spirit is still evolving, the universe is still evolving. If man recognizes the biological value of moral action and the organic nature of personal relationships he can see that the human spirit or human consciousness is evolving both individually and collectively.[10] Teilhard says that

> . . . the moral and social development of humanity is indeed the authentic and 'natural' consequence of organic evolution.[11]

Without entering into a lengthy discussion of morality at this point we must note that the basis of morality is to be found in man's obligation to respond to the opportunity to develop himself and the universe through thought and action. Morality is a direct extension of the biological and organic sphere; it completes thought and freedom in a manner similar to that by which they complete the psychological awakening of life.[12] Evolution, which has rebounded upon itself reflectively in man, acquires morality in order to advance further. Ethical principles are not superimposed from without on the laws of biology but are literally a condition of survival for mankind. Further advances in the complexification of matter (necessary to promote human development) cannot occur unless the human mind not only directs technical organization but also provides evolution with purpose and direction. Beyond a certain minimal level technical progress necessarily and functionally adds moral progress to itself. The pursuit of knowledge is a power of reflective arrangement and as such at a certain point automatically includes internal obligations which curb and direct it while also engendering new spiritual needs.[13]

Modern man, aware of evolution and the reality of transformism, is conscious of his moral responsibility and of the cosmic dimension of his actions. He recognizes himself as born of and developing as a part of a cosmic movement. He must act to foster the movement of the whole because his individual destiny is dependent on a universal destiny. His life in one sense is no longer strictly private. If he refuses to share in the task of conserving, increasing and transmitting the goods of the world part of the whole creative effort will be lacking in the future. The moralization and sanctification of the universe are the real evolutionary progress. And what is even more significant, neither moralization nor sanctification constitute a break with human effort; they are a purification which neither rejects the least fragment of legitimate human effort nor overlooks the fundamental unity of the whole of creation.[14]

In 1924 Teilhard sketched in a few lines the basic thread of evolution prior and subsequent to the appearance of man. He was concerned to show that evolution occurs now in the souls of men and *in their union* through the energy of love. He says:

> The true evolution of the world takes place in souls and in their union. Its inner factors are not mechanistic but psychological and moral. That, as we shall again have occasion to note, is why the further, physical, developments of mankind — the true continuations, that is, of its planetary, biological, evolution — will be found in the increased consciousness obtained by the activation of psychical forces of unification.[15]

It must be noted that in this passage analyzing how human activity fosters evolution there is an emphasis on the role of interiority or spirit as well as on union through convergence. This emphasis provides an inherent direction and an end toward which evolution moves.

III. *Science and Technology as Instruments of Evolution*

At this point in the exposition of our processive world view for pragmatic christians it is necessary to analyze the role of technology, research and invention as tools or instruments which enable men to achieve self-realization, a reality which includes religious experience. Ultimately science must be understood in its relation to religion. And since research and all other forms of work take on a special significance for the christian who attains heaven through fulfilling the earth, part of this discussion concerning science, technical advances and work must be withheld until we have introduced the religious dimension of our vision. Therefore, our present analysis will limit itself to showing their function within the process of socialization.

Science and technology are *instruments* and as such imply *ends, purposes* or *ideals outside of themselves* which control them and to whose purpose they are used. Man is purposive and responsible; he sets the goals and ends of science and technology. If they have not promoted authentic human and social development, man, not technology, is responsible. Science and technology have ideal value only insofar as they are instruments which enable man to gain control of the processes which help him achieve the values that give meaning to life. Man's natural organs enable him to approach nature, and science can be regarded as an extension of his natural organs insofar as it extends his insight and understanding by bringing relations in nature into view.[16]

In order to understand the role of science and technology in biological evolution we must overcome the tendency to divide reality into opposing compartments, that is, the tendency to establish dualisms between the natural and artificial, the physical and moral, the organic and juridical. From the point of view of expanding life there is no great difference

85

between the vertebrate equipping its wings with feathers and the aviator providing himself with wings in order to fly. Artifice is nature humanized. Man must recognize the real analogies between the bird and aeroplane, the fish and submarine. Not only in social forms but also in technical accomplishments the artificial, moral and juridical are hominized versions of the natural, physical and organic. All methods of mass communication, besides enhancing business transactions, create for humanity a true nervous system and develop a mass common consciousness for humanity. All such technical activity is the continuation of biological evolution on a higher scale by creative means.[17] Once one is willing to recognize the organic nature of humanity one can see that as one organism it can be compared to an ellipse the two foci of which are technical organization and psychic knowledge. By this very fact one can conclude, according to the law of complexity-consciousness, that technology plays a vital role not only in maintaining but also in furthering the degree of consciousness of humanity considered as one organism.[18]

The law of complexity-consciousness can be applied much further. Man-as-individual and man-as-species (noosphere) can be represented in terms of two ellipses each having a focus of material arrangement and of consciousness. For the individual these foci represent the complexity of the person and individual reflexion; for the noosphere they represent the level of technical arrangement of the earth and the level of co-reflexion of humanity. The big difference between the individual and humanity is their respective lengths of life. The human ellipse lasts for a brief period; that representing humanity maintains itself as a kind of stationary (but not static) wave extending beyond the constantly changing machines and thoughts which constitute its foci at any moment. Through the succession of persons and machines that make up this wave "humanity" can be said to actually increase and a relatively permanent arrangement takes shape over a period of generations. This process is a very flexible form of heredity, a form of educative transmission through which individuals of succeeding generations are gradually enriched.[19]

What is at stake here is the additive quality of life itself. Education is one form of the very process of evolution. What has been slowly added to humanity over the centuries has become an organic part of it. Mankind's collective experience has resulted in an "added element" which, for each person, is a sort of matrix just as real as his mother's womb.[20] No human starts, as it were, from zero; through the accumulated effect of co-reflexion each generation begins on a higher turn of the spiral. Teilhard is so insistent upon this point that he denies that it is permissible to compare two men who are from different epochs.[21] To do so would be to fail to take into account the added 'noospherical' qualities not available to the man of the earlier era. Modern man truly stands on the shoulders of his forefathers; to move forward he must understand and respect the past.

Scientific progress, planning of collective organisms, the awakening of humanitarian feelings and sympathy with the universal are not merely *quantitative* progress, merely added knowledge. Such realities are true *qualitative* and *organic* progress which bring about an *entitative* transformation of *both* the *persons* involved *and* their *environment*. Teilhard maintains that:

> *Every increase of consciousness inevitably transforms* the monads and the world *in their physical being.* The fantastic enlargement, therefore, of our view of the cosmos as presented to our senses, the incessant multiplication of 'unitary' relationships in every order of things, inevitably represent an *entitative* aggrandisement of the universe.[22]

Since man is reflective and responsible for the arrangement on which the process of evolution continues, choices must be made. Evolution cannot continue in the noosphere by chance;

responsibility itself evolves as technology evolves and as planetary compression and the radius of individual action increase.[23] In fact, technology necessarily forces men to choose between a materialistic or spiritualistic ideology. Teilhard finds the former (which emphasizes organization more than consciousness or spiritualization), inadequate because it fails to give evolution a direction. The maximum of organization is not necessarily a move toward the optimum for mankind. In fact, Teilhard sees a materialistic ideology leading to total death because the more an arrangement is complex the more reversible and unstable it is. Man, however, must move in an irreversible direction or he will lose his taste for action. A spiritualistic ideology, on the other hand, emphasizes the pole of consciousness which, in turn, controls material organization. Under these circumstances means of judging good from bad arrangements are available, and life can continue to center itself and move in an irreversible direction.[24] Modern man must frequently remind himself, in order to overcome materialism and naturalism, that although the laws of evolution in the noosphere naturally bring about improvements in human living conditions,

> . . . it is not *well-being* but a hunger for *more-being* which, of psychological necessity, can alone preserve the thinking earth from the *taedium vitae*. And this makes fully plain . . . that it is upon its point (or super-structure) of spiritual concentration, and not on its base (or infra-structure) of material arrangement, that the equilibrium of mankind biologically depends.[25]

The law of complexity-consciousness indicates that invention is not restricted to the human level alone. Invention is an analogous concept. All of life invents; it organizes itself in the direction of ever greater consciousness, but man's power of projecting or inventing objectives and the degree of attraction that the world exercises over him are both greater than in the lower forms of life. In man the attraction of the future substitutes itself little by little for a simple effort to survive so that the unachieved, the unforeseen and the ideal tend to take a greater and greater part in the ideas and affections of men considered individually and collectively. The power of invention enables consciousness to take charge of the progress of material arrangement in the universe, and man is motivated to seek and invent in order to *be more,* to *be better* and to *be more conscious.*[26]

Research, considered as the effort to feel one's way toward continually better biological arrangements, is a fundamental property of all living matter. When defined more strictly as *reflective* groping it is a specifically human activity, yet in the fullness of its operations it is a very recent development resulting from planetary compression and the increased release of human energy. John Dewey defines scientific method, in its most generic sense, as a general method of inquiry in which the senses are the source of knowledge and conclusions remain tentative and subject to further testing. In this general sense it is far from having reached maturity. It must be developed further and expanded to attain human goals in ethics, esthetics, religious, social and economic matters.[27]

At present the concerns of scientific inquiry are limited and its effects are partial, often exaggerated and sometimes evil. New methods and results have been applied to the *means* of life rather than to its ends. Human ideals have been influenced only accidentally and change has been primarily technical rather than human or moral, economic rather than social. Many areas of political, religious and economic conditions have not been touched by serious scientific investigation so that whole realms of human experience still remain under the control of pre-scientific influences. Science is bringing about many social consequences, yet these consequences are not controlled because advanced techniques are not brought to bear on social matters. Change is occurring at an extraordinary rate in physical applications of science, but the range of *rapid change* does not extend to intellectual and moral attitudes nor to personal relations. The scientific mentality is still restricted to "the scientists;" and is not brought to bear on most daily problems. To adopt the scientific attitude and apply it in human affairs would mean a revolutionary change in industry, politics, religion and morals.[28]

Science and technology are the moving forces of our era and their resources must be brought to exercise a liberating function in human activities. As early as 1930 Dewey described man as moving rapidly into a corporate era in which the individualism based on the keen competition associated with building oneself a financial empire for *private* economic gain was beginning to be submerged. He also saw at least the beginnings of the downfall of extreme individualism in economics and politics. He recognized that the coming era was a critical point of transformation because as the old individualism crumbled men were left without the loyalties which had held them together and given them support, direction and a unified outlook on life. Not even the economic leaders held any common opinion as to the meaning of economics and industry in civilization as a whole; and because of this Dewey said they could not even possess their own souls. Their leadership was that of impersonal and socially undirected economic forces and their satisfaction was gained from putting social consequences to private profit. As a result workers were dehumanized by being reduced to "hands" only, acting without engaging their hearts and imaginations. Science and technology were not contributing to the evolution of civilization because they were subjected to the end of private gain and not the solution of real human problems.[29]

Dewey's criticisms of economic policies and industrial and political leadership in the thirties are equally valid and even more relevant today. Rapid advances in technology have pushed us forward into an electronic era and created the global village in which we live. Present conditions demand that we constantly re-examine the ends and ideals towards which we direct technological developments. Man must project more pervasive, far-reaching (but concrete) objectives and goals, yet a rather narrow nationalistic spirit and an over-emphasis on profit making still dominate many of our policies. Too frequently our pragmatic decisions in politics, economics and industry as a whole are made in the light of short-term objectives and immediate consequences rather than in terms of more far-reaching consequences for all nations and for our world environment. The results of these present policies are often conflicting and depersonalizing.

In one summary statement Dewey described the misuse of science and began to indicate how it can be used effectively to promote the evolution of all men.

> At present, the application of physical science is rather *to* human concerns than *in* them. That is, it is external, made in the interests of its consequences for a possessing and acquisitive class. Application *in* life would signify that science was absorbed and distributed; that it was the instrumentality of that common understanding and thorough communication which is the precondition of the existence of a genuine and effective public. . . . In consequence, man has suffered the impact of an enormously enlarged control of physical energies without any corresponding ability to control himself and his own affairs.[30]

The material is instrumental to the good life. All men must be concerned with the evolution of

> . . . a social organization that will make possible effective liberty and opportunity for personal growth in mind and spirit in all individuals.[31]

Economic prosperity must be favoured and fostered insofar as it gives the material security necessary for men to share in cultural resources. Economic organization must assure a secure basis for an ordered expression of individual capacity and for the satisfaction of men's needs in *non-economic areas*. Men must commit themselves to material production in such a way that it does not exhaust all their energies but provides a basis for the liberation of intellectual, esthetic and social values. Science and technology have liberated man from spending all his time at material production and thus have made this ideal possible.[32]

Science and technology are such important factors in our civilization that only by understanding and using them effectively can a new individualism consistent with modern culture be developed. The resources of science and technology must be controlled and made to serve expanding concepts of the human and social. At present man has physical control of these resources, but to be able to control power by means of machines is not necessarily to control the machines. Control is relative to consequences and values. Men are, in fact, controlled by their machines because they have not really begun to manage physical power for the sake of projected purposes and prospective goods. They subject revolutionary instruments to the service of traditional individualistic values rather than to organizing individual purposes and satisfactions and choosing specific social goals which enrich and liberate human life.[33]

An industrial civilization can be converted into an instrument for liberating men's minds and refining their emotions. Of itself industrialization will not produce a new culture; men must humanize both science and technology and make them serve the hope and faith of democracy. Social phenomena cannot be understood without an understanding of the physical laws involved in their interactions. Expert scientific knowledge is necessary, therefore, for advancing the study of socio-cultural phenomena.[34]

The responsibility for achieving human goals falls on man; he must decide the ends to which science is to be directed. Only a society committed to fostering human evolution will use scientific method to effect this end.

Such a society would meet the demand for a science that is humanistic, and not just physical and technical. "Solutions" of the problem of the relation of the material and the spiritual, of the ideal and the actual, are merely conceptual and at best prophetic unless material conditions are idealized by contributing to cultural consequences. Science is a potential tool of such a liberating spiritualization; the arts, including that of social control, are its fruition.[35]

If science and technology do not assist in effecting this spiritualization it is because man, lacking in social awareness and insight into the individual and collective consummatory experience that industrial work can bring about, does not use it to its full advantage. It can be an instrument for a new individualism and a new culture for all.

There is a constant increase in the number of persons devoting their lives to research and in the degree of organization and coordination among them, yet there is an urgent need for more extensive co-operative research, especially on the international level. Man must not attempt to curb the irreversible tide of technology and cybernetics, which unfortunately leaves large numbers of persons unemployed. It is essential that steps be taken to transform this released energy into further research. This is possible and practical because research is the native and natural form assumed by human energy at the moment of its release. In Teilhard's perspective modern collective research is moving toward ever increased cerebration on the scale of the whole noosphere (the thinking layer of the earth). In fact, this movement is the main axis of zoological evolution today. This increased cerebration is capable of foreseeing and planning its own future evolution.[36]

We have seen that the role of technology, research and invention in the present compressive phase of socialization has been to forward the process of co-reflexion. As the thinking envelope of the earth continues to coil in upon itself and tighten its network around the earth in what can be called the super-organization of matter, there is a further liberation of consciousness. On the basis of scientific evidence we can extrapolate in order to determine the outcome of evolution. We have already seen Teilhard speak of this outcome in terms of increased cerebration. He also describes the maximal radiation of thought, which will coincide with the planetary arrangement of humanity, as the "planetization of mankind," as "human totalization" and as "ultra- or super-hominization."[37] Before concentrating on this state of ultra-personalization it will be profitable to describe the present critical period, the causes for it and the general requirements and necessary conditions for the advance of evolution. Some of these conditions will be considered briefly and others, such as the role of love energy which effects union and therefore personalization, must be dealt with separately in considerable detail.

IV. *The Present Critical Period: Requirements and Conditions for Advance*

Just as in the lives of individuals there are moments of sudden transformation which result in critical moments of conscious choice between commitment or infidelity to life, so too in the general development of human consciousness there are such moments. The temptation to revolt is as old as thought and constantly grows and changes as consciousness develops. This being so, the present era of change is necessarily a critical time in which men are tempted to revolt against life and the effort necessary to maintain evolution. The present change is one leading to a new corporate experience in living; the crisis is one of finding new meaning and purpose for the individual and his activity. Teilhard describes the situation in terms of a great game in which men are the cards, players and stakes. They are conscious of the fact that what is developing is by means of them, possibly at their expense, and terminable by an act of their will. They realize that nothing can force them to commit themselves to its continuation. If they are to continue men must be convinced that the effort is worthwhile.[38] What specifically brought about this consciousness and anxiety and what will make the game worth continuing?

The primary factor which brought about a rather sudden increase in consciousness was man's recognition of evolution and his recent harsh encounters with the realities it involves. Humanity is going through an experience like awakening all alone in the night. The individual (whether one person, family or nation) has always had someone else to reassure him, but humanity which is just recognizing itself as one, is alone and anxious as it finds itself pressing upon itself on an increasingly contracting globe.[39] The change in phase from socialization of expansion to that of contraction is the major factor in bringing about a radical change in structure and climate which in turn is re-shaping men's outlook and activity.

Under the increasing pressure of human totalization men are experiencing various anxieties associated in one way or another with their desire to survive and transcend. They feel threatened in a world in which men are forced together yet remain hostile or closed to one another. They feel repulsion for one another and see the totalization of humanity leading to a materialization in some areas of the world so that the human quality in man is being degraded. At the same time they feel lost and crushed in the immensity of the world recognized for the first time with our modern perception of the indefinite extent of space and the conic curvature of time. In this new cosmic setting man is being forced to transpose his knowledge of physics, biology, ethics and even religion, a transformation which influences action and involves adjusting values. Men fear that mankind as a whole can be reduced to immobility and become incapable of further development even if its universe is directed toward some summit of consciousness. Some also fear that the universe is not open-ended but closed in or reversible so that progress and effort are meaningless.[40] Teilhard was very sensitive to these anxieties and set out to outline the conditions and requirements necessary to overcome them and preserve the process of evolution. One such requirement is faith in the future of mankind.

A. *Faith in the Future of Mankind*

In 1929 Teilhard wrote that thought and action can lead only to faith in the progress of thought or of spirit, a progress which of necessity demands the destruction of all that has outlived its time. By "faith" here he is referring to a psychological act, an intellectual adherence to a general view of the universe; believing is effecting an intellectual synthesis.[41] In his later writings he maintained the necessity of this faith in the progress of thought, but broadened his concept to include faith in the future achievement of a higher or super-life for mankind regarded as an organic and organized whole. In both the thought of Teilhard and this present work faith in mankind's future *includes* worship of God. Nevertheless it is evident that today the perennial temptation for mankind to worship itself is entering a critical phase on account of man's rapid conquest of matter. This absolutizing of mankind by men is a matter for optimistic concern. Unfortunately the advocates of a faith in mankind which includes faith in God do not always show sufficient initiative in promoting earthly progress, a factor which is causing an increasing polarization between them and the advocates of worship of mankind. A solution to the problem arising from this polarization can be found in the fact that modern man is experiencing an ever increasing need for greater unity based on a *solid foundation*. Unity is achieved through cooperation in common enterprises and through response to common fears, but such unity is external and temporary. Unity can also be achieved through the formulation of a common philosophy acceptable to all men of good will. But modern man, unprepared for such a philosophy, is only able to formulate propositions which could hinder or restrict progress and unification.[42]

The starting point on which to achieve unity must be the basic pre-christian or pre-materialistic faith in man and his future. This basis is common to all men of good will. So long as even the extreme adherents to democracy, communism or fascism retain some faith in man, or, in other words, some desire for an upward surge towards spirit, they have some common basis. The adherents of all three viewpoints possess at least to some degree the aspirations which characterize faith in the future: a passion for the future, for the universal and for the individual person. This basic faith in man is so elementary and universal that it is not a formula but rather a general atmosphere or environment of union in which the more elaborate and even opposing forms of faith can grow and come together. This assertion is not just an optimistic hope; it is a conviction based upon the principle that everything that is faith must rise and what rises must converge.[43]

Mankind can and must cut across political and ideological lines to form a *human front*. Such a front would divide mankind into two camps: those who stake everything on faith in a future greater than themselves — those who possess "a great hope held in common" — and those who have lost the desire to progress. Once the basis of separation is clearly defined the emphasis on opposing ideologies in the world diminishes to the extent that men of good will can see that their duty is to recognize that which is universal in all ideologies and to pursue and push to the very end that which is most universal in their own ideology. In that frame of mind they can cooperate in raising the level of consciousness on the earth. Scientific evidence indicates that the concept of raising consciousness to a level of super-consciousness is well founded and necessary in order to preserve men's will to act. Furthermore, this idea, pushed to its extreme, is the only idea capable of bringing men together in *one* unified impulse of worship combining the de-

sires to conquer the world and be united with God. These desires must be united because faith in mankind involves worship of God and the further technical and scientific advances
necessary to conquer the world require faith in mankind.[44] A
second condition necessary to overcome the anxieties of our
present crisis is the acceptance of a modern philosophy of
knowledge and action.

B. *Modern Philosophy of Knowledge and Action and its Consequences*

Ancient philosophy tended to ascribe to knowledge the role
of enlightening man speculatively concerning the ready-made,
given objects in his environment and equated increased knowledge with increased being because "to be" was essentially "to
know." Modern philosophers, on the other hand, have introduced a new dynamism into our concepts of knowing and
being. Knowing or discovering, in a sense, is bringing something new into existence. Intellectual discovery and synthesis
are not merely speculation but creation. Some physical consummation of things is connected with the perception man
makes of them. Knowledge is for its own sake, but even more,
knowledge is power. The corpus of knowledge has always increased due to the stimulation of particular problems of life.
Humanity develops in the direction of conquering matter in
order to put it to the service of increasing human consciousness. Knowledge, therefore, is for power, but increased power
is for increased action and increased action is ultimately for
increased being. "To be" has lost its static connotations and
is synonymous with "to grow" and "to become."[45]

The corresponding morality of movement confronts the problem of how to guide man in the direction of his anticipated
fulfillments so that the personality of humanity may be fully
released. The moralist directs and builds up the spiritual energies of the earth. The highest morality is that which will

best develop nature to its highest limits, and "the best" is what assures the highest development of the spiritual powers of the earth. From the point of view of establishing a science of human activity there is no real necessity to distinguish between what we ordinarily call physical energy and moral power; the realm of human energy is the physico-moral. The supreme law governing morality and human activity would be to try everything to its conclusion for the purpose of constantly increasing knowledge and power.[46]

In this philosophy of action or maximum activance "the real" must not only be fully intelligible to reason, it must also be endlessly actable and activating to man's will. In every conceivable aspect the universe must contain a maximum of truth and attractive power in relation to man's abilities to understand and create. There would be an ontological imbalance in the universe if man's capacity to desire or to act were greater in any way than the possibilities offered by the universe. If, therefore, man observes his own actions and isolates the fundamental milieu in which each motive to act is born and sustained he can distinguish the general conditions which the universe must fulfill if he is not to be stifled and his action cease. The world must be open; the process of evolution must be irreversible and therefore personalizing, and a work of absolute value must be accomplished through mankind.[47] A brief analysis of these conditions, which may also be referred to as *futurism, universalism* and *personalism*, will further clarify the consequences of the modern philosophy of action.

Evolution progresses by virtue of an internal preference for survival which in man is a zest for life. Teilhard is aware of the critical quality of mind of modern man and his lack of any guarantee of a tomorrow. He is also aware that man will not take a step to move in a direction which is blocked. The possibility of total death immediately destroys the motivation behind conscious activity. The end of thought can only consist in not having a limit. Man will only put forth the effort to continue evolution on the condition that the world is open so that through effort he can develop to his utmost limits. He will continue to press on only if the universe possesses the properties which fulfill the functional needs of reflective action. Once evolution has reached the conscious level it must know itself to be irreversible, transcendent or immortal. And once mankind has seen the possibilities of rebounding on itself and attaining some future term of super-human organization it will not press forward if its progress can end in failure. The future must also be so comprehensive as not to exclude any positive elements presently included in the universe. There must be a totality toward which mankind is progressing. It must be able to believe in the absolute value of something in its effort, and that is possible only if the world in its development is maturing something that is absolute.

Finally, the universe must be a personalizing one. The spiritual totality toward which evolution is moving must be a reality in which both the universe and each of its personal elements will be fully self-centered. Evolution is a movement of centration or personalization extended irreversibly beyond the individual elements, and such a process of synthesis demands a super-personal and super-personalizing Center in which all the individual elements will be centered. The universe cannot fulfill all the intrinsic and extrinsic requirements for mankind's ultimate self-realization unless it increasingly becomes a convergent psychic milieu and unless there is a transcendent active pole of super-consciousness in which all the individual persons will survive. Teilhard calls this pole, arrived at by means of philosophical reflection, Omega Point.[48]

Most of the fundamental conditions necessary if evolution is to continue have been examined. The main exception is the necessity of men to unite as personal centers, and this requires a separate treatment of the role of love energy in evolution, a study which will be made later in our vision. Having examined the conditions necessary if evolution is to continue, we shall turn now to an analysis of that by which evolution is fostered, namely, the various modes of human experience.

FOOTNOTES

1. *Experience and Nature,* pp. 286, 288, 370-71.
2. *Experience and Nature,* pp. 276-79, 285-86, 290-91.
3. *Experience and Nature,* p. 280.
4. *Experience and Nature,* p. xiii.
5. "Les Singularités de l'espèce humaine, . . . ," *AppH,* pp. 329-31 [Eng. trans. pp. 237-38]; *PHN,* pp. 124-25 [Eng. trans. pp. 85-87].
6. Pierre Teilhard de Chardin, "Un Sommaire de ma perspective 'phénoménologique' du monde," *Les Études Philosophiques,* 10 (1955), p. 570; "La Question de l'homme fossile," *AppH,* p. 174 [Eng. trans. p. 125]; "La Structure phylétique du groupe humain," *AppH,* pp. 214-16 [Eng. trans. pp. 154-56]; "Les Singularités de l'espèce humaine, . . . ," *AppH,* p. 329 [Eng. trans. p. 237]; *PH,* Résumé, pp. 339-40 [Eng. trans. pp. 305-06].
7. *PHN,* pp. 118-19 [Eng. trans. pp. 81-82]; "La Structure phylétique du groupe humain," *AppH,* pp. 217-18 [Eng. trans. pp. 157-58].
8. *PHN,* pp. 139-44 [Eng. trans. pp. 96-100]; "La Structure phylétique du groupe humain," *AppH,* pp. 218-20 [Eng. trans. p. 158-60]; "Du Pré-humain à l'ultra-humain," *AH,* pp. 382-83 [Eng. trans. p. 294].
9. "La Place de l'homme dans la nature," *VP,* pp. 254-56 [Eng. trans. pp. 181-82]; *PH,* pp. 244-45 [Eng. trans. pp. 220-21]. The term "noogenesis" refers not only to the appearance of man, but also to the continued development of mankind. In his *Lexique: Teilhard de Chardin,* p. 63, Claude Cuénot defines noogenesis as ". . . a movement of the universe which consists in a gradual concentration of its physico-chemical elements in more and more complex cores, each subsequent degree of concentration and of material differentiation being accompanied by a more advanced form of spontaneity and of psychism."
10. "L'Hominisation," *VP,* pp. 105-06 [Eng. trans. pp. 74-75]; "La Place de l'homme dans la nature," *VP,* pp. 255-56 [Eng. trans. p. 182]; "Note sur le progrès," *AH,* pp. 27-28 [Eng. trans. p. 15].
11. Pierre Teilhard de Chardin, *Genèse d'une pensée, lettres 1914-1919* (Paris: Bernard Grasset, 1961), Letter, July 10, 1916, p. 140 [Eng. trans. pp. 110-11], hereafter cited *GP.*
12. *GP,* Letter, January 29, 1917, p. 228 [Eng. trans. p. 176].
13. "Le Rebondissement humain de l'évolution et ses consequénces," *AH,* pp. 261-62, 267-68 [Eng. trans. pp. 203-04, 209].
14. "Les Fondements et le fond de l'idée d'évolution," *VP,* pp. 191-92 [Eng. trans. p. 137]; "L'Esprit de la terre," *ÉH,* p. 36 [Eng. trans. p. 29]; *GP,* Letter, January 9, 1917, pp. 214-15 [Eng. trans. p. 166].
15. "Mon Univers," *SC,* pp. 76-77 [Eng. trans. pp. 48-49].
16. John Dewey, "Philosophy and the Social Order," *Characters*

101

and Events: Essays in Social and Political Philosophy by John Dewey,
ed. by Joseph Ratner (2 vol.; New York: Henry Holt and Co., 1929),
II, pp. 440-42; John Dewey, *Individualism, Old and New* (New York:
Capricorn Books, 1962), p. 97.

17. *PH,* p. 246 [Eng. trans. p. 222]; "L'Hominisation," *VP,* pp.
86-89 [Eng. trans. pp. 58-61].

18. "Place de la technique dans une biologie générale de l'humanité," *AÉ,* pp 165-67 [Eng. trans. pp. 159-61].

19. "Les Singularités de l'espèce humaine, . . . ," *AppH,* pp. 334-
36 [Eng. trans. pp. 241-42].

20. "Hérédité sociale et progrès," *AH,* pp. 41-49 [Eng. trans. pp.
25-32].

21. "Les Singularités de l'espèce humaine, . . . ," *AppH,* pp. 336-
37 [Eng. trans. pp. 242-44]; "Note sur le progrès," *AH,* pp. 29-30 [Eng.
trans. pp. 17-18].

22. "Mon Univers," *SC,* p. 111 [Eng. trans. p. 82].

23. "L'Évolution de la responsibilité dans le monde," *AÉ,* pp. 211-
21 [Eng. trans. pp. 205-14].

24. "Place de la technique dans une biologie générale de l'humanité," *AÉ,* p. 168 [Eng. trans. pp. 161-62].

25. "La Fin de l'espèce, *AH,* p. 395 [Eng. trans. p. 303].

26. "L'Hominisation," *VP,* pp. 102-03 [Eng. trans. p. 72]; "L'Énergie
d'évolution," *AÉ,* pp. 386-87 [Eng. trans. pp. 366-67].

27. *Problems of Men,* pp. 10-12. For a detailed analysis of the
generic and specific senses of "science" in Dewey's thought see: Robert
J. Roth, *John Dewey and Self-Realization* (Englewood Cliffs, New Jersey: Prentice-Hall, 1962), p. 49.

28. *Reconstruction in Philosophy,* pp. xxv, 42-43; *Individualism,
Old and New,* pp. 154-55, 161; *Problems of Men,* pp. 29, 173-74; John
Dewey, *The Quest for Certainty: A Study of the Relation of Knowl-
edge and Action* (New York: G. P. Putnam's Sons, 1960), pp. 168-69;
John Dewey, *Philosophy and Civilization* (New York: Capricorn Books,
1963), p. 328.

29. *Individualism, Old and New,* pp. 31, 51-54, 71-72, 131-32; *Problems of Men,* pp. 174-75.

30. John Dewey, *The Public and Its Problems* (Denver: Alan Swal-
low, 1954), pp. 174-75.

31. John Dewey, *Liberalism and Social Action* (New York: Capricorn Books, 1963, p. 57.

32. *Liberalism and Social Action,* pp. 57, 88-89.

33. *Individualism, Old and New,* pp. 92-100.

34. *Individualism, Old and New,* pp. 29-30, 123-26, 137-38, 144-
45; *Problems of Men,* p. 33; John Dewey, *Logic: The Theory of Inquiry* (New York: Holt, Rinehart and Winston, 1938), pp. 491-92;
Philosophy and Civilization, pp. 329-30.

35. *Individualism, Old and New,* p. 138. See also: *Philosophy and
Civilization,* pp. 319-23.

36. *PHN,* pp. 150-54 [Eng. trans. pp. 104-07]; "La Structure phylétique du groupe humain," *AppH,* p. 224 [Eng. trans. p. 163].

37. *PHN*, n. 1, p. 157, indicates that ultra-hominize is used by analogy with ultra-violet simply to describe the concept of a human prolonged beyond itself in a more organized form than that which we experience today. [Eng. trans. n. 1, p. 109].

38. *PH*, p. 255 [Eng. trans. p. 230].

39. "Les Singularités de l'espèce humaine, . . . ," *AppH*, pp. 327-28 [Eng. trans. pp. 235-36].

40. For a discussion of all these anxieties see: *PH*, pp. 251-54, 282-86 [Eng. trans. pp. 226-29, 254-57]; "La Grande Option," *AH*, pp. 79-80 [Eng. trans. pp. 58-59]; "L'Esprit nouveau," *AH*, pp. 109-10, 116-17 [Eng. trans. pp. 82-83, 88-89]; *PHN*, pp. 148-50 [Eng. trans. pp. 103-04]; "Les Singularités de l'espèce humaine, . . . ," *AppH*, pp. 295-97, 326 [Eng. trans. pp. 208-10, 234].

41. "Comment je crois," *CJC* p. 119 [Eng. trans. pp. 98-99]; *LV* Letter, January 8, 1929, p. 117 [Eng. trans. p. 150].

42. "La Foi en l'homme," *AH*, pp. 235-41 [Eng. trans. pp. 185-91].

43. Pierre Teilhard de Chardin, "Construire la terre," *Construire la terre*, Cahier I, extraits d'oeuvres inédits (Paris: Éditions du Seuil, 1958), pp. 16-17 [Eng. trans. pp. 50-51], hereafter cited *CT*; "La Foi en l'homme," *AH*, pp. 242-43 [Eng. trans. pp. 191-92]; "Sauvons l'humanité," *SC*, pp. 184-85 [Eng. trans. pp. 142-43].

44. "Réflexions sur le progrès," *AH*, pp. 96-97, 105-06 [Eng. trans. pp. 72, 80-81]; "Le Rebondissement humain de l'évolution et ses conséquences," *AH*, p. 271 [Eng. trans. pp. 212-13]; "Sauvons l'humanité," *SC*, pp. 185-87 [Eng. trans. pp. 144-46]; "Universalisation et union," *AÉ*, pp. 98-101 [Eng. trans. pp. 92-95]; "Construire la terre," *CT*, pp. 40-44 [Eng. trans. pp. 74-78].

45. *PH*, pp. 276-77 [Eng. trans. pp. 248-49]; "Action et activation," *SC*, p. 221 [Eng. trans. p. 174].

46. "Le Phénomène spirituel," *ÉH*, pp. 131-35 [Eng. trans. pp. 105-08]; "L'Énergie humaine," *ÉH*, pp. 157-58 [Eng. trans. pp. 125-26]; "L'Énergie d'évolution," *AÉ*, p. 393 [Eng. trans. p. 372].

47. "Action et activation," *SC*, pp. 221-25 [Eng. trans. pp. 174-78].

48. For a treatment of all these conditions see: *PH*, pp. 254-57 [Eng. trans. pp. 229-32]; "L'Hominisation," *VP*, pp. 108-10 [Eng. trans. pp. 76-78]; "Mon Univers," *SC*, pp. 70-71 [Eng. trans. pp. 42-43]; "Sauvons l'humanité," *SC*, pp. 175-78 [Eng. trans. pp. 134-37]; "Super-humanité, super-Christ, super-charité," *SC*, pp. 205-08 [Eng. trans. pp. 161-64]; "Action et activation," *SC*, pp. 227-29 [Eng. trans. pp. 180-82]; "La Biologie, poussée à fond, peut-elle nous conduire à émerger dans le transcendant?," *SC*, pp. 279-80 [Eng. trans. pp. 212-13]; "Les Conditions psychologiques de l'unification humaine," *AÉ*, pp. 179-81 [Eng. trans. pp. 173-75]; "Le Rebondissement humain de l'évolution et ses conséquences," *AH*, pp. 263-66 [Eng. trans. pp. 205-07]; "Comment je crois," *CJC*, pp. 129-33 [Eng. trans. pp. 108-13].

CHAPTER 5

EVOLUTION OCCURS THROUGH
HUMAN EXPERIENCE

We have already indicated that cosmic evolution after the appeareance of man occurs through advances in such things as morality, knowledge, scientific research and technology, in short, through the various modes of human experience. Man and human achievements are within nature, and nature is not a complete reality to be accepted, submitted to and enjoyed just as it is. It is incomplete, consisting of a connected series of histories the term of one being the beginning of another; it possesses beginnings, endings and some sort of direction. In one sense, then, nature is an extensive human affair with man at the rudder. The emphasis, therefore, must be on human experience, present meanings and uses and the responsibility of man to control the processes of change in nature (which include, of course, all human interactions). As such, nature is a challenge and opportunity for man; it must be modified and controlled.

Teilhard neither analyses experience philosophically nor develops a detailed description of nature. In this area his cosmic vision provides only a few skeletal ideas and is in need of further development. The vision we are proposing here, starting as it does on the phenomenological level with observation and firsthand experience of reality and indicating that evolution occurs through experience, must necessarily include a developed analysis of experience. This is especially imperative because it is a vision of reality for christians many of whom place more emphasis on reason and principles than on experi-

104

ence. In fact, in many traditions within Christianity reason and experience are regarded as if they opposed each other. Some christians fear and distrust experience because the concept "experience" is not clearly defined and is used to cover anything from a fleeting emotion to histories inclusive of a number of consummations. In recent years christian moralists have proposed that experience, rather than principles, be the starting point for ethical reflection, and much of the controversy and confusion in ethics today is caused by inadequate and conflicting concepts of what constitutes *a human experience.*

Dewey's notion of experience is rich and has a great deal to offer our vision. Experience denotes the interaction of man with his environment. Man is within nature and experience is *in* and *of* nature. Man experiences nature; experience is his method of penetrating it so that in return it can enrich his future experience. In nature man finds an ally enabling him to realize his ideals and achieve authentic human goods. In and through the interaction between man and his environment both are brought to new consummations, new levels of development or integration. Experience is evolutionary, encompassing the process of encountering a problematic situation, inquiring into it systematically and transforming it into a determinate one, bringing it to a consummation of esthetic quality.

In any vision of an evolving universe in which nature as well as man achieves fulfillment through mutual interaction the concept of *nature* which is operative is very important. It is impossible, therefore, to plunge directly into an extensive analysis of experience without first analyzing in further detail the specific concept of nature operative in this vision. We have already seen that there are different concepts of "process," and that there are significant differences in the way "process" is conceived by various process philosophers.[1] So too there are different ways of understanding the teleology within nature, its origins, endings, potentiality and other inherent qualities. Man must gain insight into how nature directs itself to endings or fulfillments apart from human intervention if he is going to act in such a way as to bring both himself and his environment to fuller realization.

Although there are numerous valuable insights in Dewey's thought on these topics there are many aspects of his approach which are incompatible with the over-all type of process we are proposing. Thus it is not possible to flesh out our vision by merely incorporating Dewey's unaltered reflections within it. Some of his major principles must be rejected whereas others are functional *in toto*. Thus many selected highlights of his thought on nature will be modified and balanced with specifics in Teilhard's vision to develop a third type of process in nature which is compatible with our over-all vision.

I. *The Teleology of Nature*

The study of teleology is a philosophical inquiry into the evidence of design in nature, an inquiry to determine to what extent and how beings are directed toward an end or shaped by a purpose. How is nature itself purposive apart from the direction given it by man?

We have already proposed that nature is processive, that is, undergoing modification or change; and every change has a beginning and ending. An event has a beginning which may be characterized as an indeterminate situation which, through interaction, proceeds to some sort of resolution or ending. Scientific investigation reveals that there are neither isolated occurrences nor permanent, unchanging things in nature. Even a mountain is an event to a geologist, a history of birth, growth and decay. Since nature is constituted by events which can be described only in terms of beginnings, movement and endings it necessarily involves some sort of teleology.[2]

Although Dewey never denies the existence of things with material boundaries which limit them and mark them off from each other, he avoids any detailed discussion of things as being and even denies any interior principle in them. In the world view we are proposing we have already emphasized the fact that in its overt activity a thing manifests its interior in such a way that it can and must be observed and taken into consideration if the thing is to be observed and known adequately. Thus in chapter two we indicated the necessity of achieving a balance in examining reality by considering things *both as events and as beings with an interiority* which constitutes them as the precise beings they are and qualifies their modes of interacting with their environing conditions.

The balance between conceiving of a thing as an event open to and modified by environmental changes around it and as a being with a unique interior which determines and directs, to a considerable extent, the type of change which it can undergo is extremely important in determining both the type of teleology in nature and the kind of over-all process that is occurring. We have already indicated that Teilhard's law of complexity-consciousness is the underlying law of evolution operative in this vision and pointed out that this law implies but does not emphasize the constant interaction between organisms and their environments without which evolution could not occur. The whole evolutionary process by which things ascend in the direction of increased complexity and consciousness presupposes that organisms interact with and assimilate what is outside of them. Energies which are foreign to an organism become part of it and the re-organization of the whole that is involved at such a time may well effect a critical change in it. Therefore, the approach to teleology which we are about to propose will be consistent with the law of complexity-consciousness enriched by rather detailed insights concerning the way organisms interact with their environments.

As indicated above things are never static; nature is precarious and perilous. The world is unstable, unpredictable and incomplete. The very conditions and processes of nature generate uncertainty and risks as well as security. The union of the precarious and stable, the incomplete and recurrent, in nature is the condition of problems, satisfactions and novelty in life. Morals, politics, art, religion and science as inquiry or discovery have their origin and meaning in this union in nature of the stable and hazardous. And ends, regarded as projected consequences or consummations, are possible only in such a universe.[3]

The terminus of one sequential order may be the beginning of another sequence or history. A thing as it exists at any moment, a "this," sums up one history and simultaneously begins another; it is a fulfillment and an opportunity. In a sense, therefore, every "this" is transitive, in process of being modified or becoming a "that." In its movement it is preparing the conditions for what is to come. Nature does not have to be just accepted, submitted to or enjoyed just as it is, but can be modified and controlled. As it exists at any moment it is not a completion, but a challenge in that it provides starting points and opportunities, not final ends. An end is both static and dynamic. As an ending of one process it is static, but as the beginning of another it is transitive or dynamic.[4]

Simple ends of natural transactions apart from human intervention may be consummations but they may also be mere arrests of nature, stoppages or closures so that such endings need not necessarily be identified with the greatest attainable good, value or perfection. Ends in nature need not be what should be chosen by mature persons. Natural ends which have not been deliberately chosen and striven for need have no intrinsic eulogistic value because they may be mere stoppages due to failure or exhaustion. In the sense that a thing is a conclusion, that is, recognized because of its goodness to be worthy of attainment and effort, it is an end-in-view. Such ends are usually brought into existence by an action which modifies the surroundings. Thus a projected set of consequences or end-in-view, which has been actualized, is the consummation of a controlled activity or experience.[5]

Recognizing numerous ends in nature apart from human activity as bare arrests of nature and not as conclusions which must be recognized as good and valuable is a means of reducing determinisms, freeing man to manipulate natural transactions, and giving him the responsibility to control such transactions for his own purposes. All natural processes are open at least to some degree to human direction so that human purposes can be furthered and greater goods achieved. Man's immense capacity to manipulate nature today gives him tremendous responsibilities. The approach presented here which balances the need to interact and effect change with an emphasis on the interiority of things (which gives them a nature and therefore some inherent purpose and direction) will provide some guidelines concerning the extent to which man can reasonably alter the processes in nature through deliberate intervention.

Both things as endings and qualities of things are immediately experienced by man. As such they are final, just what they are in existence. Dewey describes this immediate experience of them by saying that they are immediately *had*, that is, undergone, enjoyed or suffered. He distinguishes this mode of experiencing things from knowing or understanding them, and stresses the fact that as long as man puts the emphasis on objects and qualities as finalities or completions to be possessed and appreciated, potentialities are not developed and nature is not brought to completion. Man defeats his own purposes and acts against nature in over-emphasizing the finality of immediate objects because this aspect of things does not effect change.[6] The fact that qualities of things are had and to be enjoyed but not clung to (since excessive possessiveness hinders subsequent interaction and change) shows at a very fundamental level how nature itself is constituted in such a way as to encourage man to balance his moments of appreciation with a willingness to detach himself from the immediate good in order to pursue a greater good. The intimate connection between the precariousness and stability of nature also reveals how continued possession of a quality or thing at a certain stage of development is futile. Thus the materialistic, possessive urge in man, if given way to, is inherently damaging.

There is also a deep continuity revealed here between the process of nature itself and the balance between possession and use of things and ultimate detachment from them proposed by Christianity.

From what has been stated it is evident that an over-all analysis of causality is controlled by the basic principle that existence is historic. A cause is not merely an antecedent; it is that which, if in interaction with other things, or if manipulated, regulates the occurrence of the consequent. Existentially, cause and effect are parts of the one historical process each possessing immediate quality and serial connection. For purposes of knowing one must distinguish cause and effect as portions of the process, but one must also recognize that each is incomplete in itself. Having recognized this it becomes more evident why causality consists in the sequential order itself involving both initiation and finality.[7]

Further analysis of the process of causality necessarily involves a description of the concepts of potentiality and tendency, and what will be said concerning these concepts will be influenced not only by the reflections above on causality, but also by the balance we have struck between a thing as an event and as a being.

All things, precisely because they are beings with a specific interiority or consciousness which determines their specific nature and causes them to be what they are, possess an immanent causal force or dynamism which we shall refer to as potentiality. The notion of potentiality signifies that at any stage of its development a thing is incomplete, possessing limited present powers capable of further development. It also indicates that all things are capable of developing and manifesting new powers under different conditions. This is always possible, and indeed necessary, because of the continuous interaction between the material complexity and consciousness within things, an interaction made possible and flexible through the continuous interaction of things with their environing conditions. Potentiality, therefore, implies the possibility of both

110

further development and diversification of a thing in a specific direction.

The tendency in all things to move, interact and develop in a specific direction may be furthered or frustrated. Through a study of things in their relationships with each other man can become conscious of the goal or possible goals of individual existences. This consciousness of the possible goals of things in interaction with each other is, in fact, perception of the meanings of things. And when man perceives meanings he can manipulate environing conditions and add flexibility to the direction of a thing's development. In this way the end of a thing, which, once again, can only be understood in terms of both its specific interiority and its interaction with environing conditions, is an end-in-view capable of considerable modification and in need of constant re-assessment. An end-in-view is not a terminal point external to the conditions which led up to it. It is certainly determined in part by the inherent causal force within the thing, but this inherent dynamism is not so limited or deterministic as to necessarily move the thing toward a pre-arranged goal independent of surrounding conditions and on-going interactions. An end-in-view for a thing is the continually developing meaning of its tendencies, which, when they are directed, become means of its development.[8]

The approach to potentiality and tendency in things being presented here rejects a conception of nature as a system that develops in a very set way which can be discovered and rigidly mapped out so that man can know antecedently in detail how nature will continue to unfold and where she will direct herself without exception in the future. It is an attempt to get away from either a mechanistic or biological determinism but in no way denies that all things have specific natures or essences. The essence of a thing, however, is not static, but on-going. Recognizing that ends in nature are not necessarily good and to be chosen by man has the effect of forcing man to take the evolution of all things, including himself, more seriously. He is forced to recognize the limitations of a statement like "every dog is like the first dog," and becomes very wary of drawing conclusions regarding the purposes and activities of a dog on the basis of what it did in the past. He is also made aware of the real element of untruth in such a statement as "every man is like the first man," because it does not take into consideration man's entire past. The additive qualities accruing from education and the changes resulting from centuries of human evolution are not accidental to man. These changes have altered him essentially. What were regarded as natural endings of both natural and human processes in the past need not be regarded as necessarily natural and good today. Thus some deliberate alterations of them by man in the light of reasonably projected consequences need not be regarded as either unnatural or evil. The scope of man's responsibility for determining and directing nature can be greatly extended through deliberate intervention in its processes.

Goals and processes are open to constant reconstruction, but this does not imply that man is free to manipulate nature arbitrarily or force things to develop in any direction whatsoever. He is a co-creator sharing in the Creator's over-all plan for the fulfillment of the universe through his powers of reason and choice. In his reasonable determination of goals and direction he must always be guided by the fact that the whole evolutionary process is primarily a psychic one, a process of spiritualization, which is another way of saying that it is a process of centration or unification directed toward a specific end, namely, a point of total psychic convergence.

Not every type of human intervention in natural processes necessarily results in the unification or centration of the organisms involved or even in a deeper integration of man and his environment. If man is to further evolution he certainly cannot disregard the natures of the organisms with which he is interacting, which means that in all his relations with nature he must take into consideration the specific interiorities of organisms because their interiority enables them to become what

112

they are. The dynamic is the psychic element in things, their consciousness or spirit. The particular type of consciousness of any being is responsible for the specific way its material complexity is organized and united to form a unique unit within a specific species. The psychic centers of things are the primary sources of the dynamism involved in all interactions. Because even the most elementary forms of reality have at least some type of interior psychism there is some direction and purposiveness in nature before and apart from the appearance of man and his intervention. In the lower forms where there is a high degree of multiplicity and less unity (therefore, a weaker psychic interior) chance plays a larger part in the formation of complexes. In the higher forms of living beings the degree of purposiveness and direction is increased in direct proportion to their increased consciousness. With the appearance of reflection spirit predominates and man must be characterized as a purposive being.

The specific consciousness of a thing determines to a great extent its potentiality and its tendency to evolve in a set direction as well as being responsible for the particular responses it makes in any interaction. The consciousness of a thing, therefore, determines to a considerable extent its capacity to respond but also its ability to alter that response. When a being evolves part of that evolution is a change in its interior psychism, and this change in its interior is primarily responsible for its new responses. Nevertheless, *interiority alone* does not effect the evolution of a being nor cause it to adapt its responses to varying circumstances. Changes in environment are also instrumental in promoting change in a thing and in causing it to alter its mode of response. The total dynamism or spontaneity involved in interaction is partially due to the tension or intensity of the interacting situation. Thus the outcome of any interaction between an organism and its environment will depend upon the interplay between the dynamism of the organism itself and the dynamism created by the unique intensity of the situation. These dynamics complement one another, but the former dominates. The latter dynamic may well alter the course of a thing's evolution, yet the thing's interiority remains its principle of unity and ensures continuity in its development and activities.

In the light of the above it is evident that a *realistic* consideration of the over-all potentiality of a thing to realize itself must take into account *not only* its *inherent capacity* to develop along certain lines, *but also* the *additional "potentiality"* it receives *through* its *interaction* with its environment. A seed can only realize its inherent potentiality to become a plant when it is grounded in moist soil open to light. An infant can only develop his inner potential to become a reasonable, loving person if he too is grounded in an adequate human and cultural environment from which he receives love, understanding and support. The inner dynamism of any being can only be developed through appropriate interactions with realities external to it.[9] This realistic approach to potentiality is in complete conformity with what has previously been described as the matter-spirit slope and the ethical connotations associated with it. This fact needs to be mentioned here because it points out the moral dimension that is necessarily involved in all man's interactions with nature.

There are limits, therefore, concerning both the manner and extent to which man can intervene in the natural processes occurring within and around him. Everything that *can be done* ought *not necessarily be done.* Man is the responsible agent of evolution; he must use his reason to determine what ought to be done, to decide what actions will or will not promote the over-all process of centration or spiritualization of the whole of reality. In doing this he must respect the natural law, which when understood accurately does not conceive of the natures of things as static completions whose patterns must be observed and conformed to slavishly. Man acts according to his nature because it shares in reason which is open to the Infinite. The dignity of human nature flows from its capacity to determine itself reasonably, that is, its capacity to follow reason. We cannot delve into the specifics of how man ought to determine what is reasonable intervention or unwarranted interference in specific instances in which he is presently transforming natural processes. We shall merely point out that this is an area of vital concern today. In the research being done in the areas of genetic control and the development of human life outside the womb the whole future of mankind may well be at stake. The principles set forth above leave room for cautious research in genetics, but certainly show that man cannot proceed in a moral fashion by merely deciding to do all that he can do technologically.

Thus far we have concentrated on describing the interactions which take place in nature and showing that man has an instrumental role in bringing both nature and himself to fulfillment. Much more must be said regarding these fundamental concerns, but to accomplish this we must switch the emphasis from teleology to the concept of experience. The previous analysis has provided the context in which this can be done effectively since experience denotes the interaction of man with his environment. The analysis of experience which will be set forth concerns the basic principles applicable to all experience, although it must be recognized from the beginning that there is no such thing as experience in general, but only *an* experience, particular experiences.

II. *Experience Denotes the Interaction of Man with his Environment*

In order to establish human experience within nature and to reveal its basic pattern it must be linked with the processes of life on the biological level. A theory of experience must proceed by first integrating it with the processes and functions of life as these are disclosed in biological science; human experience has a biological basis. Organic life is a process of activity involving an environment[10] by means of which the organism lives. The processes of living are enacted by the

115

organism and environment which form an integration. Life itself involves phases in which the organism falls out of step with the movement of things around it and once again achieves harmony with them. Where there is *growth* the balance achieved never represents a regression to an earlier state; rather the temporary disharmony is a transition to a more extensive balance of the energies of the organism and its surrounding conditions. This evolutionary process may be referred to as *organic adaptation through expansion.* Whenever a stable but moving equilibrium is attained form is achieved. Changes interlock and sustain one another so that order arises from interactions themselves and the stability necessary for life is maintained.[11]

Human experience is not reduced, however, to the biological. The biological is incorporated into the human in such an intimate manner that biological laws remain and are operative, *in a transformed way,* in human experience. The biological provides the operative basis for what is specifically human. Such statements as "organic life is a process" and "an organism lives by means of an environment" are not statements about human experience as such, but statements about the *conditions of human experience.* There is definitely continuity but also a clear distinction between organic interaction and human experience. Experience is what it is because of man's capacity to develop definite means of intercommunication, personal sharing and culture. There is some determination or limitation placed on human experience, but the biological paradigm for experience does not make it overly deterministic nor reductionistic.[12]

Dewey was very concerned with developing an integral concept of experience, one which recognized distinctions within it, but avoided unnecessary and harmful dualisms. Thus he took over and developed William James' idea that experience is a double-barrelled word. It not only includes *what* men do, suffer and believe, but also *how* they act and are acted upon. Experience, therefore, does not recognize, *in its primary integrity,* any separation between act and material or between subject and object, but contains both in an *unanalyzed totality.*

The concept "experience" suggests a focusing of the world at one point in such a way as to produce one focus of immediate apparency. To distinguish "thing" and "thought" or "subject" and "object" is to refer to realities which have already been set apart from primary experience by reflection; such terms are single-barrelled. Experience of itself is neither subjective nor objective; there is an objective world which enters into men's actions and is modified by their responses to it. "Objective" and "subjective" are necessary distinctions instituted *within* experience.[13]

As indicated earlier man and his environment are not regarded as independent entities facing each other statically. Emphasis is placed on the primary integrity of their interrelationship; they affect each other mutually in such a way that one cannot understand them in isolation from each other. In short, one does not know man and his environment as separate from each other and then interacting; they are known as interacting.[14]

The outstanding highlight in Dewey's concept of experience is his insight into the dynamic within the interaction which constitutes it. It is possible to understand experience only when one recognizes that it includes an intimate combination of *activity* and *passivity* (the word "passivity" derives from the Latin *passio* which means suffer or undergo). These elements are an integral part of *every interaction*. Experience is *doing and undergoing*. In experiencing something man acts upon it and his action effects consequences in the thing. In return these consequences react upon man and his activities. Man suffers the consequences of his own activity. The close connection between doing and undergoing constitutes experience and is the measure of its fruitfulness. Neither mere activity, disconnected action nor disconnected suffering constitute experience. The change effected by the action involved in experience is meaningless transition if it is not consciously connected with the consequences which in turn affect the agent. Whenever this connection is present the change becomes significant and

117

learning occurs. Experience is a cumulative process. Man learns from it when he makes backward and forward connections between his actions and the enjoyment or suffering they cause. Under these circumstances doing becomes trying, an experiment, and undergoing becomes instruction, the discovery of connections.[15]

This element of suffering is even an integral part of esthetic experience. Although struggle and conflict may well be painful, they may be enjoyed when they are experienced as means of developing an experience. The phase of undergoing or suffering is present in every experience or there can be no assimilation of what preceded. This phase involves reconstruction which is frequently painful; nevertheless, whether it is painful or pleasurable depends on specific conditions and is indifferent to the total esthetic quality of the experience. Few intense esthetic experiences, however, are wholly pleasurable. Many such experiences involve suffering, which, as part of a greater whole, is consistent with the *complete enjoyable experience*.[16] The dynamic described here, which constitutes all human experience, is of immense significance for our vision for christians because such persons are concerned with both evolution and sanctification. When we examine the added significance that work, and indeed all evolutionary activity, has for the christian, we shall see that the dynamic involved in all redemptive activity is identical to that of all authentic human experience.

Experience, to be authentically human, must not be fragmentary, but must have *internal* principles of connection and organization. There must be continuity not only within an experience but among experiences. Persons live in a series of successive situations, and something is carried over from one to the next. This transition does not involve an experience of finding oneself in a "new world;" rather one's "old world" (environment) expands. Experience is given temporal continuity by content and by operations. Habits, impulses, and social organization enable an on-going type of organization and continuity to prevail.[17] However, the fundamental principle of continuity and organization within and among experiences is the inherent principle of continuity (interiority) within all things. What has been said previously regarding the human spirit (both in its origin and functioning) reveals its necessity for the on-going process of evolution. Man is characterized as such by his spirit and experience must be of the spirit if it is to be truly human, that is, if it is to lead to further centration, harmony and wholeness.

Dewey reveals the continuity among the various phases of experience by developing James' comparison of it to the alternate flights and perchings of a bird. In the process of experience gains must be periodically consolidated in the light of further advance. Movement which is too rapid permits the agent to surpass the body of accrued meanings and his experience becomes thin and confused. Remaining complacent without advance after having made a gain also destroys experience which is an affair of histories.[18] One of the primary purposes of the book, *Art as Experience,* is to restore continuity to experience and

> . . . to restore continuity between the refined and intensified forms of experience that are works of art and the everyday events, doings, and sufferings that are universally recognized to constitute experience.[19]

Concern for the continuity of an ever-expanding experience within history is accompanied by concern for experience which is future oriented. The present vision appears to place more emphasis on the future than it does on either the present or the past; yet we shall see that their significance is not neglected. Experience is a temporal process; *man lives forward.* The supreme interests in life are achieving good and averting evil; thus success in modifying the environment or creating a new world is a primary concern for man. Anticipation, projection of consequences and the imaginative forecast of the future

119

are of paramount importance given the kind of world in which men live. An empirical approach to experience is future oriented. The adjustment of an organism to its environment is a continuing process in which each step is conditioned by further changes which it effects. Every event is a challenge not only because the person involved can alter the outcome but also because every event opens or stretches the person to meet what is coming. In brief, experience is a future implicated in a present.[20]

Emphasis is placed on experience as future oriented because it is the future and not the past which dominates man's imagination and because a pragmatic intelligence is creative, not routine. Experience is a liberating power capable of enabling man to effect a deliberate control of his environment and overcome the limitations of the past. Faith in experience reduces the possibility of a slavish adherence to the past, and promotes discovery of new facts and truths as well as concern for progress.[21] Nevertheless, one must not overlook the importance of the past or present. "The ideal of using the present simply to get ready for the future contradicts itself."[22] The present cannot lead to the future if it is not lived fully now, nor can an experience expand and develop the future if it has not been enriched through incorporation of past experience. Experience is not isolated and fragmentary. Continuity demands that an experience assimilate something from preceding experiences and modify in some way the quality of those that succeed it.[23] Nor is experience a private affair shut up within a person's feelings or imaginings. It is objective, public and social, the richest experience being that signifying complete inter-penetration of the self and the whole world of objects and events. The aim of such experience is not just the further development of man's environment nor merely the greater well-being of man (measured in terms of material and social accomplishments), but primarily the greater development of man himself (an increase in his very being).

The above analysis provides the basic insights necessary for a fruitful examination of the common patterns in various experiences, patterns which recur no matter how unlike the experiences are in the details of their subject matter. This examination will focus on the instrumental role of experience in bringing nature and man to fulfillment, but its greatest emphasis will be on the instrumental role of intelligence within experience.

III. *The Common Patterns in Experiences*

There are common patterns in all experiences because there are *conditions which must be met if an experience is to come to be*. The basic outline of this common pattern is determined by the fact that every experience is a process which must continue until a mutual adaptation of the person and environing conditions occurs bringing the experience to a satisfactory ending. Otherwise the experience is fragmented, terminating in a mere stoppage. The doing and undergoing mentioned earlier must be specifically related in perception so that meaning can accrue. Some process of inquiry is invariably necessary in order that the original situation be transformed into a satisfactory one and the experience be brought to a consummation.[24]

An instantaneous experience is a biological and psychological imposibility. *An* experience is a product of cumulative interaction of the self and the world marked by a beginning and ending.[25] Dewey introduced *Essays in Experimental Logic* by saying:

> The key to understanding the doctrine of the essays . . .
> lies in the passages regarding the temporal development of experience.[26]

He develops the distinction between a casual or immediate encounter with reality, which he calls "immediate," "primary," "immature" experience or "having an experience," "*an* experience" which is a cognitive encounter with nature resulting in knowledge and the solution of a problematic situation. Merely having an experience may be just an experiencing of things in such a way that they are not composed into an experience.[27]

Primary experience is an encounter with the gross, crude subject matter of every day life. The subject matter in such experience is immediately had, possessed and enjoyed. Insofar as there is possession and enjoyment there is consummation in primary experience, but possession and enjoyment pass imperceptibly into appraisal of that which is enjoyed. In his initial encounters man is often content to settle for enjoyment, but invariably enjoyment ceases to be a given and becomes problematic. As a problem it initiates intelligent inquiry into its consequences and the conditions under which it can become an object of value; it initiates criticism. This is a continuous process because values are not static since the things which possess them are contingent and changeable and the forces which effect change are indifferent to man's enjoyments.[28] Primary experience, therefore, is by no means final; in fact, it leads to the process of appraisal, which, when carried to its term, is "secondary" or integral experience.

The distinction between primary or immature experience as a casual or immediate encounter with reality and secondary experience as the objectivising process with a temporal spread is an insightful one which can help many christians overcome their mistrust of experience. The superficial, subjective and fleeting quality of primary experience is too often equated with integral experience and confidence in it is lost. The distinction between immediate, unenlightened enjoyment and possession in primary experience and the enlightened enjoyment and possession attainable through integral experience is also a beneficial insight for the christian evolutionist. It leads him to a deeper awareness of the fact that his immediate encounters with the crude subject matter of life are inadequate for him as a person. In order to become himself he must move beyond this superficial level of experiencing life and search for the deeper di-

mensions of things, a process which requires continual re-
appraisal, criticism and a search for meaning and value. Not
every manner of possessing and enjoying reality is adequate
for him.

The first phase of the temporal process which constitutes an
experience is a *problematic situation,* possibly a fresh encounter with a particular aspect of reality or any development
in which there is a certain lack of harmony, the relations among
the elements not being congruent. One must inquire further,
however, into the precise nature of a situation. A "situation"
designates a contextual whole,

> . . . something inclusive of a large number of diverse
> elements existing across wide areas of space and long
> periods of time, but which, nevertheless, have their
> own unity.[29]

It is dominated by an immediately pervasive quality which
unites and modifies all the constituents and relations within
the situation making it unique and unduplicable. It cannot be
known or expressed verbally because it is felt or immediately
had. If the underlying quality is indeterminate there is not
mere tension at large in the situation, but a particularized tension which characterizes the whole. The indeterminate situation marks off what Dewey calls "a universe of experience"
from which the discourse necessary to solve the problem arises
and by which it is controlled.[30]

The best evidence for the existence of the undefined pervasive
quality of an experience is man's immediate sense of things as
belonging or not belonging. This quality provides him with a
guide to subsequent reflection. The sense of an underlying
whole is both the context of every experience and the essence
of sanity; without it things are isolated and incoherent.[31] The
insight that a situation is a contextual whole which usually
embraces elements extended over a considerable expanse of
space and time is particularly enlightening. It is imperative to-

day that in making decisions men realize that the elements involved extend far beyond the immediate relations and inter-actions which constitute their own private lives. Such relations and interactions are not only affected by, but affect, relations on a much broader scale. Major decisions in even personal matters have national, international and even global conse-quences, and to gain insight into the present interactions and relations among men on a global scale one must also study the past and look to the future.

The most expansive contextual whole in which men act and of which they must be aware in making major decisions is the whole evolutionary process itself. Only when we examine our present situation and decisions in the light of the whole global movement are we capable of seeing their real significance for mankind as a whole. Failure to give adequate consideration to the expanded context in which decisions must be made has been one of the tragic weaknesses of many of the leading writers in the field of contextual or situation ethics. By restrict-ing their vision of the situation in which decisions are made to immediate elements (often as if the factors that constitute a situation are directly observable or given and not arrived at only after extensive analysis) they have drawn conclusions which are short-sighted and irresponsible.

Recognizing that the elements in any situation are held to-gether by an immediately pervasive quality enables a person to respect the particularity or unique quality of every situation and to see the connections among the diverse elements in it while at the same time recognizing its similarity to other si-tuations both past and present. Observing that a problematic situation is not characterized by tension at large but by *one* particular tension provides man with the possibility of solving the problem. Where everything conceived as constituting one situation is problematic man cannot cope with it; it is too difficult to isolate a starting point. Elements of different situa-tions overlap and man must analyze and separate the situations through his reflection on them before he can proceed to make decisions. Certainly no clearcut solutions as to how to do this have been given in what has been said above, but helpful insights for persons who desire to give the situational element its rightful place in moral decision-making have been set forth. This is an area in ethics which will require much more investigation as christians tend to move farther away from a dominantly legalistic approach to morality.

Since a problematic situation leads to a process of inquiry by which it can be resolved, knowledge finds its place as an instrument within experience. Therefore, no sharp contrast should be drawn between experience and reason or between action and thought, but between experience which is free, funded with thought, and responsible and that which is meaningless, slavish and undirected. Experience is not to be set off in opposition to knowledge or reason. It is not primarily a matter of knowing; nor is knowing the only or major form of experience. It is, however, one mode of experience, a mode which marks a transitional re-direction and re-arrangement of reality; it is both intermediate and instrumental insofar as it occurs between a casual, accidental experience and a relatively defined or settled one.[32]

All experience of worth is not purely cognitive experience. Other modes of qualitative experience such as practical, moral, esthetic and religious experience are too frequently regarded disparagingly. As a result objects of experience which cannot be reduced to properties of objects of knowledge are often regarded as purely subjective, and harmful dualisms are set up between man's various modes of experience.[33] Knowing is instrumental in all forms of experience, which, if they are complete, culminate in a consummation which is esthetic in quality. Knowledge, therefore, is man's primary means of controlling nature. All experience contains some element of thought although only some of man's experiences are dominantly intellectual.

The assertion that there are two kinds of experience, one occupied with uncontrolled change, the other with directed change, indicates that reason is method; it is operative. Its relations and universals are valuable because they apply to individual things with spatio-temporal existence. In thought concepts are abstracted or detached from individualized reality in order that they might be applied again to it. Intelligence designates methods of observation, experiment and reflective reasoning which remake the conditions of life and enable man to project and realize a desirable future.[34] Where this approach is taken knowledge is a mode of doing and all knowledge has far-reaching consequences which make it moral. The process of inquiry is

> . . . the controlled or directed transformation of an in-
> determinate situation into one that is so determinate
> in its constituent distinctions and relations as to con-
> vert the elements of the original situation into a unified
> whole.[35]

This process is open to investigation. Logic is the theory of inquiry which sets out to examine the *methods* of inquiry so as to guide man in achieving better inquiries which in turn will reconstruct his experience more effectively. Logic is empirically founded and experimentally applied. Only when it concerns itself with the origin and use of thought in daily life and in science can it follow the natural history of thinking as a life process,[36] and only then can it fulfill its true evolutionary function.

The process of thinking, therefore, is not something purely mental, apart from action. The scientific method establishes doing at the very heart of knowing. Evolution is inevitable and man *must participate* in it to his advantage or destruction. When he uses reflection and inference to project future results and directs events to desired consequences, he achieves *controlled participation*. He discovers the hidden links and relations in nature itself and controls them so as to promote the on-going process which is nature. He directs change toward ends compatible with the principles of life and applies natural energy to satisfy concrete human wants. Man learns to control natural forces so that he is freed from fear to strive to secure an ample and *liberal life for all men*.[37]

Joseph Ratner points out the very intimate relationship between "controlling" and "controlled by" in any process of scientific inquiry. Man is controlled by the problem at the beginning and by the test at the end, but at the end he controls the problem.[38] Any theories, ideas or systems developed in the process of inquiry, no matter how self-consistent and successful they are, are hypotheses to be accepted as bases for actions and not as finalities.[39] Even solutions remain tentative and open to test and further investigation. The ultimate measure of intelligence, therefore, is conceived in terms of establishing a desirable future and searching for the means to effect it progressively; this is the slow co-operative work of mankind.[40] Progress demands increase of present meaning, and considering the experience of mankind, historical progress is found in the complication and extension of the significance found within experience. Man must always act so as to increase the meaning of each present experience.[41]

The final aspect of knowing which must be examined in this analysis of the common patterns within experience is the fact that it is directed toward a consummatory experience. If this were not so, knowledge could neither be truly intermediate, instrumental nor evolutionary. It leads to a fulfillment which is esthetic in quality. The significance of this fulfillment is stressed by the statement that knowing is

> . . . instrumental to the enrichment of the immediate significance of subsequent experiences, and it may well be that this by-product, . . . , is incomparably more valuable for living a life than is the primary and intended result of control, essential as is that control to having a life to live."[42]

The final element in any integral experience, therefore, is a fulfillment or consummation. Even the most intellectual experience must possess an esthetic quality if it is to be a complete experience.[43] The satisfaction or completion of an integral experience is not a subjective or private affair; rather it is an objective thing with objective conditions attained only after fulfilling the demands of objective factors.[44] A consummation is a natural ending in that it is realized within an experience and is not imposed from outside of it. It is immediately had or enjoyed as was the pervasive quality which characterized and united the problematic situation from which it developed.

Our analysis of the common patterns in experience highlights the fact that experience is *in* and *of nature*. It is not experience or the process of experiencing which man experiences, but nature. Experience penetrates nature in depth and breadth; it is also the method of penetrating nature, which when made known in an empirical manner, enriches and directs subsequent experience.[45] In this perspective, as Dewey points out,

> . . . nature signifies nothing less than the whole complex of the results of the interaction of man, with his memories and hopes, understanding and desire, with that world to which one-sided philosophy confines, "nature."[46]

A great deal of emphasis has been placed on the role of the empirical method as being a central on-going force in the evolutionary process. It must be recognized that when we speak of scientific method we are not referring to specialized scientific techniques, but to a general method of inquiry which begins with observation and provides conclusions which are tentative and subject to further testing. At present this method is neither adequately developed nor universally applied. The empirical method is an approach directed toward improving the quality of life because it effects a continuous reconstruction of nature and a transformation of man. Through its consistent application experience can become self-corrective. Neither our analysis of experience nor our over-all world view imply, however, that the empirical method is the only method of thought nor is it capable of answering all men's problems in spite of the fact that empiricists make numerous assertions that it can. Empirical knowledge must be complemented by the knowledge of revelation if the total cosmic picture available to mankind is to be seen and the elements consistently co-ordinated. Philosophical and theological methods, which incorporate the data of science, are necessary, and they must retain their own distinct methodologies.

Another area in which the above analysis of experience has qualified Dewey's concept of experience is in the fact that it is open to religious experience through which man encounters a personal God who transcends the limits of the cosmos and the capabilities of strictly empirical evidence. Dewey limits all human experience to that of the phenomenological universe and denies that man can transcend his sense experience. He has built these limitations right into his philosophy of experience[47] and regards anything that transcends sense experience as anti-natural. The view presented here rejects Dewey's principle that man must confine his inquiries and projected ends to the limits of the natural totality described as the universe. It does so on the grounds that the transformation which occurred at the appearance of man effected a radical difference between man's interiority and that of all other things. Man's spirit is a part of the natural universe, and because it animates the whole person, is the subject of sense experience; nevertheless, it transcends sense experience.

Man is unique *within nature* but at the same time his transcendent spirit and ability to reflect on his own knowledge give him a distance from it; it can never fully encompass him. A person who rejects the transcendence of the human spirit, may well argue that affirming transcendence re-affirms a radical dualism between man and nature. Once again man and his environment are isolated things set off from each other so that man acts on nature rather than interacts with it. Any emphasis placed on the role of the human spirit in modifying and uniting the material might convince him that interaction in Dewey's sense is impossible; man merely confronts nature so as to effect desired changes in it.

In order to meet these objections one need only recall that Dewey rejects all purposiveness in nature apart from that given by human intelligence. Yet his emphatic rejection of any inherent direction in evolution apart from thought and any inherent principle in things is a major factor which prevented him from attaining an adequate degree of precision and detail in his explanation of *how* the successive plateaus in the evolutionary process appeared. Although Dewey claims that man is within nature and nature is without direction until thought appears, he never accounts adequately for the appearance of this directive force in man. He rejects the human spirit because he feels it destroys man's *continuity* with nature. But one can certainly question whether he is as true to his principle of continuity as he might be, and ask whether, in reality, any principle of continuity is even possible without recognizing some sort of interiority in all things and spirit in man.

It is also worth noting that two Dewey scholars, Robert C. Pollock and Robert J. Roth, maintain that in spite of Dewey's explicit statements to the contrary he has not succeeded in eliminating all evidence of a directive striving or purposiveness at the heart of things, a striving which goes beyond what his own philosophical premises will allow.[48] In the view presented in this work the incomplete and mutually dependent qualities of man and nature are respected; man is not isolated from nature. Being within created nature, he too is radically relational and processive. Yet in this conception of the interaction between man and his environment there is a sense in which man confronts nature although he remains in it throughout the entire interaction. This fact must be recognized because man, an intelligent, free agent, intervenes to direct natural processes to deeper, more extensive consummations than they could achieve on their own. Interaction, therefore, involves an element of man's action upon nature, yet interaction remains basically mutual as do its effects.

By way of summarizing some of the main points set forth in our analysis of experience as evolutionary, that is, as man's way of becoming himself and developing nature, we shall emphasize the fact that this approach to experience shows great respect for the past. Old experience suggests aims and methods for developing new, improved experience in the future. Imaginative, creative recovery of the past is necessary for successful development of the future, but this does not involve isolating the past or absolutizing its methods or knowledge. When men recognize reason as instrumental within experience they become capable of determining the conditions under which the funded experience of the past and creative intelligence can interact effectively; then they project realistic programs of action for the future. To the extent that this is done experience becomes *constructively self-regulative and expansive.*[49] Because it is instrumental and within experience thought transforms and develops experience.

> Development does not mean just getting something out of the mind. It is a development out of experience and into experience that is really desired.[50]

Thought enables experience to be evolutionary and to develop nature. And as Robert J. Roth points out, nature cannot be regarded solely in terms of a universe facing man nor in terms of interaction with him; its meaning must be expanded to not only what *has* but what *will* come into existence through interaction.[51]

Experience is the driving and directing force effecting evolution. The identification between evolving and becoming or achieving wholeness has been established, as has the fact that this is achieved through consummatory experiences in ever-increasing spheres of activity. Man's various modes of experience, such as scientific, moral, esthetic and religious, are his ways of becoming himself. He can commit himself to these and in so doing promote evolution or withdraw from the process and isolate himself. If he does the latter neither he nor the rest of nature will achieve fulfillment.

FOOTNOTES

1. Eugene Fontinell refers very briefly to the difference between process in pragmatism and other process philosophies according to the interpretation of John Herman Randall, Jr. He indicates that in the pragmatic approach the process of reality cannot be known or experienced as a single, unified whole yet it allows man to think of or believe in reality as a single process. On these grounds Fontinell distinguishes the pragmatic approach (presumably Dewey's approach) from that of Teilhard. Eugene Fontinell, *Toward a Reconstruction of Religion: A Philosophical Probe* (Garden City, New York: Doubleday and Co., Inc., 1970), p. 189.

2. John Dewey, *Logic: The Theory of Inquiry* (New York: Holt, Rinehart and Winston, 1938), pp. 222-23.

3. *Experience and Nature*, pp. 41-42, 47-48, 117, 395-96; *The Quest for Certainty*, pp. 243-44.

4. *Experience and Nature*, pp. 100, 352-53; *The Quest for Certainty*, p. 100.

5. The approach presented here differs from that of Dewey insofar as he regards all simple ends of natural transactions as mere arrests of nature which cannot be identified with good, being, value or perfection. No natural end which has not been striven for has any intrinsic eulogistic value. *Experience and Nature*, pp. 101-04, 112, 351-52, 395-96. Dewey also maintains that nature has no end apart from the goals given it by man. Up to the point where nature produced an intelligent being it had no regard for value. Nature's teleology is achieved in thinking and not apart from it. John Dewey, "Ethics and Physical Science," *The Andover Review*, 7 (1887), pp. 579-80, as quoted by James Collins, "The Genesis of Dewey's Naturalism," *John Dewey: His Thought and Influence*, ed. by John Blewett (New York: Fordham University Press, 1960), pp. 12-13; "Nature and Its Good: A Conversation," *The Influence of Darwin on Philosophy*, pp. 43-44; *The Quest for Certainty*, pp. 210-11, 214-15.

6. The basic insight of Dewey is incorporated in our approach but the thought differs at least to the extent that we attribute qualities to things whereas Dewey tends to stress qualities as properties of interactions. *Experience and Nature*, pp. 86, 96-97, 108-09, 129-32.

7. *Experience and Nature*, pp. 99-100, 109.

8. The approach to potentiality and tendency outlined here rejects many of Dewey's ideas on this topic while modifying and incorporating others. For his specific thought see: Richard J. Bernstein, ed., "The Subject Matter of Metaphysical Inquiry," *On Experience, Nature, and Freedom* (New York: Bobbs-Merrill Co., Inc., 1960), pp. 220-21; *Experience and Nature*, p. 373.

9. For a much more developed treatment of this notion see: Eulalio R. Baltazar, *Teilhard and the Supernatural* (Baltimore: Helican Press, 1966), pp. 121-39.

133

10. "Environment" is not something around or about a person or human activities in an external sense. A person is not "in" either a situation or an environment as a penny is "in" a can. Environment is the milieu or medium of human activities in the sense in which a medium is intermediate in carrying them out, the channel through which they move and the vehicle by which they progress. Proximity does not necessarily determine environment; things remote in space and time may form part of a person's environment. Environment consists of whatever *conditions* interact with personal needs and purposes to create an experience. It includes all the conditions which enter into human activity and sustain or frustrate it. See: John Dewey, *Experience and Education* (New York: Collier Books, 1967), pp. 43-44; *Democracy and Education*, pp. 11-12; John Dewey and Arthur F. Bentley, *Knowing and the Known* (Boston: Beacon Press, 1960), p. 272.

11. *Logic*, pp. 25-27; *Art as Experience*, pp. 14-15; "The Need for a Recovery of Philosophy," *On Experience, Nature, and Freedom*, pp. 24-25.

12. John Dewey, "Experience, Knowledge and Value: A Rejoinder," *The Philosophy of John Dewey*, ed. by Paul Arthur Schilpp (2nd. ed.; New York: Tuder Publishing Co., 1951), p. 530; *Art as Experience*, pp. 22-23.

13. *Experience and Nature*, p. 8; *Essays in Experimental Logic*, pp. 7-8.

14. John Dewey and Arthur F. Bentley, *A Philosophical Correspondence, 1932-1951*, ed. by Sidney Ratner and Jules Altman (New Jersey: Rutgers University Press, 1964), Letter, July 2, 1942, p. 115, Letter, February 1, 1944, pp. 207-08.

15. *Democracy and Education*, pp. 139-40, 166, 273-74; *Reconstruction in Philosophy*, pp. 84-87; "The Need for a Recovery of Philosophy," *On Experience, Nature, and Freedom*, pp. 25-26; *Art as Experience*, p. 246; "Experience, Knowledge and Value: A Rejoinder," *The Philosophy of John Dewey*, p. 532.

16. *Art as Experience*, p. 41.

17. *Experience and Education*, p. 44; *Logic*, pp. 245-46; *Reconstruction in Philosophy*, pp. 91-92; John Dewey, *Human Nature and Conduct* (New York: Henry Holt and Co., 1922), pp. 178-80; "The Need for a Recovery of Philosophy," *On Experience, Nature, and Freedom*, pp. 23, 28-30, 40-47. Dewey rejects the human spirit which he regards as super-natural or super-empirical, and maintains that such a reality destroys man's continuity with nature. In "Experience, Knowledge and Value: A Rejoinder," *The Philosophy of John Dewey*, p. 542, he says that "the word 'subject,' if it is to be used at all, has the organism for its proper *designatum*. Hence it refers to an *agency* of doing, not to a knower, mind, consciousness or whatever." Nevertheless, Richard J. Bernstein criticizes Dewey's principle of continuity, pointing out that he never gives a detailed, systematic analysis of continuity and uses the principle with more of an emotive and normative meaning than a descriptive one. Richard J. Bernstein, *John*

Dewey (New York: Washington Square Press, 1966), p. 180. There is certainly evidence in Dewey's writings on which to base this criticism. This basic weakness pointed out by Bernstein has been overcome in the present work in which interiority or spirit plays a dominant role in maintaining both continuity and distinction in every phase of the evolutionary process.

18. *Art as Experience*, p. 56.

19. *Art as Experience*, p. 3.

20. "The Need for a Recovery of Philosophy," *On Experience, Nature, and Freedom*, p. 27.

21. *Reconstruction in Philosophy*, pp. 48, 93-94; "The Need for a Recovery of Philosophy," *On Experience, Nature, and Freedom*, p. 65.

22. *Experience and Education*, p. 49.

23. *Experience and Education*, pp. 16, 35, 77.

24. *Art as Experience*, pp. 43-45.

25. *Art as Experience*, p. 220.

26. *Essays in Experimental Logic*, p. 1.

27. *Art as Experience*, p. 35.

28. *Experience and Nature*, pp. 398-99.

29. *Knowing and the Known*, p. 315; "In Defense of the Theory of Inquiry," *On Experience, Nature, and Freedom*, p. 135.

30. *Logic*, pp. 66-68, 70; *Essays in Experimental Logic*, pp. 35, 122-23, 137-38; "In Defense of the Theory of Inquiry," *On Experience, Nature, and Freedom*, pp. 135-36; "Qualitative Thought," *On Experience, Nature, and Freedom*, pp. 180-84.

31. *Art as Experience*, pp. 194-95.

32. *The Quest for Certainty*, p. 219.

33. *The Quest for Certainty*, pp. 295-96; *Experience and Nature*, p. 435; "The Need for a Recovery of Philosophy," *On Experience, Nature, and Freedom*, pp. 53-54; "Experience, Knowledge and Value: A Rejoinder," *The Philosophy of John Dewey*, p. 524.

34. *The Quest for Certainty*, p. 83; *Experience and Nature*, pp. 435-36; *Democracy and Education*, pp. 343-44; *Liberalism and Social Action*, p. 50.

35. *Logic*, pp. 104-05.

36. John Dewey, *Studies in Logical Theory* (Chicago: The University of Chicago Press, 1903), p. 13; *Essays in Experimental Logic*, p. 103; *Reconstruction in Philosophy*, p. 138. Richard J. Bernstein states the functions of logic in Dewey's thought. "Inquiry as a mode of conduct is accessible to objective study, and the function of logic is to discern the methods and patterns of inquiry in order to provide us with a guide for better and more successful inquiries. Logic as the theory of inquiry is therefore descriptive and prescriptive, or normative; it is descriptive insofar as it is concerned with the ways in which men actually do inquire; it is normative because its aim is to isolate, appraise and evaluate those norms and standards that are most successful in achieving warranted knowledge claims." *John Dewey*, p. 102.

37. *The Quest for Certainty*, pp. 36-37, 83-84; *Reconstruction in*

Philosophy, pp. 112-17; *Experience and Nature*, pp. 137-38; *Logic*, pp. 116-17; *Liberalism and Social Action*, p. 56; *Essays in Experimental Logic*, pp. 135, 183; "The Need for a Recovery of Philosophy," *On Experience, Nature, and Freedom*, pp. 33-36; "Intelligence and Morals," *The Influence of Darwin on Philosophy*, p. 58. Eugene Fontinell quotes Dewey who insists that the meaning of the emphasis on scientific method has little to do with specialized laboratory technique. *Experience and Education*, p. 87-88. Fontinell points out that Dewey has an analogical rather than a univocal understanding of scientific method. Eugene Fontinell, "Religious Truth in a Relational and Processive World," *Cross Currents*, 17 (Summer, 1967), p. 298.

38. Joseph Ratner, ed. *Intelligence in the Modern World: John Dewey's Philosophy* (New York: Random House, 1939), pp. 124-25.

39. *Reconstruction in Philosophy*, pp. 144-45.

40. "The Need for a Recovery of Philosophy," *On Experience, Nature, and Freedom*, p. 39.

41. *Human Nature and Conduct*, p. 283.

42. *Essays in Experimental Logic*, pp. 17-18.

43. *Art as Experience*, p. 38.

44. *Experience and Nature*, p. 64.

45. *Experience and Nature*, pp. x, 2a, 4a, 11.

46. *Art as Experience*, p. 152.

47. George R. Geiger, *John Dewey in Perspective* (New York: Oxford University Press, 1958), pp. 17-18.

48. Robert J. Roth, *John Dewey and Self-Realization*, pp. 134-39; Robert C. Pollock, "Process and Experience," *John Dewey: His Thought and Influence*, p. 173.

49. *Reconstruction in Philosophy*, pp. 94-97, 101-02; "The Need for a Recovery of Philosophy," *On Experience, Nature, and Freedom*, p. 28.

50. John Dewey, *The Child and the Curriculum and the School and Society* (Chicago: The University of Chicago Press, 1966), p. 18.

51. Robert J. Roth, *John Dewey and Self-Realization*, p. 81.

Chapter 6

THE EVOLUTIONARY FUNCTION
OF KNOWLEDGE

I. *Scientific Knowledge as Evolutionary*

A. *The Relation between Common Sense and Science*

A convenient starting point in our analysis of the evolutionary function of knowledge will be the relationship between common sense and science which complement one another in a manner that furthers evolution. Common sense, which tends to be an undefinable reality, is taken here to have as its concern the daily conduct of living in an immediate community. Its distinguishing quality is a direct "acquaintance knowledge" of both the persons and conditions encountered in the immediate environment. Problems to be faced in common sense inquiries have as their frame of reference the immediate use and enjoyment of objects, activities and products of the community. In brief, therefore, common sense is the name for a body of basic facts concerning the immediate use and enjoyment of all the realities in the immediate environment of which man obtains an acquaintance knowledge. Systematic attention must be given to this body of knowledge if science is to exist and if philosophy is to have a foundation in reality and a field of application. The source or point of departure of science is necessarily the qualitative matter of objects and processes of the common sense world although its approach and concern with these realities is different from that of common sense inquiries. Both common sense and scientific inquiries are important, practical, human activities characterized by knowing and doing, but the latter are a form of practical human activity concerned with advancing knowledge apart from interest in the practical affairs of immediate use and enjoyment. Science, therefore, is a concern which grows out of and eventually returns into other more primary human affairs.[1]

The subject matter of science differs from that of common sense, yet unless the material of science can be traced back to those of common sense inquiries, science can have no matter for concern. Because it involves abstraction, scientific inquiry is liberated from the concrete and particular; the outcome of this liberation can be a transformation of the affairs of common sense. Both scientific *methods* and *conclusions* are brought back and applied to the uses and enjoyments of daily life so that a transformation of the judgments, emotions, preferences and aversions of ordinary, non-scientific men accrues.[2] This fact is stated summarily and its evolutionary thrust is made clear in the following statement:

(1) Scientific subject-matter and procedures grow out of the direct problems and methods of common sense, of practical uses and enjoyments, and (2) react into the latter in a way that enormously refines, expands and liberates the contents and the agencies at the disposal of common sense. . . . Scientific subject-matter is intermediate, not final and complete in itself.[3]

Science is made by man for man; the physical sciences must continue to liberate and extend the range of ends open to common sense and increase the scope and power of the means available for attaining these ends. Men do not train themselves to observe fruitfully so that their knowledge is inaccurate and a source of conflicts. The approach by which the fruits of scientific inquiry are deliberately and consistently fed back into common sense knowledge so as to refine it and overcome the conflicts within it is a most practical way of furthering the general evolution of thought and practice. It is also compatible with the criteria of homogeneity and coherence for all knowledge which will be proposed later.

Even today, common sense is still divided within itself because many of its meanings and procedures antedate science and scientific methods. The resulting division within common sense is evident in the religious, economic, political, legal and artistic phases of life. Science has had more influence on the actual *conditions* of ordinary life than on the ordinary habits of belief and inquiry in these areas. According to Dewey what is needed to overcome the social conditions which prevent the return of scientific conclusions and methods into common sense is a *unified theory of inquiry*. Once a fundamental unity is achieved in the *structure of inquiry* in both common sense and science the split within common sense itself and the division between it and science will be more effectively overcome and science will be more effective in its intermediary role because it will be applied in the common sense situations from which it arises.

B. *The Process of Inquiry*

A great deal of Dewey's life was devoted to achieving a fundamental unity in the structure of inquiry; the result was his theory of knowledge or inquiry. A detailed presentation of his thought on this topic is beyond the scope of the present work. In fact, since not all his thought is compatible with the present author's view, some of his ideas have been rejected and others will appear here in a modified form. We shall examine a number of the theoretical highlights concerning the process of inquiry in such a way as to show that its pragmatic quality is compatible with our over-all vision and that inquiry is an instrument of evolution.

We have already touched upon the problem of knowing

and inquiring in earlier sections of this work where we discussed "seeing reality as processive or historical," "the modern philosophy of knowledge and action," and "the common patterns in experience." Thus a number of points have already been established which we shall recall because they provide a context for our further thought. There is no dualism between the ontological order and the order of knowing; things are made in the same pattern as that in which experience unfolds them. Knowledge is instrumental within experience which enables man to know reality as it is. All knowledge begins with phenomenological observation, is operational and public. It reveals reality, not as static, but as an historical process of development. Since the scientific approach to reality is the historical approach, we have discussed the additive and reconstructive functions of knowing and spoken of learning in terms of creation, affirming that some physical consummation occurs. Knowing is not mere speculation; doing is at the heart of knowing because it is an event in which something new comes into existence. A reconstruction of both existing conditions and the organism occurs; so that knowing is truly evolutionary.

Some form of evolution or process is inevitable; thought enables man to control his participation in it. Inquiry enables man to interact with his material surroundings and put them in the service of increasing human consciousness. This has been expressed most succinctly in the statement that knowledge is directed toward increased power, increased power is for increased action and increased action for increased being.

In the context outlined here it is evident that all thinking involves a natural history. The procedure in thought or inquiry is not only operational and public, it is also temporally intermediate between the problematic situation out of which it arose and its solution. Thus it is also instrumental in achieving that solution. According to Dewey, when any of these aspects of the thought process are overlooked or denied men forget 1) that the essential function of thinking is controlling the environment to bring about human progress and well-being, and 2) that the modification thought effects is a physical one.[5] In the context of our vision we would take the emphasis off *controlling or conquering the environment* because our past experience ought to show us that this emphasis has led man to interfere with natural processes in such a way as to do irreparable damage to his environment. The human progress and well-being we tend to pursue are measured in terms of increased productivity, more and better commodities for men to consume. These goals have proven themselves to be inadequate.

The function of inquiry is not merely to enable man to control nature, but more accurately, to enable him to interact with it, to investigate it in such a way as to plumb its deepest secrets and gain insight into its extensive processes and interactions so that he can interact with it in a manner that is compatible with its own inherent dynamisms. In this way he will not frustrate nature and destroy both his environment and himself. The modifications that thought brings about are physical and affect man and nature simultaneously. Certainly Dewey recognized this fact, but his thought (to the extent that it has influenced our North American attitudes and procedures) has not led men to stop exploiting nature in their interactions with it. We maintain that the deficiency in Dewey's thought lay not only in the fact that he de-emphasized the interiority and purposiveness within things apart from human thought, but also in his denial of man's interiority, transcendence and ability to ask ultimate questions. These limitations are at least partially responsible for the erroneous ideas that human progress can be measured in terms of increased productivity and that human well-being is identical with greater being. Dewey, of course, would not subscribe to these inadequate notions himself.

Before we can see the full significance of this shift in emphasis we must discuss the pragmatic and naturalistic characteristics of the process of inquiry. Dewey characterizes his theory of inquiry as pragmatic, insisting on its practicality, yet denying that as such a practical approach to knowing reduces it to promoting "definite utilities of a material or bread-and-butter type"[6] or the "preservation and grosser well-being of the body."[7] On the other hand, "pragmatic" stresses the need to refer to consequences as the final meaning and test of all thinking. Since these consequences may be esthetic, moral, religious or political, the process of inquiry is to be applied to all human activities which need regulation.[8]

Our exposition of a processive world view for christians must certainly address itself to the pragmatic character of the process of inquiry as set forth by Dewey not only because this quality of thought is fully developed by him, but primarily because we North American christians think and act pragmatically. Whether we are aware of it or not, pragmatic criteria are operative in the processes by which we arrive at most of our decisions.

Dewey's thought is most enlightening in his denial that utility is identical with practicality. Pragmatism is not utilitarianism. To determine the validity of a goal or event in terms of its consequences is not to reduce the limits of one's inquiry to the scope of either immediate or even long-term usefulness. An examination of the consequences of an act can, and ideed *must*, extend far beyond all the possible, positive useful effects it can produce. The most significant consequences of men's actions and goals are those which affect them specifically as persons, consequences which develop their character and either fragment or integrate them as persons. Very frequently such consequences cannot be measured in terms of utility.

For instance, it would be extremely difficult if not impossible to justify martyrdom, giving up one's life to maintain one's integrity by bearing witness to the validity of a principle or truth, if the criterion by which one judged the act were merely utilitarian. Nevertheless, such an act can be not merely justified but may even be regarded as morally necessary according to the pragmatic criterion of examining *all* the foreseeable consequences in the alternative choices available in a given situation. Historically many men have been confronted with a demand to either face execution or perform an action which in their judgment would fragment them and destroy their personal integrity. In such a situation pragmatic criteria for evaluating moral action and truth may well lead an individual to decide that to perform this particular action to which he cannot commit himself conscientiously is equivalent to destroying himself. That is to say that for him the consequences of performing the act would be paramount to death. Thus he may determine that accepting death at the hands of another is the only meaningful alternative open to him because it enables him to maintain his integrity and exercise his freedom.

The world view presented here maintains the validity and the necessity for using pragmatic criteria in all processes of inquiry. It affirms that there is *a type of pragmatic test* by which even the various practices of religion and the dogmatic expressions of religious faith can and ought to be examined. The christian must confront the tenets of his faith with a serious inquiry into what they mean *in the world* here and now. He must search to find the meaning, the fittingness and the consequences of his faith in relation to his secular learning and activities if he is to develop as a person and christian simultaneously. This is not to imply that the process of inquiry into religious matters will be identical to the process of inquiry into empirical matters. Nor is it to affirm the need to refer to consequences as the *final meaning* and test of *all* thinking even in scientific investigations. We wish to set forth the pragmatic criterion of truth as one useful and necessary criterion to be used in conjunction with other criteria. (Further discussion of this matter will occur when we examine the meaning and criteria of truth.) At present we shall examine the naturalistic character of inquiry which in most North American thought is intimately connected with the pragmatic.

It is not accidental that the naturalistic and pragmatic characteristics of inquiry are closely connected. It has been pointed out by George Grant that pragmatism is the end result achieved through the continued process of secularizing certain trends of Protestant theology.[9] Thus, it is not surprising to find that the most thorough expositions of the pragmatic process of inquiry are at one and the same time thoroughly naturalistic, that is, they not only state that all thinking must have its foundation in natural functions and structures, they also reject the validity of any inquiry which exceeds the limits of man's sense experience. They deny the reality of the transcendent, including a personal God in the traditional sense.

The present author maintains that christians have always thought and acted, to some extent at least, in a pragmatic fashion. Although many of the most mature insights of pragmatism have developed in a secularist milieu, many facets of pragmatic thought need not be absolutized and isolated from the christian tradition. They can be incorporated within christian thought and practice in such a way as to enable especially North American christians to appreciate the richness of their christian way of life as a very feasible, integral one. The present work also maintains that the process of secularization is necessary and beneficial. The christian must respect the relative or relational autonomy of all earthly things; nevertheless, their autonomy is not absolute. Secularization and secularism are not identical; the process of secularization need not lead to secularism. Our view also affirms that there is a naturalistic foundation for knowledge but denies that man's knowledge and experience are restricted to the empirical. Man can experience the revelation of a transcendent, personal God and can ask ultimate questions.

A general theory of inquiry is naturalistic insofar as it has its natural foundation or matrix in the biological. Biological functions and structures prepare the way for inquiry and foreshadow its pattern. Rational operations grow out of organic activities, but are not identical with them. Man's environment is not just physical; the biological, as we have seen earlier, is incorporated into man's more inclusive social and cultural environment. Problems causing inquiry grow out of cultural conditions and are directed toward their modification.[10] In fact in a broad sense culture may be spoken of as "the capacity for constantly expanding the range and accuracy of one's perception of meanings."[11] Thus its on-going aspect and the central position of inquiry in expanding and achieving new meanings are emphasized. The deeper man inquires into nature the more he must be sensitive to its structures and dynamism. He must learn to observe, but his inquiry must not be *overly determined* by the biological. He must take full account of what is specifically human.

Inquiry is only free and impartial when no limitations regarding its end are established antecedently. Thinking must have its own value and its own esthetic and moral interest or it is easily subordinated to pre-determined ends and private advantage. In order that the process of inquiry might culminate in instituting conditions which can be characterized by the terms "truth" or "warranted assertibility," the strictly naturalistic philosopher maintains that all dogmatic statements, that is, statements claiming to possess inherent, self-evident truth, must be relativized and tested in terms of their consequences. Any form of absolutizing or pretending to give any knowledge a privileged relation to reality is incompatible with a consistent theory of inquiry. In fact, Dewey criticizes the "religious," and "idolatrous" atmosphere which has built up around science or physical knowledge as well as around religious dogma.[12]

Certainly the christian must agree with the naturalist that all inquiry must be free, which not only precludes the possibility of an answer being known prior to inquiry, but also calls into question the far too common practice of subordinating new knowledge to old goals, objectives or ideals. Inquiry is restricted and progress is stifled whenever men refuse to admit that their present humanistic and social goals and ideals are limited and in need of re-evaluation, expansion and even rejection. The christian, however, cannot agree with the naturalist who maintains that there is only one valid method or approach to reality, namely, the empirical. Reality must also be examined according to the specific methods of philosophy and theology. These methods differ from the empirical method and go beyond its scope; yet their investigations cannot be executed without respect for and an accurate knowledge of empirical data. Knowledge gained through revelation must be brought into relation with scientific knowledge. Any theological approach which fails to give scientific knowledge of nature full scope or tends to limit or restrict research is suspect and to be condemned.

Too frequently the naturalist uses the argument that inquiry must be free and impartial in order to do away with or invalidate all religious dogma and dogmatic assumptions. The christian must disagree. The rejection of dogmatic assumptions (assumptions made on the basis of revealed knowledge) is a real limitation to naturalistic thought, because to reject certain assumptions entails rejecting whole areas of thought and possibilities which flow from them. The use of such assumptions is valid on the grounds that basic assumptions cannot be proven right or wrong prior to inquiry. Their truth, validity or warranted assertibility can be determined by observing the coherence of their consequences with knowledge attained from other sources.

As indicated above, the knowledge of revelation can be put to a type of pragmatic test. One can inquire into the pragmatic meaning of God, the Trinity, the resurrection, etc., in such a way as to show their fittingness without attempting to give any empirical proof for them. Whereas the naturalist rejects anything transcending sense experience and seeks complete openness to truth by an initial rejection of dogma and dogmatic assumptions, the christian seeks the same openness by accepting the possible validity of dogmatic assumptions and then demonstrating their fittingness in terms of their coherence with thought arising from other sources.

Scientific inquiry, in either its broadest sense (which is

equivalent to the theory of inquiry under discussion) or in its specialized method, has as its outcome a settled state of affairs which the scientist is willing to act upon. This settled conclusion has no guarantee of permanency, but is open to further investigation. The criterion of knowledge is settled in such a way as to be available as a resource in further inquiry yet not so settled as to eliminate the possibility of further revision. Attaining settled knowledge is a progressive affair. The universality of scientific theories lies not in an inherent, fixed content, but rather in range of applicability; they are capable of taking seemingly isolated events and ordering them into systems resulting in the kind of change which is growth.[13] What is said here of scientific inquiry is also true, at least in a limited sense, of biblical and theological studies each of which has its own scentific methods. Biblical interpretation is constantly in need of revision by means of the detailed procedure of exegesis, historical and literary criticism, etc. And theologians are only too aware of the fact that their statements or propositions expressing the faith of the christian community are limited, historically conditioned and in need of further development and interpretation.

The naturalist and christian agree that all inquiry is specific in origin and aim because problems are concrete and specific. Questions arise within the historical continuum, and knowledge arises out of particular problems in need of solutions. Yet they disagree regarding the possibility of asking ultimate questions. Dewey's rejection of the possibility of man being able to ask ultimate questions or attain any answers to ultimate concerns appears to be closely connected with his theory of intelligence. As indicated above, the succession of concrete problems keeps thought alive; the function of the mind is to project new, more complex ends and to free experience from routine. Intelligence is inherently forward-looking and creative.[14] Thus to affirm that man could ever achieve a relatively certain universal conception of the whole universe and answers to ultimate questions is incompatible with maintaining a living intelligence and the unending process of growth which is the only end Dewey will acknowledge for the cosmic process.

Both the naturalist and christian experience a deep need to achieve unity in their over-all outlook on reality. In one sense this is a very specific problem, and yet in its full scope it is an ultimate question whose answer extends to the whole of reality and whose consequences affect the other specific questions in life. One cannot help but feel that the naturalist who rejects ultimate questions does so because the limits of his naturalism require it, yet he must concern himself with such questions in spite of this if he is to attain any in-depth insight into more specific human questions. For instance, when Dewey regards philosophical thought as criticism he necessarily involves himself in ultimate questions, in things that are not merely instrumental.

The christian can affirm that knowledge enables man to overcome fears and be free to secure an ample, liberal life for all men. Unity and wholeness are the goals of thought. He can maintain creative intelligence and the drive to advance toward a desirable future at the same time as he affirms the necessity of a certain knowledge of an ultimate goal and a divine guarantee that ultimately evolution will succeed, a guarantee which cannot be had on the basis of empirical knowledge. In fact the christian can maintain that the direction, certainty and relative security afforded by revelation are necessary if man is to persevere in promoting further inquiries and pushing ahead. A balance between temporal and specifically christian goals can be maintained, because, according to the christian tradition, the goal to which the whole cosmic process is directed requires the full and continued use of all man's faculties and yet extends beyond man's powers of attainment unaided by the love of God. Such a goal heightens rather than weakens man's need to apply creative intelligence and wholehearted commitment to the task of fostering evolution.

Historically there have been inadequate theologies of the Incarnation and Redemption which have in fact dampened the incentive of many christians to commit themselves whole-heartedly to fostering temporal concerns. Certain theologies have given the impression that a man's redemption has already been completed or at least guaranteed once he acknowledges Christ as Saviour and does his best to avoid seriously sinful action. Naturalists are certainly justified in pointing out that such an attitude is destructive of what is most creative and on-going in man. It allows him unwarranted opportunity for complacency with himself and the status quo in society and weakens his drive to pursue temporal concerns.

The theology of both the Incarnation and Redemption to be presented in this work achieves a much healthier balance between "the already" (that which has already been accomplished by Christ's passion-death-resurrection) and "the not yet" (that which is still in process of becoming). Man is redeemed and yet must commit himself to the whole task of working out his salvation which includes the work of fostering evolution as a necessary but insufficient precondition of the second coming of Christ. He cannot use his faith in Christ's redeeming love to justify lack of industry in the pursuit of his temporal responsibilities.

We have pointed out that both the re-evaluation of present ends, goals or ideals and the development of new ones are an integral part of man's processes of inquiry and necessary for evolution. Thus we shall examine the development of ideals in an evolutionary perspective.

C. Developing Ideals in an Evolutionary Context

There is no doubt that the ideals held by men in a world in process of development are of crucial significance for both the individual and the whole. There is also no doubt that in such a milieu man's ideals must be on-going; processes of technological and social advance force him to alter both his immediate, specific ideals or aims and his long-term, more comprehensive goals. It is also very difficult for man, who is within the evolutionary process, to examine reality and develop ideals on the basis of this examination which will be adequate norms by which he can turn round and evaluate the very process out of which the ideals were developed. Yet if we affirm that man is an inherent part of nature and that the mental, spiritual and ideal are not epiphenomena of nature, we are forced to admit that this is what must be done.

The very fact that various schools of philosophy have been characterized as "idealistic" and "realistic" indicates that the problem is not new although it undoubtedly takes on added dimensions in process philosophy. The fact that large numbers of persons today have "given up" on ideals and regard them as unrelated to reality heightens the need to highlight the connection between the actual and the ideal. John Dewey's approach to ideals does this and can be developed further to consistently include ideals which have been promulgated specifically by Christ.

An object as it exists and is known has value, but is also open to possible development and therefore increased value. *The actual,* therefore, is a set of present conditions. *The possible* is the ends or consequences which the actual may bring into existence if it is used or interacted with in specific ways. *The possible,* therefore, *is the ideal* for that situation. In other words, the ideal is the intelligently thought-out possibilities of the real or actual which may be used as methods for improving it. Thus ideals are continuous with natural events; they do not exist in a superior realm apart from actual conditions in such a way that they are merely imposed on the real from above. An idea, in its intellectual content, is a suggestion of something to be done and a method or plan of action. Having ideals is one aspect of existence made possible because reality, being both precarious and incomplete, needs to be brought to fulfillment by means of intelligent interaction.[15] If men were unable to form ideals they would be incapable of bringing nature to fulfillment.

There is an intimate connection between *the material* and *the ideal*. The material is a condition of the existence of something else. To disregard the effective means of change (material conditions) is to disregard the spiritual or ideal because the ideal is the consummation of conditions, the fulfillment of means. Nature, because it involves matter, has mechanism; but nature is *not only mechanism*. Because there are interactions and connections within it which are mechanistic (that is, relatively constant and uniform) inference, calculation, prediction and control of nature are possible. The application of mechanical formulae enable man to know nature, to develop it and put it to human use. Tools are things in which a sequential bond of nature is embodied, and their ability to help man interact with and realize nature depends upon the mechanical aspect of nature itself. The mechanization of nature by man is the condition of a practical, progressive idealism in action, the condition of framing new ideals and progressing systematically to achieve them.[16]

Dewey goes on to show how science and art, which are concerned with ideals and values, are not only within nature but are instrumental in modifying it and bringing it to fulfillment. Thus they are also instrumental in assisting men to formulate and realize ideals. We have already seen that according to the underlying evolutionary principle operative in this work (the law of complexity-consciousness) the spiritual is never separate from but rather co-extensive with its material base. The material and spiritual develop in intimate connection and in proportion with one another. It is not difficult, therefore, to see how Dewey's detailed analysis concerning science, the practical arts and art is compatible with our over-all view of evolution.

Scientific knowledge enables man to know experienced objects in terms of their relations and to interact with these relations for the purpose of directing change, bringing about new ends and realizing new possibilities. It opens up nature to human purposes and desires, modifies the connection between the energies and acts which compose nature, and regulates the appearance of immediate qualities in nature. Experimental science is an art of development, and nature is the material to be reshaped. Yet both science and the practical arts are within nature in such a way that new objects of imagination and projected ends are really continuations of the natural process itself. The laws of nature are convenient formulations of chosen portions of change registered in such a way that they become methods of subsequent procedure. They flow from interactions within nature and return to regulate future interactions. The discovery of each law of nature and the accompanying increase of control increases man's responsibility to direct nature toward its fuller good or realization.[17] He does this through science and particularly through art.

Although we shall not discuss esthetic experience in detail now the relationship between science and art and the role of art in man's self-realization will be analyzed briefly in order to show how art is connected with the process of achieving ideals. The significance of the esthetic in man's spiritual fulfillment will be developed further when we show the intimate connection between esthetic and mystical experience.

Intelligence and science are also instrumental in directing natural events to meanings capable of immediate possession and enjoyment; that is, they are instrumental in operative art. Art is

> . . . the mode of activity that is charged with meaning capable of immediately enjoyed possession.[18]

It is "the complete culmination of nature," and science is a handmaiden which directs natural events to such a consummation. In art the ordered phase and the incomplete, particular phase of nature are united; thus art is a natural event in which nature comes fully to itself. At the same time art both distinguishes man from nature and unites him to it. He is distinguishable from it because he can intentionally use its materials to develop his own life. Yet he is concretely united to nature because he achieves this expansion in accord with the structure of his own biological organism. Art is, therefore, both *the complete culmination of nature* and one of the most efficacious means of personal self-realization.[19] In this way it assists man in developing and realizing ideals.

The approach to ideals set forth above need not be restricted to natural aims, but can be extended within the christian context to include the transcendent ideals known to man through revelation and achieved by the grace of Christ. There need be no opposition or dichotomy between authentic humanistic ideals and christian religious ideals because grace does not destroy but builds on nature. Christ did not come to take His disciples out of the world, but that they may "have life and have it to the full." The realistic ideal He offered mankind was the fullness of human life and even more. Human powers to love, serve, heal and build community are extended or perfected beyond the natural capacities of man because they have been transformed by the indwelling Spirit of God acting as an interior divine principle or source of life and activity in man.

Man's *actual* situation, therefore, is an on-going, problematic one, but one to which he brings all his human capabilities perfected by the grace of Christ. The *possible* or the *ideal* for which man can strive is not only the full realization of the earthly community, but the realization of universal brotherhood in the life of Christ. The promise of resurrection means that this brotherhood, which human powers aided and transformed by grace can realistically strive for here and now, will be brought to its consummation in eternity. Christian ideals, therefore, need not distract man from temporal ideals because to become fully christian man must become fully human; and God has promised him the inspiration, motivation and love to achieve this ideal. In relating and comparing humanistic and christian ideals, therefore, one must consider which is more adequate on the basis of 1) whether it takes into account *all* the phenomena whose functions are active in evolution now, and 2) whether it includes within itself *all* the forces necessary to accomplish the task of building a universal community based on brotherhood and love.

D. *The Means - Ends Relation within Activity*

A study of the means-ends relation within activity finds a place in the discussion of scientific knowledge as evolutionary because the process in which ends and means are determined is a deliberative process which involves the acquisition and use of scientific knowledge. As well, it is not only intimately connected with the determination of ideals, but also with the process of inquiry because knowing is doing.

A means is never to be conceived as a mere means, separate from and merely instrumental in achieving an end. The *process* in which aims or ends are formed begins with a wish or an emotional reaction against existing conditions and a hope for change. This process is a deliberative one, and the proposed end or end-in-view must be worked out in terms of the concrete conditions which are available as means to realize it. The end-in-view, therefore, is really a set of foreseen consequences or the "what" of that which is to be enacted. These consequences influence and guide the process of deliberation and bring it to a conclusion by providing adequate motivation to move the agent to overt action. Ends are not "things" beyond activity; they are "terminals of deliberations," and therefore, turning points in activity. They give activity *meaning* and *direct its further course*; thus they should never be regarded as ends of action separate from or independent of the means by which they were achieved. Means are the specific conditions which can be actively used to attain foreseen consequences in the most effective way.[20]

Within the whole process of deliberation the consequences or the "what" are an integral component of the "how," the procedure or means of knowing. Any acceptance of an end-in-

154

itself apart from its means 1) takes attention away from examining consequences and purposes, 2) leads to carelessness in inspecting present conditions, 3) turns man back to act upon past habits, 4) connotes that *ideals* are fixed ends beyond activity, and 5) gives ideas a static connotation as well.[21] In Dewey's thought

> Ideas are largely the obverse side of action; a perception of what might be, but is not. . . .[22]

The intimate connection between means and ends can be developed further. Means are always causal conditions which have been *freely* used *because of their connection with chosen consequences*. To choose and accomplish anything as an end is to commit oneself at the same time to the same love and care for the acts and events that are its means. Or, one can say that one wills the end in the means. Ends are effects only when thought has perceived and chosen the conditions and processes that can bring them about.[23]

Means and ends or consequences are temporally connected, but their connection cannot be reduced to time alone. The means is not past when the end is achieved. Both the means and the consequences of having chosen this particular means live on in the end. Within the temporal process there is a deposit *at each stage* which enters *cumulatively* and *constitutively* into the outcome. Whenever means and ends are regarded as separate (not intimately connected *within* the one process) one performs an activity or production which is not regarded as consummatory and an end or consummation is reached which is not seen as the fulfillment of a productive process. The result of such a perspective is that means are degraded and regarded as inferior to ends.[24] Such a separation is invalid; consequences develop throughout the whole process of transforming the undesirable situation into a more acceptable one and means remain as part of the transformed situation. As Richard Bernstein put it, in Dewey's thought means and ends refer to the same reality conceived from different perspectives. They form one continuum, at any point the means being in the end in its present stage of realization.[25]

This entire approach to the means-ends relationship is particularly significant because it takes the emphasis off attaining or *possessing things* as ends and places it on liberating activity. There is no doubt that the way to define an activity is to place before oneself the *object* in which it terminates, but the *object* is only a sign or mark by which the mind specifies the *activity* to be performed. Dewey illustrates this point by the example of shooting at a target. Not the target, but *hitting* it is the end-in-view; both the target and gun sight are means by which one takes aim. If the target is a rabbit, the rabbit by itself apart from the activity is not the desired end. The rabbit is a factor in activity; the marksman may want it to eat or to show as a sign of his marksmanship. It is *doing something with a thing* and not the thing in isolation which constitutes an end. The object or thing is but *one phase* of the active end. When the end is regarded as a thing to be possessed, a static reality acquired apart from the activity, *activity* becomes a *mere unavoidable means to something else,* insignificant on its own account, a necessary evil which must be gone through before the desired object can be attained. Separation of means and ends diminishes the meaning of work and reduces it to drudgery to be avoided if possible. Only when men experience realizing their end at every stage of their activity does the full realization of the end become a future sight which keeps the activity moving fully and freely. The aim or end is then a *means.*[26]

There are, however, activities and experiences which are not inherently consummatory, but which can lead to consummations. Such activities are sheer hard work for man in spite of the fact that some satisfaction is achieved through their relation to the consummation to which they are directed. According to Robert J. Roth, Dewey does not reduce even these predominantly instrumental activities to mere means. Means are "media" when they are *not just* preparatory or preliminary but are seen as *consciously related to consummatory experience.*[27] Even when regarded as "media" and not mere means these activities are not consummatory in the full sense, but such an approach to them increases man's appreciation of their meaning in his life. This is of primary significance because the characteristic human need is "the possession and appreciation of the *meaning* of things,"[28] not their mere possession.

The analysis of the means-ends relation has shed light on the significance of work in man's development and the need of finding meaning and satisfaction in all activity if it is to promote self-realization. Significance is put back in means and taken away from mere possession of material things; thus integrity is given to the very process of living. Above all, this analysis reveals the total inadequacy of determining one's ends or goals prior to the consideration of their means of attainment and the fallacy of the addage that the end justifies the means, an approach which has had disastrous consequences in decision-making in ethical matters. We shall turn now to examine the meaning of and criteria for truth.

II. *The Meaning and Criteria of Truth*

As Eugene Fontinell points out, historically three basic theories of truth or knowledge have developed: the correspondence theory, the coherence theory and the pragmatic theory. He recognizes many variations and overlappings among these theories, and suggests that any significant theory of truth combines elements involved in all three criteria.[29] A study of the thought of both Dewey and Teilhard indicates that both authors incorporate some aspects of all these criteria, yet they differ as to the relative emphasis each places on them. Dewey places almost exclusive emphasis on the pragmatic criterion, and since this world view is directed to christians whose mode of thought is frequently pragmatic, we shall outline Dewey's thought in some detail. Next we shall set forth Teilhard's concept of the various criteria and finally conclude our analysis by pointing out which of the three criteria should be dominant and what elements of the other criteria can be most effectively related to it in our world view.

Dewey's theory regarding truth flows from his theory of knowledge. Since ideas, meanings, theories and conceptions are all instruments in the active re-organization of a troubled situation, the test of their validity lies in whether they resolve the situation or not. If they succeed they are reliable, good, true; if they fail to clear up the confusion when acted upon, they are false. Truth is a name for an experienced relation, one in which intentions or purposes are examined from the point of view of the fulfillment they secure through their own operation. Verification lies in consequences; that which guides a process truly is true. Truth is demonstrated capacity to give such guidance. The quality of action an idea effects is that in which its truth or falsity lies. By their fruits you will know them — the successful hypothesis is the true one. "Truth" is an abstract noun applied to all the cases which have, do or will receive confirmation in their works and consequences; it is processes of change directed so as to achieve a desired consummation.[30]

The pragmatic concept of truth often speaks of truth in terms of satisfaction, but this is neither emotional satisfaction, private comfort nor the gratification of a strictly personal need. The satisfaction at issue is one concerning the needs and conditions of the specific problem out of which the method of action arose; thus it involves *public* and *objective conditions*. Truth when defined in terms of utility must not be reduced to use for personal profit; rather, as utility, truth means service in making the specific contribution an idea claims to be able to make in re-organizing a situation.[31] When truth is thought of as correspondence between existence and thought, the correspondence is not that of two pieces of paper of identical size and shape, but a correspondence or interadjustment between the consequences called forth by the conditions of the situation to be rectified and the consequences of the ideas or plans of action projected to rectify it.[32] This is a dynamic relation of correspondence, not conformity of thought to a static reality.

A truth arrived at in solving one problem often affords an effective method of controlling other problems so that it secures a certain permanent status. Such ideas become permanent resources, the "eternal truths" to which positive value is assigned on their own account; yet these truths are only *relatively* unchanging. When they are applied in new situations to solve new problems they *must* undergo some re-making if they are to maintain their vitality and success.[33]

This incomplete, in-process-of-developing, quality of truth as well as its inherent limitations is expressed by Dewey when, from a logical standpoint, he approvingly quotes Peirce's definition of truth.

> The opinion which is fated to be ultimately agreed to by all who investigate is what we mean by the truth, and the object represented by this opinion is the real.[34]

This same definition is further developed by Peirce and quoted by Dewey.

> Truth is that concordance of an abstract statement with the ideal limit towards which endless investigation would tend to bring scientific belief, which concordance the abstract statement may possess by virtue of the confession of its innacuracy and one-sidedness, and this confession is an essential ingredient of truth.[35]

Not only is truth always in process of undergoing modification, its limitations or inaccuracy are an essential element of the definition of truth itself; they are not merely accidental.

Teilhard aimed at a synthesis of knowledge; above all he sought to attain coherence and homogeneity in knowledge. The essential mark or criterion of truth for him was *coherence*, the power of thought to develop itself indefinitely without developing internal contradictions, but rather forming a positively construed whole in which the parts support and mutually complement each other. The more true the vision the more the various elements (physical, moral, social and religious) mutually illuminate each other indefinitely. The more successful a synthesis and the more true an idea the more they open up wider, unforeseen horizons for future inquiry. True scientific discovery consists in finding the hidden connections between areas and orders which had appeared to be radically separated; thus there is a homogeneous quality to truth. The danger of subjectivism is avoided by the balance of both coherence and homogeneity in knowledge and by insistence on the need to begin with observation. Whereas mathematics is coherent it is purely subjective so that mathematical statements are not to be called truths. In the light of the discussion of these criteria it is evident why Teilhard places as great an emphasis on research as he does and why he regards any scientific, philosophical or theological approach that limits discovery as automatically suspect and open to condemnation.[36]

Both the on-going quality of truth and its pragmatic quality are upheld because *in science and elsewhere* the test of truth is *coherence and productiveness*. The more order a theory imposes on man's cosmic vision and the more it is capable of directing and sustaining further research and construction, the more certain the theory is. The truth of an hypothesis is demonstrated by its heuristic value — its ability to provoke further development of the theory. *True theory* is to be equated with that which is most *advantageous* in the scientific pursuit of reality.[37]

Our exposition of Teilhard's reflection on truth can be concluded by examining a text which rejects a pure subjectivity but insists upon what might be described as a relational objectivity.

> The *truth* is nothing but the total coherence of the
> universe in relation to each part of itself. Why suspect

or undervalue this coherence because we are ourselves the observers? Scientists are always contrasting something they call anthropocentric illusion with something they call objective reality. The distinction does not exist. The truth of man is the truth of the universe for man, that is to say the truth, pure and simple.[38]

As indicated in chapter one Teilhard rejects a type of pure objectivity in knowledge (what he calls here "objective reality") and also a pure subjectivism (what he calls here "anthropocentric illusion"). His insistence upon the objectivity of truth and also upon its relational quality is evident from the above text. His rejection of pure subjectivity is further illustrated in a note in which he insists that where the criterion for truth is establishing a growing maximum of universal coherence the truth achieved has something objective about it which exceeds the effects of personal temperament.[39] He has rejected an older concept of objectivity compatible only with the concept of a static universe and, while avoiding the danger of pure subjectivity, sketched the basic lines for conceiving an objective, dynamic truth compatible with a dynamic, evolutionary cosmos.

The approach to the problem of subjectivity and objectivity in knowing presented in this world view has as its object to drive a mean between theories which propose either an extreme objectivism or an extreme subjectivism both of which misrepresent reality and diminish respect for experience. It rejects what might be described as a spectator conception of knowledge, that is, a conception in which the knower is set over against the world to be known so that reality is presented to him as pre-established and ready-made. The knower's job then is reduced to obtaining a transcript of reality which conforms with it as a mere existence. Our view certainly does not deny that there are things in existence prior to the beginning of the process of knowing them. But it does deny that as mere existences (and not as the conclusion of one historical event of inquiry in connection with other histories) things are the object of knowledge. The antecedent of thought is not mere existences as such, but these realities as part of a situation which is indeterminate in its components. Thus man becomes a knower; the subject of knowledge is part of the whole reality under examination.[40]

It is not necessary to conceive of reality as immutable in order to recognize that value and meaning are objective. Yet an excessive objectivism must be avoided insofar as facts and meanings are never immediately observable as if they were raw existences. They do not exist in isolation apart from a theory. Experience becomes enveloped in a series of assumptions as soon as man attempts to formulate it. There is a subjective element in interpretation in all experience. Thus we deny a pure objectivity to knowledge in the sense that things have a permanent essence which can be grasped apart from their relations with other things. And we would also maintain that the truth of a proposition does not have a type of objectivity which enables it to be understood apart from the process of inquiry from which it developed.

There is, therefore, a subjective element in all knowledge, but this does not imply an excessive subjectivism, a type of knowledge which is merely personal or characterized by a private or exclusive quality. Where the criterion of truth is establishing a universal coherence, the knowledge or truth man acquires has an objectivity which exceeds the effects of personal temperament. There is no dualism between the orders of being and knowing. Man must learn to see and develop a subjective sensitivity in interpreting reality and formulating judgments about it. The way reality is in existence is the way man experiences it, and he must not suspect the coherence he recognizes in his knowledge because he is the observer. The truth of man, as Teilhard puts it, is the truth of the universe for man.

The present world view maintains that the type of correspondence involved in truth is more complex than a mere

162

static correspondence between existence and thought. Influenced by the validity of pragmatic insights, it affirms that this correspondence is a dynamic relation of correspondence between the consequences of the conditions of the situation to be rectified and the consequences of the ideas or plans of action proposed as solutions. This *dynamic* correspondence is also evident by the fact that man must learn how to observe and approach reality in a way in which it can reveal itself as it is historically. The concept of an on-going type of correspondence is compatible with and indeed supported by the fact that *one* criteria of truth or warranted assertibility must certainly be that a statement which has achieved a permanent status in one situation be effective as a means of control in others.

The pragmatic criterion of truth is important but must be related and *subordinate* to the more essential criteria of coherence and homogeneity. The pragmatic criterion will stress the practicality involved in truth and the need to refer to consequences in determining meaning and testing thought. The satisfaction afforded by truth is the satisfaction of the needs and conditions of the problematic situation in which it arose; this satisfaction, therefore, involves public and objective conditions. If any emphasis is placed on the "utility" of truth within the larger pragmatic approach this is neither a promotion of private profit nor well-being. The utility promoted by truth is a much more extensive and inclusive usefulness which encompasses all the goods which promote authentic human life and growth in being. Immediate satisfaction and comfort must often be sacrificed in order that this criterion of truth may be fulfilled. In fact the pragmatic quality of truth is more accurately referred to in terms of productiveness than in terms of utility. In this way its intimate connection with coherence is more readily seen. The true theory is the most advantageous in the scientific pursuit of reality. The truth of an hypothesis is in proportion to its ability to provoke further development of the theory of which it is a part. This pragmatic or productive quality of truth is demonstrable not only in the realm of science but extends and is revealed in philosophical and theological approaches to reality as well.

The dominant criterion of truth is coherence; the more order a theory imposes on man's cosmic vision and the more capable it is of directing and sustaining further research and construction the more certain it is. Thought must be able to develop itself indefinitely without developing internal contradictions. It must form a positive whole in which the parts support and complement one another. The more true the vision the more its physical, moral, social and religious elements illuminate one another and the more hidden connections are seen between areas which appeared unrelated. Wider, unforeseen horizons for future inquiry continually come to light. The coherence and relative homogeneity in reality is also found in knowledge. We have demonstrated this fact throughout our work not only by showing the intimate connection between the biological and cultural but also by showing the coherence between the biological and cultural structure of reality and the structure of thought and inquiry.

In order that the coherence and homogeneity in reality and in knowledge be more evident and applied in life we have discussed the need to achieve a fundamental unity in the progress of inquiry and pointed out many of the highlights of this process. Yet we do not maintain that this is the *only* method by which reality can be approached. The empirical method must be complemented by the philosophical and theological methods. All these methods were described in chapter one in terms of meridian lines which run parallel to one another and converge only at the poles. Thus in the over-all view of reality a number of assumptions based on non-empirical evidence may be accepted and coped with and the coherence between natural and revealed knowledge can be demonstrated. According to our perspective to reject these assumptions is to place an unwarranted limitation on the coherence and scope of truth.

FOOTNOTES

1. *Logic*, pp. 60-65, 67, 76-78, 114-15; *Knowing and the Known*, pp. 272-73, 281-83.
2. *Logic*, pp. 64-66, 71, 74-75, 115-17; *Knowing and the Known*, pp. 272-73, 278-84.
3. *Logic*, p. 66.
4. *Logic*, pp. 76-79, 97-98; *Experience and Nature*, p. 382.
5. *Essays in Experimental Logic*, pp. 22, 30-31, 91-92; *Logic*, pp. 14-15; *The Quest for Certainty*, pp. 242-43.
6. *Essays in Experimental Logic*, p. 330.
7. "The Need for a Recovery of Philosophy," *On Experience, Nature, and Freedom*, p. 64.
8. *Essays in Experimental Logic*, p. 330; "The Experimental Theory of Knowledge," *The Influence of Darwin on Philosophy*, p. 109.
9. George Grant, *Philosophy in the Mass Age* (Vancouver: Copp Clark, 1966), pp. 82-84.
10. *Logic*, pp. 9-10, 18-20, 23-25, 42-44, 246.
11. *Democracy and Education*, p. 123.
12. *Reconstruction in Philosophy*, pp. 145-46; *Problems of Men*, p. 335; *The Quest for Certainty*, p. 221.
13. *Logic*, pp. 7-9; *Reconstruction in Philosophy*, xv-xvi; "Qualitative Thought," *On Experience, Nature, and Freedom*, p. 187.
14. For some insight into Dewey's thought in this area see: *The Quest for Certainty*, p. 228; *Essays in Experimental Logic*, pp. 18-20; "The Postulate of Immediate Empiricism," *The Influence of Darwin on Philosophy*, pp. 237-38; "The Need for a Recovery of Philosophy," *On Experience, Nature, and Freedom*, pp. 65-66; *Experience and Nature*, p. 406.
15. *Essays in Experimental Logic*, pp. 72, 237, 240-41; *Experience and Nature*, pp. 62-63; *The Quest for Certainty*, pp. 299-300; *Reconstruction in Philosophy*, pp. 118, 121-22.
16. *The Quest for Certainty*, pp. 247-48, 269-70; *Reconstruction in Philosophy*, pp. 70-73; *Experience and Nature*, pp. 122-23.
17. *The Quest for Certainty*, pp. 98-105, 128, 245-47; "Intelligence and Morals," *The Influence of Darwin on Philosophy*, pp. 72-74; *Experience and Nature*, pp. 128, 135-36, 413-15, 421-22.
18. *Experience and Nature*, p. 358.
19. *Art as Experience*, pp. 25-26; *Experience and Nature*, pp. 357-60.
20. "Means and Consequences — How, What, and What For," *A Philosophical Correspondence*, p. 651; *Human Nature and Conduct*, pp. 223-25, 234.
21. "Means and Consequences — How, What, and What For," *A Philosophical Correspondence*, pp. 651-52; *Human Nature and Con-*

duct, pp. 223, 232-33.

22. *Experience and Nature*, p. 350.
23. *Experience and Nature*, pp. 366-67.
24. *Experience and Nature*, p. 368.
25. Richard Bernstein, *John Dewey*, p. 153.
26. *Democracy and Education*, pp. 105-06.
27. Robert J. Roth, *John Dewey and Self-Realization*, pp. 44-47.
28. *Experience and Nature*, p. 362.
29. Eugene Fontinell, *Toward a Reconstruction of Religion*, p. 99.
30. *Reconstruction in Philosophy*, pp. 156-57; *Experience and Nature*, p. 161; "The Experimental Theory of Knowledge," *The Influence of Darwin on Philosophy*, pp. 95-96, 109-10; "The Intellectual Criterion for Truth," *The Influence of Darwin on Philosophy*, pp. 150-51; "A Short Catechism concerning Truth," *The Influence of Darwin on Philosophy*, p. 164.
31. *Reconstruction in Philosophy*, p. 157.
32. "A Short Catechism concerning Truth," *The Influence of Darwin on Philosophy*, pp. 159-60.
33. "The Intellectualist Criterion for Truth," *The Influence of Darwin on Philosophy*, pp. 147, 151-53.
34. *Logic*, n. 6, p. 345.
35. *Logic*, n. 6, p. 345.
36. "Comment je vois," (unpublished mimeographed manuscript, p. 1); "Mon Univers," *SC*, pp. 66-67 [Eng. trans. pp. 38-39]; "Action et activation," *SC*, pp. 225-26 [Eng. trans. pp. 178-79]; "Le Phénomène humain," *VP*, p. 234 [Eng. trans. p. 166]; *PH*, Prologue, p. 29 [Eng. trans. p. 35].
37. "La Place de l'homme dans l'univers: Réflexions sur la complexité," *VP*, p. 318 [Eng. trans. p. 227].
38. "Esquisse d'un univers personnel," *ÉH*, p. 71 [Eng. trans. pp. 54-55].
39. "Comment je crois," *CJC*, n. 1, p. 150 [Eng. trans. n. 12, p. 130].
40. *Experience and Nature*, pp. 156, 214-15, 230-31, 241; *The Quest for Certainty*, p. 204; *Reconstruction in Philosophy*, pp. 112, 121-22; *Essays in Experimental Logic*, pp. 38-40; "The Need for a Recovery of Philosophy," *On Experience, Nature, and Freedom*, pp. 61-62.

Chapter 7

MORAL EXPERIENCE AS EVOLUTIONARY

I. *The Origin, Scope and Approach to Morality*

A philosophical view is not formulated merely to provide men with an intellectual vision, but rather to expand their moral attitudes and give orientation to their conduct. All knowledge is directed toward action and friendship. Our intellectual vision of reality, therefore, is meant to help men see the full context in which they act so that they can determine more effectively the action required of them if they are to fulfill themselves and bring the evolutionary process to its consummation. The concept of morality presented here flows from the fundamental evolutionary tenets of the whole world view, is as extensive as the whole, and cannot be presented apart from the entire movement of the cosmos toward its spiritualization or fulfillment.

In one sense, therefore, the ethical dimension of the vision ought not to be introduced until the entire world view has been presented, because it is both dependent upon and the fruit of the whole. Yet it is impossible to complete the vision without discussing its moral dimension at this point.

A. *The Origin of Morality in the Nature of Man Himself*

We have already seen that with the appearance of man evolution emerged into the realm of liberty; free reflective energy was released into the world, an indeterminate energy capable of getting out of control. Man is not only capable of thought, he reflects on his own thinking and chooses the goals toward which his thought and action are directed. Liberty is always *for* something; it must have an end to which it is oriented and it must be guided. Freedom and thought appeared as the term of the psychic development of life, and morality is essential if free, reflective activity is to bring evolution to its consummation. Morality is a direct extension of the biological and organic sphere, and as such is at the service of evolution to direct it toward its end. The moral development of humanity is the authentic, natural consequence of organic evolution.[1]

Because evolution had to acquire morality in order to advance beyond the appearance of man, both the origin and foundation of morality can be established within the evolutionary process itself. Morality can also claim an organic function within the evolutionary process, that of coordinating and controlling the free human energy which must foster evolution. Once men recognize the biological value of moral action and the organic nature of personal and social relationships they will appreciate more fully that the moral life and ethical principles are not externally imposed from ideals or obligations independent of life, but are stimulated by the necessities of existence itself, the need to maintain and foster life.

The whole approach to morality presented here, therefore, is couched in the dynamism of cosmic evolution. The very fact that man is born and must develop himself in function of the cosmic current is the initial foundation of his obligations. The individual destinies of men depend upon a universal destiny so that the whole evolutionary process is at stake when men choose the direction of their action or refuse to act. This is the framework and condition of the gigantic problem of duty and its fulfillment. Questions concerning why and how men should act are questions of cosmic action. Since on the practical level man is the responsible heir of a large portion of the world's energy which must be conserved and extended, he has an obligation to make all the forces provided by the earth serve to advance the progress of the whole. Harnassing the forces of material energy is essential, but secondary, to his task of *promoting* the continued flow of the current of spirit in the cosmos. Man must see that respect and love for life does not decrease or waste away. This is a responsibility which increases as man's spiritual and technological evolution continue, and one which requires an intimate co-operative effort among the moral, physical, biological and social sciences. Once man sees himself as the motor and organic center of the spiritual evolution of the universe he sees his full responsibility to organize all the energies available to him in order to complete the task. Such a view requires a transformation of both his view of himself and of his morality.[2]

We have attempted to show the broadest basis for morality, man *within* nature; but in order to understand morality we must focus more specifically on man. Morality is a specifically human reality. Man can be and act morally because he is intelligent, free and social. He can think, evaluate, project ideals and make reflective choices. These capacities are conditions for moral action. But man is also moral because he is a social being to the core. We have already shown in our discussion of creation that man does not come into existence first and only secondarily, or at a later moment, enter into relationships with God and his fellow man. We defined creation in terms of God bringing man not merely into existence, but into relationship with Himself and with his fellow men. We have also seen that a man cannot be or know himself apart from his fellow men. Man is his history; he is *radically relational* or *social*.

What we are doing here is analyzing human nature, a task which is absolutely essential if we are to gain any authentic insight into morality because morality is the most humane of all subjects, that closest to human nature. Morality has traditionally been defined as what man ought to do by reason of what he is. It is grounded in the very nature or being of man as reflective, free and social. Thus we must study human nature, a reality which is neither static nor in constant flux. Human nature certainly has its own constitution, that is, it has permanent elements which are continuous and essential to it, yet it is on-going, open to further development and modification.[3]

Both Dewey and Teilhard recognize that morality is grounded in and flows from the nature of man. In fact, Dewey maintains that, because this is so, morals must be reflective and empirical. Because ethics is concerned with the healthy and efficient development of human nature it must be closely connected with a *science of human nature*. He also maintains that such a science has not been adequately developed and points out that, as a science, ethics cannot progress until a science of human nature has been developed and its methods and materials brought to bear on ethical judgments.[4]

Our concern here is not with the development of a specific science of human nature; reference to it is merely made to emphasize the intimate connection between human nature and ethics and to show that ethics must be grounded in human nature as an on-going metaphysical reality and not in mere social customs and conventions. It must also be made clear once again that throughout this work when we speak of such realities as human nature, more-being and self-realization we are speaking of metaphysical and not merely sociological realities.

Morality, therefore, has its specific origin and basis in human nature as an on-going reality understood not in abstraction from the whole cosmic process, but in its specific interactions with its environment, that is, human nature as an organic part of the whole of nature. It is evident, therefore, that what we are proposing is a type of on-going natural law ethics, but not one which is equivalent to *conforming* to static laws or patterns of nature. Man must constantly move beyond nature in the sense of moving beyond his present patterns and accomplishments. He must master the patterns by which his life is structured; this requires an in-depth knowledge of human nature, its goals and the ways it is evolving.

B. *The Development and Scope of Moral Theory*

Having shown that morality is grounded in human nature, we are in a position to discuss the manner in which moral standards and ethical theory develop. Man is born associated with other persons, but mere association cannot be equated with personal participation, sharing in the goals and lives of other persons. Personal participation and the development of community occur through the give and take of communication and mutual interaction. Active connections and customary ways of relating with each other naturally develop among men, and these mutual activities have consequences. Whenever these consequences are regarded as good a reasonable desire to maintain this activity arises. Once men have attained this level of communal sharing the necessary foundation for further moral growth is available. Continued organization of social and rational choices may be made, and these choices may be secured in terms of habits and character.[5]

Certainly men judged right and wrong before they began to develop ethical theories. Only when there is no clear belief as to what is right or wrong in a situation is there a need for further inquiry and criticism and for new criteria for criticizing accepted standards. Through such processes moral theory has arisen. It is nothing but the conscious systematic questioning of a person or group of persons who seek to solve moral conflicts reflectively. The sources to which both the perplexed individual and the moral theorist must look in order to obtain a body of dependable data and working hypotheses to assist them in developing ethical theory are extensive. They include all the codes of conduct developed by various cultures and religions, the materials of legal history and judicial decisions, the history and activities of all great human institutions, the findings of all the sciences (especially those closest to man), and the methods and conclusions characteristic of both Western and Eastern history and thought.[6]

One of the fundamental problems in the development of moral theory has been that it has tended to conceive morality as static. This tendency arose because men saw a need to protect themselves against mutual encroachments; thus morality was conceived and developed as a defense of both the individual and society. Whenever a system or organization developed which guaranteed most men what was due to them, they felt that the system had to be guaranteed against changes which might challenge accepted solutions and procedures and upset the established order of society. Thus morality was conceived as a fixed system of rights and duties designed to establish a static equilibrium among individuals. Morality has frequently maintained this equilibrium at the expense of limiting creative energies. Underlying this whole concept of the role of morality is the idea that each person represents in some way an absolute term in the world which must be protected against exterior invasions.

Without detracting from the absolute value of individual persons and the significance of their self-realization, our understanding of the role of morality can be transformed. The weaknesses in a static morality can be overcome in a processive world view in which the development of individual persons in seen in its cosmic dimension, that is, within the development of the larger collective consciousness that is in process of development.

In this perspective morality is no longer aimed primarily at preserving and protecting individuals, but at guiding them so effectively in the direction of their individual and collective fulfillments that the enormous amount of personal energy and potential left untapped at present will be fully released. Such a morality may be described as a morality of movement as opposed to a static morality. The ethicist becomes the engineer developing the spiritual energies of the whole world, and the highest morality is that which will discover the best way to develop the riches of nature to their most superior limits *by awakening and convergence.*[7]

Once men recognize that reality is processive and see the universe in the form of a common ascent toward consciousness, life will take on added meaning, connections and responsibilities. Individual men will see more clearly that their lives are not merely private and that they are not free to waste their creative potential and opportunities. The waste of human potential is not only a loss to the individual but has detrimental consequences for the whole. Each individual person is an integral part of the whole current of life, the product of an enormous creative work in which all reality has collaborated from the beginning. Whenever individuals fail in their responsibilities to promote life, a portion of the whole development of the universe is lost forever.[8]

The dynamic, reflective morality we are proposing may appear absurd to the person who does not recognize that life is a groping, an adventure toward fulfillment. But when man is seen as an integral part of nature and as the agent of evolution, the goal of morality can no longer be conceived as simply to maintain justice and balance in interpersonal interactions. Morality must guide men in the direction in which the personal emerges most assuredly. To do this it must enable them to assess the value of *all* their interactions in relation to the *whole* cosmic development. Moral action assists man in integrating himself more fully with both his fellow men and his environing conditions; in so doing it enables him to develop both simultaneously. Through moral experience men unite themselves in the pursuit of ideal ends. The more inclusive these ends the greater the possibility of self-realization. The degree of effectiveness of any action in promoting evolution can be measured in terms of the breadth and depth of the unification it promotes among the agent, his fellow men and nature. Only the richest, fullest experience possible is good enough for man and all men, not just a few moral reformers, must pursue this as their common purpose.[9]

Since the law of complexity-consciousness on the ethical level is the process of personalization, the function and goal of morality is the building of a *personal* and *personalizing universe*. The fundamental energy of the whole universe is a movement directed toward personalization; thus moral interactions cannot be restricted to an artificial or secondary domain in nature. Since the appearance of man, the cosmos is built up physically by moral advances. Therefore there cannot be a *radical separation* between the physical realm and the moral realm. There is only physico-moral energy in the universe; all energy is intimately connected with the extensive domain of human energy, the energy of personalization.[10]

As well, there ought to be no *radical distinction* between moral goods (the virtues) and natural goods (health, art, science). The dualism which has been established between them has led to compartmentalizing morality and leaving large areas of activity outside the realm of moral survey. As a result man has lost sight of the moral quality of the natural sciences and the sciences have lost their consciousness of human value. Once these dualisms have been rejected, morality can become more reflective and things intellectual and scientific can be more directly related to ethics. Any inquiry that is deeply and inclusively human enters into the area of morals and values. A detailed knowledge of all disciplines is essential for developing ethics, and no area of research falls outside its subject matter.[11] In fact, research is urgently needed today in such areas as social and international relations and international trade precisely because the spiritual, moral and physical growth of mankind as a whole depends so much on these relations. As we have already seen, beyond a certain minimal level technical and/or social progress in any area necessarily alters man's situation, creates new problems for him and calls forth moral progress.

Morality, therefore, must be placed in the service of progress. The line of progress to be pursued must be that of not only maintaining but increasing in all men the appetite for living. This goal demands a systematic effort to reduce the great losses of potential throughout society in the form of sinfulness, disordered or selfish pursuits and wasted love. Ways of assisting men to perceive and appreciate universal realities such as a sense of the world and a sense of humanity must also be devised. True progress cannot be achieved until man's urge to live is directed toward unification, not only the unification or personalization of individuals but the unification of the whole of humanity. This can be accomplished if we strive to destroy the artificial barriers which separate us and to promote the natural affinities which tend to unify us in a single organ devoted to research and to sharing the goods of the earth.[12]

We have described the whole evolutionary process as one of spiritualization by means of unification or convergence. In order that man's moral experience be truly evolutionary it must contribute to the unification of mankind into *one* living organism. Morality has always been in the service of uniting and sustaining the fundamental unit of society, the family, and also the nation. Today it must also be in the service of developing humanity as a unit in which the full consciousness of each individual and nation will be sustained by every other individual and by humanity as a whole. Men have not as yet fully realized that such things as the mass media and rapid travel have created a new situation in which *all* of mankind must strive to integrate itself into one universal community if the good of *all* is to be fostered.

It is difficult to see progress along these lines today because a consciousness sufficiently universal to encompass the whole is slow to develop and is indeed threatened by the short-term, pragmatic, economic and political policies of individual nations and the broad currents of hatred, prejudice and fear which separate men. Individual persons and nations move out beyond themselves and unite in co-operative efforts in times of mutual needs and moments of crises, but we are neither conscious of nor capable of expressing all the natural unity we must achieve if evolution is to succeed. True progress, therefore, is to be achieved by the free co-operation of all men in the moral organization which will extend the evolutionary process toward its ultimate consummation in a universal community of men developing and sharing the goods of the universe.[13]

In attempting to set forth the basic features of dynamic morality Teilhard proposes three principles which ought to define the value of human acts:

i. *only* finally good is what makes for the growth of the spirit on earth.

ii. good (at least basically and partially) is *everything* that brings a spiritual growth to the world.

iii. Finally *best* is what assures their highest development to the spiritual powers of the earth.[14]

He also points out the consequences of these principles by contrasting the demands they will make on man with those made by the more traditional ethics emphasizing equilibrium and justice. By reason of the first principle many things which were permissible in the traditional approach will be forbidden. In the traditional approach if a man did not encroach on the rights or property of others he could use as he thought best or leave dormant whatever belonged to him. In the light of this principle it is evident that no mode of acting is moral if it does not tend to utilize and develop the power within the realities involved. Accumulating wealth and possessions can no longer be justified simply on the basis of exchange and fairness; riches become good only to the extent that they work for the benefit of the spirit (the authentic human good of mankind). Morality cannot be satisfied with preventing individuals from doing harm, but must forbid neutral or inoffensive existence and foster the full autonomy and personal self-realization of men.

By reason of the second principle many actions which appeared forbidden may be permitted or even obligatory. The order to be achieved through moral activity and law has too frequently been conceived in a static way and too many creative, spiritual energies have been excluded from the framework it constructed without adequate examination of their possibilities and consequences. When justification for them was not readily available, out of timidity or safety, they were rejected or allowed to remain undeveloped. In the context proposed here everything containing or fostering an ascending force of consciousness is recognized to that extent to be good and to be developed.

Finally, by virtue of the third principle, morality is seen to have as its goal and measure the indefinite, continuous discovery and development of the animate powers of the earth. Morality is open-ended, a morality of goals, not merely of acts, one by which man sets out to explore and humanize all the energies available to him. He must move everything in the direction of the greatest consciousness, the greatest unitive energy of love. According to Teilhard's thought to limit energy and love, unless by doing so one can release even greater energy and love in another manner, is to sin.[15]

It is possible to reveal the nature of a dynamic, reflective approach to morality by further contrast with traditional morality. Although the latter does not place exclusive emphasis on customs, laws, religious codes and other standards, usually established on the basis of habit and authority, it over-emphasizes habit and authority. A dynamic, reflective approach to morality does not deny the validity of customs, laws and religious codes (man must rely on the secular and revealed wisdom of the past), but it shifts the emphasis from custom to making desires and ideals articulate in terms of reflective inquiry into their conditions and consequences. Criticism or judgment engaged in discriminating among values determines not only *what* is better and what worse, but *why* each is such. Reflective morality also attempts to discover what character traits *should* be approved and recognizes that in moral deliberation what is at stake is the worth of this or that kind of character and moral disposition. It identifies virtues with *what is approvable not* merely with *what is approved.* The basic problem in reflective morality is

> . . . that of embodying intelligence in action which shall convert casual natural goods, whose causes and effects are unknown, into goods valid for thought, right for conduct and cultivated for appreciation.[16]

As we have seen, morality is a continuing process, not a set achievement. This requires growth of conduct in meaning, and grasping the meaning of an action is achieved by observing its conditions and its consequences. Men must question the purposes which direct action and develop inclusive and enduring aims which make action more comprehensive and give it greater unity.[17]

In a problematic moral situation a judgment and choice must be made before any overt action is taken. There are conflicting desires present as well as different apparent goods. The conflict is not between desire and reason, but between a desire which lies close to natural impulse (one which wants an immediate object and immediate satisfaction) and a desire which wants an object seen by thought to occur as the result of an intervening series of conditions. The first is a want just as it presents itself in isolation; the second is one thought of in relation to other wants. Where conflicting desires are present, inquiry is required into both the make-up of the situation and the consequences of pursuing the different desires in relation to other wants. In this way ideal values, that is, those approved by reflection after wide examination of their relations, can be established. The outcome of such a value judgment is equivalent to willingly identifying oneself as the agent in promoting a certain consequence — saying "let this consequence be."[18]

Neither suppression of raw desire nor yielding to it as it first presents itself are moral substitutes for thoughtful desire. All growth in maturity consists in not giving in to immediate desire, but in re-making it through consideration of the consequences it will effect if acted upon. Thus discipline, sacrifice, renunciation and enduring hardship in the pursuit of good are natural to man and necessary for personal evolution. In order to train persons to commit themselves to fostering inclusive enduring goods every occasion to cultivate interest in and love of them must be used to advantage. Occasions for enjoying these goods must be fostered so that the experience of appreciating them is prolonged and deepened.[19] This will in turn foster such distinctively moral traits as:

Wide sympathy, keen sensitiveness, persistence in the face of the disagreeable, balance of interests enabling us to undertake the work of analysis and decision intelligently. . .[20]

Through the exercise of these traits men can constantly pursue more universal ends, and one end or goal, once it is realized, becomes the means of attaining even more inclusive ones.

Throughout our entire vision we have equated evolution with increase in being and shown that evolution occurs through a process of convergence or unification. In our discussion of morality we have seen that authentic moral action is evolutionary. It enables man to unify himself and to achieve more harmonious, integrated interactions with nature and with his fellow man. Truly moral action must be comprehensive, unified and directed toward more and more inclusive aims. But how is man to determine what goals are most comprehensive if not by means of science and the empirical method? Thus we are confronted with the question as to whether ethics is purely scientific and whether moral action can be determined on the basis of empirical evidence and method alone.

According to Dewey, ethics is scientific, and science has

intrinsic moral potentiality in that it influences the formation of the ends for which men strive. He was disturbed by the dualism in logical standpoint and method between science and morals and set out to establish a method of inquiry applicable to both science and morals.[21] Whether his ethics is strictly scientific or not, certain aspects of it are empirical. The good cannot be determined once and for all, but must be determined again and again in terms of the conditions of concrete situations. Moral principles, in a manner similar to that of legal regulations, arise out of the subject matter of ordinary transactions. Once they are formulated they become methods of judging and directing the type of activities out of which they originally arose. Both principles and laws remain relative and subject to modification.[22] Dewey also maintains an objective relativism in morality in a manner similar to that by which he maintains it in all scientific truth. Standards enable men to view their actions objectively, to differentiate the various kinds of satisfaction and to determine which are moral. They indicate that men should choose objects and find satisfaction in things which bring good or satisfaction to others.[23]

In spite of the fact that Dewey established the outlines of a scientific method of inquiry applicable to ethics and insisted that his ethics was scientific, R. J. Roth argues that Dewey's moral theory is wider than scientific method.[24] Dewey states that the scientific criterion by which one determines the value of an act in terms of its consequences is *the* final ethical criterion. This too is questionable.

Our purpose is not to resolve this particular problem of interpretation of Dewey's thought. We agree wholeheartedly with Dewey in recognizing the intrinsic moral potentiality of science, and affirm that both scientific knowledge and method must play an integral part within the process of inquiry required to arrive at particular moral decisions. Yet we deny that the entire process of moral deliberation and decision-making can restrict itself to a purely empirical method.

We do not intend to establish a dualism between speculative

and practical wisdom; they must remain intimately connected. Nevertheless, moral decisions are ultimately the work of practical reason, and it is inconceivable that all the contingencies involved can be known and the ultimate practical judgment made and tested in terms of strict empirical method and criteria. A final practical judgment cannot be arrived at by strictly logical connection .with axiomatic premises. It involves affective knowledge and inclinations which must be directed by the virtue of prudence. A purely empirical approach to making final moral judgments would ignore the role of that connatural knowledge of the requirements of virtue possessed by persons who have developed the virtue of prudence.[25]

Although we differ with Dewey concerning the type of knowledge and the kind of truth involved in final moral judgments, we do not reject the need for empirical and pragmatic criteria in making moral decisions. We agree with the naturalistic pragmatist that the good involved in particular actions cannot be determined once and for all, but must be re-examined again and again in the light of changing conditions and the new, foreseeable consequences that will result.

C. *A Qualified Growth Ethic for Christians*

Both the christian and natural pragmatist conceive of morality as on-going, and both propose a growth ethic. There are specific differences, however, in the kind of growth ethic each proposes. For the naturalist growth does not *have* an end, but *is* an end. It is relative only to more growth; therefore, growth itself is the only moral end. A moral man is one capable of living as a social being balancing what he gets from living with others with what he contributes. What he gets and gives is a widening and deepening of conscious life, a more disciplined and expanded realization of meanings. Education is not just the means for such a life but *is* such a life, and the very essence of morals is to maintain the capacity for such education.[26]

181

As indicated above, the goal of the process we are proposing is not unending growth, but rather the unification of mankind developed to its uppermost limits through the process
of coiling in on itself, centering itself on a transcendent personal pole or goal whom the christian recognizes to be God.
We propose a specific type of evolutionary process which demands a specifically *qualified* growth ethic. The goal of morality is the free, spiritual union of all men with each other in
the life of God Himself, and not merely unending human
growth. As we shall see in chapter eight, unification or growth
occurs primarily through love; and growth in love requires
the development of all the virtues which support, direct and
make love possible. Education is intimately connected with
love because of the intimate relation between knowledge and
love, but increased knowledge and increased virtue are not
identical.

There is no doubt that we attribute a validity and normative
status to revealed moral principles which the naturalist denies
them. This does not necessarily create an unbridgeable gap
between the secular ethicist and christian moralist. The judaeo-
christian revelation does not provide man with a blueprint
which maps out his ethical responses for him or provides ready-
made answers for moral problems. Revelation does not reduce
man's responsibility to start on the concrete, phenomenological
level of experience to work out solutions to moral problems.
Scientific inquiry in all areas, the re-evaluation of moral insights and the examination of long-term consequences are just
as necessary for the believer as for the non-believer.

The christian accepts the need of a personal God who is
not only an absolute goal, a lure-from-beyond, transcending
the entire evolutionary process, but also an immanent, active,
infinite principle of enlightenment and love within man. Experience indicates that when men reject the need of an infinite God in their quest for truth and pursuit of the good,
they fashion their own absolutes, such as omnipotent science,
material prosperity or an absolutized mankind. The result of

absolutizing the particular is invariably moral confusion: inability to achieve unity and universal brotherhood, excessive competition, and the revival of the biological law of the survival of the fittest.[27]

The relationship between secular ethics and christian morality can only be understood adequately in terms of the relationship of God and Christianity to the whole evolutionary process. To extend our sketch of a qualified growth ethic for christians, therefore, we must provide a few more insights regarding the relationship between secular and christian ethics. Christian morality does not reject the fundamental moral imperative that man must become what he is. Far from destroying this moral responsibility, christian morality enriches it by extending it beyond itself, giving it an ultimate goal compatible with, but exceeding, its own capabilities. Grace builds on nature.

The teaching of Christ that God has freely given man the opportunity to receive His Spirit and participate in His life and love, heightens rather than diminishes man's moral responsibilities by extending and fullfilling all of them in the single unified imperative to love all men in charity. Christ gives ethics a firmer foundation; men are not only united as members of the human race but as brothers in the shared life of Christ. The teaching of Christ gives ethics added motivation; men not only build up a temporal community through moral action, they participate in an infinite, eternal brotherhood which is totally open-ended because it is not destroyed by death. The indwelling power of the Spirit of God in men extends their power to love, and the principle or source of love in them is not merely a limited, human principle, but a human capacity healed and perfected by divine love.

Even when christian morality is regarded as conformity to the will of God, there is no opposition established between it and authentic secular ethics. The christian is not forced to remain immature or become less a man. Conforming to God's will does not abstract morality from the whole on-going evolutionary process. If man is to know the will of God for the fulfillment of the cosmos and himself he must look to on-going nature and study its inherent laws to find in these the plan of God implanted and operative there. The will of God for man is in a sense materialized or made incarnate in and manifested through the natural order of the universe in time. This is especially true of man himself who shares in the divine providence or plan by his capacity to know and love.

Conformity to the will of God does not reduce man's duty of carry out mature, intelligent research and make choices. Even in areas where the Bible reveals specific moral imperatives and directs christians to conform their actions to the actions of Christ, it does not tell man *how* to exercise the virtues of love, justice, etc. The christian remains the free, intelligent agent of all his actions. In conforming to the will of God the christian's approach to specific moral problems is not radically different from that of the non-believer although he brings a new power of divine enlightenment and love to the task. He remains fully responsible for fostering the entire evolutionary process, and indeed, the scope of his morality is deepened because a new transcendent dimension has been added in the light of his faith. There is an added urgency which ought to motivate the christian, therefore, because the stakes are greater and more can be lost if men act irresponsibly.

II. *Moral Experience Contributes to Self-Realization*

It is possible to examine still further how morality contributes to evolution by showing specifically how moral experience fosters self-realization. Morality must enable man to use all his powers of initiative and creativity in the common responsibility of being true to nature and furthering its development. In dong this man realizes himself. This is not an egoistic concern because self-realization occurs through fostering values shared by all for the good of all. An appropriate point of departure for our discussion is the relationship between character and action.

A. *The Relationship between Character and Action*

There is an intimate relationship a) among the acts a person performs, and b) between his actions and character. The concept of human *conduct* expresses *continuity* of action. Where there is human conduct there is not merely a succession of disconnected acts; each action performed carries forward an underlying tendency and intention and conducts or leads to a final consummation. In human conduct every act, regardless of how trivial it may appear, has potential moral significance because through its consequences it is part of a larger behavioral whole. Many trivial acts are, in fact, the supports for acts involving definite moral considerations. Human action, therefore, involves a series and not merely a succession of acts.[28]

One action not only leads to another as its effect, but also leaves an enduring impression on the person by either strengthening or weakening the tendency in him to act in that way. Such tendencies are habits which extend to the very structure of the self. Actions are united to form conduct, therefore, because of their common relation to character or the self as the abiding unity in which actions leave their effects. When a person gives in to an impulse and performs an action he strengthens the impulse and to that extent commits himself to both the individual act and to a line of behavior. Thus consequences of a moral kind enter into and form the self and the self enters into consequences. In matters of choice the existing self is revealed and the future self formed because deliberation concerns not only the relative value of ends, but also the type of person the agent wants to be.[29]

When we state that the tendencies built up in man to act

185

in a certain way are habits we do not identify habits and virtues. The term "habit" refers to an inclination to act in a certain way which is acquired through repetition. It implies, therefore, an activity which becomes automatic to the point of lacking creativity. Habitual acts of his sort do not engage man's reason and will. To the extent that such acts are performed automatically they are somewhat less than fully human acts. The traditional concept of virtue is much more complex than this.

> It is an active quality which disposes a man to produce the maximum of what he is able to do on the moral plane, which gives to his reason and will conjoined, the power to accomplish the most perfect moral actions, actions, that is, of the highest value. . . . Virtue makes the one who possesses it good and renders good his work. Virtue permits a man to perform a perfect moral act and renders the man himself perfect.[30]

The creative power of virtue surpasses the pure repetition of material acts. Virtue is acquired by the repetition of acts and furthers such repetition, yet it is a disposition that enables man to perform acts which are not merely repetitive, but creative and imaginative. It enables him to use his intellect and will to their fullest capacity in moral action. To understand the working of virtue one must recognize that there are two distinct phases of activity involved in any complete human or virtuous action, namely, the interior and exterior phases. The interior phase or act is that of the practical reason and the will; the exterior act, that of all the other faculties of the body executing the material action determined and commanded by the intellect and will.[31]

Virtue is engendered primarily by repetition of interior acts of mastery over oneself. For instance, the virtue of fortitude (mastery of the intellect and will over action in the face of danger) is acquired through repeated, but not automatic, interior acts of direction and control over audacity, fear and discouragement. Under different circumstances the interior act will command different, and even contrary, external acts to be performed. In one instance the exercise of fortitude may require the person to advance; in other circumstances it may require either remaining constant or withdrawing.[32]

Thus it is evident that the repetition of interior acts necessary to acquire virtue is a series of spiritual inventions (the exercise of practical reason and the power of choice) determining what must be done in every set of circumstances. The repeated interior acts themselves are not automatic because they are acts of reason and volition; and the exterior acts they command are even more varied. Although virtue is acquired primarily through the repetition of the interior acts mentioned above, these acts are only the first phase in a complete human action. The exterior, material act must also be executed before a virtuous action is accomplished. Since virtue cannot be acquired through the exercise of intellect and will alone, the execution of repeated, exterior acts is also necessary for acquiring it.[33]

The development of virtue demands that *all man's faculties* be put in motion under the guidance and control of intellect and will. The repetition of *exterior* acts causes active dispositions, inclinations or reflexes, which resemble automatisms, to be developed in man's sensible and bodily faculties. These reflexes are never entirely unconscious. Therefore, they are not identical with, but rather akin to habits, as we have defined "habit" above. These reflexes are the product of man's spiritual faculties which have shaped and penetrated his sense appetites and corporeal faculties so that they are transformed into perfect instruments. Thus, the whole man acts harmoniously in the exercise of virtue. Virtues enable him to act with ease, facility and joy.[34]

The concept of virtue described here enables us to see that it is the acquisition of virtue that enables man to invent and carry out actions that are at the same time creative, evolutionary and morally good. Virtue does not reduce man to a sterile spiritual automatism nor to routine. On the contrary, the development of all the virtues and especially that of prudence, is absolutely essential if human behavior is to be spiritualized and if authentic evolution is to occur through moral experience.

Through the development of the virtues the character of the person is formed. The consequences of both the interior judgments and choices men make and the exterior actions they perform reflect directly on their very persons and develop them for better or for worse. Both the immediate and long term consequences of men's acts also influence their environing conditions which in turn act upon men and influence their future actions. Therefore, the emphasis placed by the pragmatist on the consideration of both short and long term consequences of acts is of equal significance in our vision. Actions flow from the character of the agent and also mold his character; they develop the *interiority* of the person. A spiritualistic evolutionary process which is identical with a process of becoming authentically human cannot continue unless the agents of evolution are men of stable, virtuous character.

A reflective, on-going morality, recognizing the intimate connection between character and action, affirms that the moral law is more accurately expressed in terms of "be this" than "do this." The self cannot stand still, but is becoming for better or worse. Attention must be placed on the process of evolution, the constant movement in the direction of the good, rather than on the new possession of certain goods. Man must constantly choose between the interests of the "old self" and the need and opportunity to go beyond himself, that is, beyond the desires and habits of his past. The good person is the man most conscious of this choice and most concerned with finding opportunities for developing himself, because he is not really exercising virtue if he fails to respond to the demand and opportunities for growth. The "lower" and "higher" self are to be distinguished in terms of a step beyond one's attained state so that the self remains dynamic. On these grounds the moral law becomes an injunction to identify oneself on every possible occasion with the new growth possible in the situation.[35]

In this context obedience is intimately connected with moral freedom. It not only involves an enlightened, free response to the commands of authorities, but also requires that all men a) take initiative in assessing the situations in which they find themselves, b) share the responsibility for determining what must be done to improve these situations, and c) adapt their own personal desires, aims and actions in such a way as to respond to the objective demands of these situations. When obedience is regarded as not merely submitting to commands and laws, but also as adapting one's own goals and desires so that one's actions are responses to the needs one sees in one's society, obedience is seen in terms of *adaptability* and its scope is extended.

To possess virtue, therefore, is not to have cultivated a few isolated traits, but to be fully what one is capable of becoming in and through association with others in all aspects of life. Virtues are not isolated entities to be attained and possessed as ends. The dynamic and inter-related quality of the virtues is of paramount importance in a morality which calls for a constantly expanding and changing sense of what concrete human relations demand.[36]

In the light of the intimate connection between conduct and character we can also comment on the controversy between those who maintain that motives alone are of moral import and those who place all the emphasis on consequences or the objective content of the act in its effect on others. Both views are one-sided because each is dealing with different poles of the same thing. Some of the consequences of any action cannot be foreseen. This fact limits intention, yet one's motive and will to perform an act cannot be separated from the realistic projection of its consequences and the effort to bring these desired consequences into existence.[37] Both the agent's intention and the objective outcome (the work itself) have moral significance. When a person intends an action he intends to bring a certain set of consequences into existence.

B. *Growth in Freedom and Responsibility*

With the appearance of man both reflection and freedom were introduced into the cosmos. Both arose within the whole current of evolution and must be seen within the scope of the entire movement. Freedom presents man with two intimately connected problems: a) a problem of meaning or purpose, that is, a problem concerning his ultimate end or his power of self-realization, and b) a problem of choosing means which will enable him to achieve this goal. To be free is an act of the spirit, an act by which man is master of his judgments. Thus freedom involves not only the power of knowing the truth but also the power of willing or choosing the good. Both of these powers, because they are powers of man's spirit, are directed toward the universal or absolute, that is, toward infinite truth and goodness.

Men are born free, capable of voluntarily following the tendency of their nature to strive, individually and collectively, to search for the truth and pursue the good. Freedom, therefore, is an oriented power. It is not given to man for its own sake or for any end which might please him. It is neither independence from everything nor a power of absolute autonomy. Man is given freedom to be free from evil in order to do good. Freedom is achieved in giving oneself to ends or goals which are greater than oneself, in realizing oneself by self-dedication to the task of developing humanity and the universe according to the call of God implanted in our very nature. In the pursuit of goodness and truth men realize themselves and bring the whole cosmic process to its fulfillment.

Men, therefore, can abuse their freedom. Forgetting that freedom is for the pursuit of authentic self-realization in goodness and truth, they can reject the tendency of their nature and pursue such ends as power, pleasure or financial gain as if these were their final goal. They can forget that choosing also means renouncing. In choosing man defines his own person by integrating that thing or action he has chosen into his own person. This implies that at the same time he must resolutely abandon what he has not willed to integrate into his personality by that choice.

Once again, therefore, we see that man's freedom involves both his intellect and his will. In his acts of choice man releases the stream of cosmic energy and life and orients them in a set direction. By his intelligent, free choices he is truly the agent of cosmic evolution. He is free, therefore, to pursue the only ultimate goal which will adequately satisfy all his spiritual aspirations and those of the universe and to choose the means which will attain this end most effectively.

Freedom is neither a fully developed power given to men at birth nor a static reality. It appeared in the world as the result of a long process of increased complexity and interiorization, and further increases in both individual and collective freedom are achieved in conjunction with continued increases in complexity and interiorization. This is not to imply that the development of either individual or collective freedom occurs automatically or necessarily.

The root of man's freedom is in his power of reason. He is the intelligent agent of evolution capable of apprehending and relating ends and means and deciding the goals he will pursue. It is evident, therefore, that man's capacity for liberty increases with increased scientific and technical knowledge and with increases in cultural, economic and sociological organization. Greater knowledge and social organization expand his choices and the scope of his activity and power. But this is not all that is involved in the development of freedom. Primarily freedom is a power of choosing (a power of the will which selects and executes the greatest good presented to it by the intellect). Precisely because freedom is a power of choice it cannot evolve independently of increases in man's power of self-mastery which requires the development of all the virtues.

There are conditions necessary for the growth of personal freedom. Its development is slow and difficult, and is dependent upon the long struggle involved in achieving personal and social integration and unification. Along with increases in consciousness, material organization and unity in society there are increases in both the intensity and quantity of evil, personal sinfulness and the capacity and temptation to abuse freedom. Authentic evolution occurs only when men comprehend and internalize the good to be achieved so that they pursue it freely. Men are free when what they want to do is identical with what they ought to do to promote the entire process of unifying or spiritualizing reality.

The law of complexity-consciousness, which is the underlying law of the evolutionary process, certainly indicates that mankind's capacity for freedom evolves with increases in individual and collective consciousness and advances in the technical, economic and cultural organization of society. Nevertheless, it does not imply that these occur independently of man's development and exercise of freedom nor that freedom evolves automatically. It does not propose a type of *evolutionism*. The law of complexity-consciousness reveals the process by which new, more complex situations are developed in which mankind's capacity for freedom is enlarged. If men, in fact, use this increased capacity by freely acting in a moral manner, evolution will continue according to the same underlying principles explained in the law.

Every increase in man's capacity to achieve good is accompanied by a corresponding increase in his responsibility to do so. Responsibility is defined and measured in terms of the use a person makes of his full ability a) to respond in concrete situations to the needs and claims of other persons, and b) to utilize all his opportunities to promote personal growth and foster community. Responsibility increases with increased stages of personal interiorization. Both individual and collective responsibility increase proportionally with increases in freedom, so that the responsibility of an individual or a society is proportionate to its present stage of development. In a sense, therefore, one's degree of responsibility is dependent upon one's freedom to act at that time. This does not imply, however, that either individuals or groups of persons are free of responsibility in present situations in which they are incapable of making an adequate moral response due to their past abuse of and failure to develop their freedom.

Neither freedom nor responsibility are strictly individual realities; individuals grow in freedom and responsibility conjointly with other persons. The realization that the whole cosmos is one converging process and the effects of rapid advances in technology and socialization have made modern man very aware of the constantly expanding influence and consequences of all his actions. The mutual interpenetration and interdependence of all nations today is forcing all men to recognize their collective responsibility to break down the artificial barriers which prevent them from using all the world's energies, and especially love, to prolong and expand life. We find ourselves tied by the very foundation of our being to the responsible task of perfecting everything in the cosmos for the good of the whole, and this responsibility will continue to increase.

The development of the material powers of the earth is a mammoth accomplishment. We have come a long way in developing a composite nervous system and brain for mankind through the development of electronics. But we must ask ourselves if this process can continue if we do not move beyond the interests of restricted groups and through a global mastery of thought and love find the common heart of mankind.

The evolution of responsibility, therefore, is an inherent part of the over-all evolutionary process. Responsibility automatically increases and intensifies to the dimensions and to the rhythm of cosmic evolution. If the laws underlying the whole process are merely conventions established more or less arbitrarily by man, men can justify compromising them. But now that we have recognized that the underlying laws are organic links established by the process of socialization itself, we are forced to admit that they cannot be violated without serious consequences for the whole of mankind. A sort of general ultra-responsibility involving all of men's actions accompanies the evolutionary process by cosmic necessity.[38]

FOOTNOTES

1. "Le Christianisme dans le monde," *SC*, p. 132 [Eng. trans. p. 99]; *GP*, Letter, July 14, 1916, p. 140, Letter, January 29, 1917, p. 228 [Eng. trans. pp. 110-11, 176].

2. "Le Phénomène humain," *SC*, p. 127 [Eng. trans. p. 96]; "L'Esprit de la terre," *ÉH*, p. 36 [Eng. trans. p. 29]; "Le Phénomène spirituel," *ÉH*, p. 131 [Eng. trans. p. 105]; "Quelques Réflexions sur le retentissement spirituel de la bombe atomique," *AH*, p. 184 [Eng. trans. p. 145].

3. In "Does Human Nature Change?" Dewey states that human nature has its own constitution, that is, some tendencies are so integrally a part of it that there could be no such thing as human nature if they changed. In this fundamental sense human nature does not change or evolve. The manifestation of these tendencies or needs does change, however, because they are affected by tradition and custom. The permanent elements of human nature can find expression in radically different ways from those operative today. Habits, not original human nature, keep things moving as they did in the past. Economic institutions and human relations are manifestations of human nature which are very susceptible to change. The great variety of social institutions and relations in the history of mankind evidences the plasticity of human nature. Without this capacity for change in human nature, education would be impossible; with it the problem becomes one of deciding how to modify human nature under set conditions in the most effective way — the problem of education in its widest sense. *Problems of Men*, pp. 184-92. This approach to human nature is, of course, significant with regard to the possibilities of moral experience effecting evolution.

4. *Human Nature and Conduct*, pp. 3-13, 295-96, 321-22, 324.

5. John Dewey, *Theory of the Moral Life* (New York: Holt, Rinehart and Winston, 1960), pp. viii-xii, 68-70, 174-76; *The Public and its Problems*, pp. 22-25, 148-55; *Human Nature and Conduct*, p. 329; *Reconstruction in Philosophy*, pp. 205-06.

6. John Dewey, *Construction and Criticism* (New York: Columbia University Press, 1930), p. 23; *Theory of the Moral Life*, pp. 5-6, 22-25.

7. "Le Phénomène spirituel," *ÉH*, pp. 131-32 [Eng. trans. pp. 105-06]; "L'Esprit de la terre," *ÉH*, pp. 37-39 [Eng. trans. pp. 29-31].

8. "Les Fondements et le fond de l'idée d'évolution," *VP*, pp. 191-92 [Eng. trans. pp. 137-38].

9. *Experience and Nature*, p. 142.

10. "Esquisse d'un univers personnel," *ÉH*, pp. 89-90 [Eng. trans. pp. 71-72]; "L'Énergie humaine," *ÉH*, pp. 157-58 [Eng. trans. pp. 125-26].

11. *Reconstruction in Philosophy*, pp. xxvi, 172-74; "Intelligence and Morals," *The Influence of Darwin on Philosophy*, p. 69; *Theory of the Moral Life*, pp. 121-22; *Human Nature and Conduct*, pp. 187-88, 279-80.

12. "Le Phénomène humain," *VP*, pp. 241-42 [Eng. trans. 172-73].

13. "L'Énergie humaine," *ÉH*, p. 156 [Eng. trans. pp. 124-25]; "Note sur le progrès," *AH*, pp. 33-34 [Eng. trans. pp. 21-22]; *GP*, Letter, January 9, 1917, pp. 214-15 [Eng. trans. p. 166].

14. "Le Phénomène spirituel," *ÉH*, pp. 132-33 [Eng. trans. pp. 106-07].

15. "Le Phénomène spirituel," *ÉH*, pp. 133-34 [Eng. trans. pp. 107-8].

16. *Experience and Nature*, p. 407.

17. John Dewey, *Freedom and Culture* (New York: Capricorn Books, 1963) p. 170; *Human Nature and Conduct*, p. 280; *Theory of the Moral Life*, pp. 29-30.

18. John Dewey, *Theory of Valuation*, International Encyclopedia of Unified Science, II, No. 4 (Chicago: University of Chicago Press, 1969), pp. 29-30, 33-37, 45; *Reconstruction in Philosophy*, pp. 163-64; *Theory of the Moral Life*, pp. 31-37, 54-55, 60-62; *Essays in Experimental Logic*, pp. 358-60; *The Quest for Certainty*, pp. 259-60, 263; *Construction and Criticism*, pp. 11-12; *Experience and Nature*, pp. 420-21.

19. *Theory of the Moral Life*, pp. 33, 35-36, 56-57, 59; *Theory of Valuation*, p. 30.

20. *Reconstruction in Philosophy*, p. 164.

21. *Freedom and Culture*, pp. 153-54; "From Absolutism to Experimentalism," *On Experience, Nature, and Freedom*, pp. 14-15; *Problems of Men*, pp. 211-12.

22. *Theory of the Moral Life*, pp. 62, 136-37, 141-45; *Logic*, pp. 17, 101-02, 280; *Problems of Men*, p. 156; *Human Nature and Conduct*, pp. 239, 244-45.

23. *Human Nature and Conduct*, pp. 51-53, 57; *Problems of Men*, pp. 250-72; *Theory of the Moral Life*, pp. 101-04.

24. R. J. Roth, "Naturalistic Ethics: Problem of Method," *The New Scholasticism*, 40 (July, 1966), pp. 285-311.

25. Yves Simon, "Introduction to the Study of Practical Wisdom," *New Scholasticism*, 35 (January, 1961), pp. 1-40.

26. *Reconstruction in Philosophy*, pp. 177, 183-86; *Democracy and Education*, pp. 49-51, 359-60; *Experience and Nature*, p. 431.

27. "La Maîtrise du monde et le règne de Dieu," *ÉTG*, pp. 78-79 [Eng. trans. pp. 85-86].

28. *Theory of the Moral Life*, pp. 9-12.

29. *Theory of the Moral Life*, pp. 9, 13-14, 148-51.

30. Servais Pinckaers, "Virtue is Not a Habit," *Cross Currents*, 12 (Winter, 1962), p. 70.

31. Pinckaers, "Virtue is Not a Habit," pp. 70-72.

32. Pinckaers, "Virtue is Not a Habit," p. 73.

33. Pinckaers, "Virtue is Not a Habit," pp. 74-75.

34. Pinckaers, "Virtue is Not a Habit," pp. 76-77.

35. *Theory of the Moral Life*, pp. 172-74.

36. *Theory of the Moral Life*, pp. 112-17, 167; *Democracy and Education*, p. 358.

37. *Theory of the Moral Life*, pp. 16, 18-19. For a further analysis of motives in Dewey's thought see: *Theory of the Moral Life*, pp. 151-56.

38. "L'Évolution de la responsibilité dans le monde," *AÉ*, pp. 216-21 [Eng. trans. pp. 210-14].

Chapter 8

EVOLUTION OCCURS THROUGH PERSONAL UNION

Throughout the preceding chapter we have seen that moral experience is directed toward the development of authentic persons in community, that is, toward the process of personalization. Man must *become what he is* through his interactions with his fellow man and nature. Now we shall show that personalization occurs through the union of persons and indicate the role of love in this process. In order to do this we shall work from Teilhard's universally valid law of experimental recurrence or complexity-consciousness which is operative throughout the entire process of cosmic evolution. Because this law is a universally operative principle Teilhard was able to find consistence and continuity within the whole evolutionary process, and was able to develop what he called "a realistic ultra-physics of union," a philosophy of union which is verifiable on the phenomenal level.

On the basis of this same universal law Teilhard was able to extrapolate to the extent of time and space and show that evolution in a converging universe not only results in the personalization of individual humans but also in the super-personalization of humanity centered in an infinitely personal point which he called Omega. In this chapter, therefore, we shall examine a) the role of love energy in personalization, b) the goal toward which it is moving, and c) those qualities which can be attributed, on the basis of philosophical reflection, to the personal point in whom the whole process converges.

197

I. *Personalization through Union: The Role and Goal of Love Energy*

Regarded as *energy, love* is an *analogous concept.* In its full biological reality it is the affinity of being for being, a force or energy of center-to-center union. On the levels of the pre-living and pre-reflective the *radial energy* which causes imperfectly centered material particles to adhere to one another, even in an incomplete manner, *is love in its most rudimentary form.* In this most elementary sense love is a general property of all reality, and as such is operative in varying degrees in all the forms adopted by organized matter. On its most *elementary level* this energy, which causes particles to unite center-to-center, *creates,* because complete disunion of the cosmic stuff is nothingness. If the presence of an internal propensity to unite were not to be found on the lower levels of being it would be physically impossible for love to appear on the human level.[1]

Thus Teilhard, speaking of love as energy, and therefore, as an analogous concept, has defined it as follows:

> Love is power of producing inter-centric relationship. It is present, therefore (at least in a rudimentary state), in all the natural centres, living and pre-living, which make up the world; and it represents, too, the most profound, most direct, and most creative form of interaction that it is possible to conceive between those centres. Love, in fact, is the expression and the agent of universal synthesis.[2]

It is evident from this definition that love energy is the energy of cosmic evolution. Teilhard refers to it almost exclusively as radial energy on the lower levels, but radial energy is love energy in the strictly human sense of love after the appearance of man.

The same law of convergence through union, which brought

about the appearance of man by organizing matter under the control of spirit, is still operative. Increases in inner unity bring about the progressive personalization of man. There are three complementary aspects or phases in this process of personalization which occur simultaneously. The first is directed toward man's continued development as a personal center. In order to enhance his own interior unification man must cultivate himself physically, intellectually and morally. To become fully himself he must strive to bring more unity or harmony to his ideas, emotions and conduct; that is, he must unify himself by directing his whole person toward more inclusive spiritual goals.[3] In this way he develops meaning and stability in his life.

The person who recognizes his capacity for centration will not fear union. Every individual person has the capacity to center *everything* partially upon himself, that is, the ability to go out to all things, know and interact with them in such a way as to assimilate them and make them become part of his life. Secondly, he has the capacity to constantly center himself upon himself. He remains a personal center who can continue to integrate reality within himself without becoming fragmented or losing his personal identity. Finally, he has the capacity to be brought by virtue of this super-centration more *into association with all other centers* around him.[4]

The process of loving oneself and developing one's own interior personal center is not an egoistic pursuit which isolates man. Man's very capacity to center himself in himself finds its fulfillment in taking him beyond himself and uniting him with his fellow man and the universe. It not only provides a basis for personal identity, but also enables persons to develop a sense of solidarity within a group. Man cannot achieve identity or wholeness except in solidarity with all men, past, present and future.

The union achieved by genuine love is a center-to-center union, that is, one which unites persons by what is most incommunicable and spiritual in them. Such a love seeks contact; it begins on the basis of sensible encounter and knowledge and does not reject the physical. Yet it is not a love based exclusively or even primarily on physical union or material expressions of love; it involves a deep mutual commitment and presence, a sharing in each other's lives. When physical union is isolated and not integrated into a deeper personal union it cannot achieve its aim. The more men attempt to unite on any level other than the personal, the more they become isolated from each other and turned back in on themselves. We must love each other in spirit if we are to unite; progress in union must be sought in the higher zones of man's being where increases in union correspond to higher degrees of spiritualization.[5]

Precisely because it is an agent of universal synthesis, that is, of organic center-to-center union, love does not confuse or destroy the elements it unites but differentiates them. On the level of simple life union differentiates the elements involved; on the level of man it personalizes through differentiation. Love does not absorb the personalities of the partners, but develops them. Personal love involves mutual self-giving, but by nature a person can only give himself *as a person* as long as he remains a *distinct* self-conscious unity. Union arouses a person's most unique qualities and creative powers through the mutual fertilization and adaptation entailed; it unites persons by what is deepest and most incommunicable in them and by so doing fulfills them. Persons no longer associate and react to each other primarily to preserve the species, but rather to create a common consciousness. To-day, individuals are confronted, in an increasingly urgent way, with the double necessity to deepen themselves and simultaneously to associate themselves ever more widely with all of mankind and with their environment. Provided this increased association is based on true union it will not choke the individual but will lead to a higher spirituality and therefore greater freedom.[6]

At the same time as man achieves interior unification or personalization by integrating or centering himself in himself he must de-center himself by uniting himself with other individuals and humanity as a whole. The power of love brings about an increase in the consciousness of the persons united. Teilhard speaks of the unique center of each person as the "personal universal;" what is most interior in each man is also that which makes him one with all other men. At the very core of his being is an infinite capacity to love and unite with all men and the entire universe. This capacity to realize oneself in conjunction with the whole is a fundamental aspect of the law of convergence and must be followed if man is to remain faithful to himself as the agent of a world in evolution.[7]

The final or most extensive phase of personalization, therefore, involves becoming fully oneself by uniting with the totality of humanity which is in process of coiling in on itself and developing what Teilhard calls a super-humanity[8] centered on Omega, a supreme personal point who is both active and attainable at present as well as being transcendent. The individual, as one conscious person, incorporates himself into this collectivized totality centered in Omega.

It is through personal union with this supreme Personality, this ultimate Center of centers beyond all the particular objects of love in the universe, that man can develop a truly universal or cosmic love which can be both universal and specific. When human love is oriented toward an infinite, personal object of love, its ability to extend itself to the universal is enhanced. Man can maintain contact with the particular beings around him and maintain a warm human affection for them. The focus of his love is ultimately the single active Center of all convergence, but he attains this Center by uniting himself to the particular beings at the foundation of which this Center is present. Thus Teilhard affirms that the *natural* phases of personalization in its full cosmic sense are to *be* (to integrate oneself), to *love* (to de-center oneself), and to *adore* (to open oneself to Infinite Personhood).[9]

We have examined the whole process of personalization in its cosmic dimension, recognizing that love energy is the humanized form of the energy of cosmic evolution itself. Love energy is a power of inter-centric relationship, the most creative form of interaction possible among persons. Now we can shed further light on the role and goal of love energy by examining some of the moral problems and attitudes related to it.

Existentially there is an ambivalence in man insofar as we find in him both the blindness of bias and preference and the openness and plasticity of needs and likings. He tends to isolate and refuse to reveal his inner self, yet at the same time moves toward union and continuity with nature and his fellow men. Whenever the tendency to isolation dominates, he detaches himself from the affairs of life and deludes himself regarding the superiority of his own inner private life. Yet through love and other forms of communication, science and art, he moves out beyond himself to other people. In fact, whenever a person freely chooses to communicate with another on a deep personal basis or to re-make environing conditions in accord with reasonable desire, he must surrender his old self. Willingness to put off the old self and to take the risks inherent in developing a new self and a better world are a necessary part of every search for truth and the growth involved in personalization through love.[10]

The tendency in man which leads him to set his own self off in isolation from the world is the tendency to possess or cling to himself at his present stage of development as if he were a ready-made, completed self. This is the tendency not to surrender oneself and not to face the risks involved in growth. Self-love and self-pity imply that acts of love and pity are turned back on the self, performed on behalf of the self considered as a completed existence. But acts of love and pity are acts of adventure in developing a self which will be more inclusive than the present self.[11] Although love of self is legitimate and necessary for personal growth, self-love in the pejorative sense described above is destructive. What is at stake is not egoism or altruism but two concepts of the self, one being a completed self, the other a relational self in process of becoming. The action associated with the first concept is directed at benefiting the self directly; that associated with the second surrenders the present self in the process of interaction with other persons so that union occurs.

An act is neither right nor wrong because it is altruistic or egoistic; it is wrong if it is unfair or inconsiderate of the rights of others. The real moral issue is not egoism or altruism, but the kind of self being formed through the action. The kind of object chosen is also of moral significance; whether it resides in the agent or in another person does not necessarily alter the moral quality of the act. Interest is always present in human action, but interest which is morally approvable or "disinterested" is that which is intellectually fair, valuing a thing equally whether it affects the welfare of the agent or that of another.[12]

Personal growth consists in expanding interests and emotions which are narrow and transient by bringing consideration of relations and consequences to bear on them. If one recalls that the self exists only in and through association with other persons, one can see why this must be so. In this perspective one can also understand why neither egoism, altruism nor a combination of the two can be an adequate moral principle to regulate action. As Dewey puts it

. . . regard for self and regard for others are both of them secondary phases of a more normal and complete interest: regard for the welfare and integrity of the social groups of which we form a part.[13]

Interest in the social group of which a person is a member necessarily involves interest in one's own self and growth. Nevertheless, in an association the members *exist in relations to one another,* and each person must get direction for his action by reflecting on the whole group and his place in it rather than by considering his action strictly in terms of either egoism or altruism. Regard for self and others must become active forces which lead men to consider objects and consequences which would otherwise be overlooked. Then these objects and consequences, which have concrete *human relations* as their material, constitute the *interest* which motivates action.[14] In this way a common regard for both self and others can more readily become the active force leading persons to concentrate their interests on human relations rather than on possession of things.

Taking the emphasis off analyzing one's actions primarily in terms of egoism or altruism can act as a corrective to many christian devotional writings in which we too frequently find an over-emphasis on altruism at the expense of the self. Man cannot concern himself with the good of others exclusively without regard for his own person and its growth. Attempts at such behavior lead to inadequate personal relationships and leave the person unfulfilled so that he is in danger of reverting to a very pervasive egoism even if this is not consciously recognized or admitted.

The above analysis points out very clearly that there is a great deal of suffering, detachment and renunciation *inherently* involved in the process of personalization in a world attaining psychic concentration. The evolution entailed in personalization involves plurality which is a source of great pain to man. Externally, friction and environmental disorders cause pain; internally, lack of unity makes man fragile and subject to countless sufferings. Union differentiates, but this very process of differentiation is also a cause of hardship and renunciation. The process of union is always "a climb" and therefore laborious: so much union, so much suffering. Finally, the most bitterly felt suffering is that involved in metamorphosis. Inherent in the process of personalization is reaching new limits of concentration and being faced with thresholds leading to spheres of action involving more complex centers. Man must constantly fight inertia and surrender himself to transformations which involve severance, detachment and the destruction of earlier bonds. Growth demands change, losing oneself in a totalized humanity and facing the final agony involved in death which is a transition from the experience to which we are accustomed to the experience of centering oneself totally in God.[15]

The intimate connection between all facets of moral growth and personalization through love can also be seen when we recognize that moral growth entails developing the affection of sympathy. A *moral judgment,* although intellectual, *must be coloured with feeling* if it is to influence action. Affection is a necessary part of all operative knowledge of the good, so that the *reasonable* act and the *generous* one are closely related. Without the capacity for sympathetic response a person's consideration of consequences and his moral judgments are reduced to the confined outlook involved in narrow calculation. Such a person lacks a spontaneous sense of the claims of other persons. Sympathy carries thought beyond the self to the universal; truly general thought is generous thought. To achieve objectivity in one's moral outlook it is necessary to attempt to put oneself in the position of others so that one's claims are on the level of an impartial, sympathetic observer. The sympathetic standpoint is the most efficacious intellectual standpoint for resolving complex situations; it helps the moral agent to attain the mean between sentimentality and cold calculation while retaining a broad, open outlook which fosters personal union and community.[16]

A constant concern of ethical theory is the growth of the self so that each person in the society will participate freely and fully in shared experience and in fostering the common or general good. The concern of ethics is to bring all the instrumentalities of business, science and the arts to bear on developing intelligent methods to improve man's common lot.[17] Improvement of social conditions is a prime concern in the effort to develop men's personalities. The moral value of social arrangements must be judged in terms of the contribution they make in leading people to find their happiness in objects which

bring happiness to others. Education, therefore, must have as
its aim fostering an interest in furthering the common good
so that people will find their personal happiness in actions
directed at improving the conditions of others.[18]

Dewey identifies self-realization (personalization) with broad
concern and generous action in promoting the good of all.

> The *kind* of self which is formed through action which
> is faithful to relations with others will be a fuller and
> broader self than one which is cultivated in isolation
> from or in opposition to the purposes and needs of
> others. In contrast, the kind of self which results from
> generous breadth of interest may be said alone to cons-
> titute a development and fulfillment of self, while the
> other way of life stunts and starves selfhood by cut-
> ting it off from the connections necessary to its
> growth.[19]

We have here a functional definition of personhood and the
moral attitudes and actions which achieve it spelled out in
terms of love, because to love another is to will the good for
that person and to actively pursue it.

There is an intimate connection, therefore, between the interests a person cultivates, the kind of personality he develops
and his attainment of happiness. Happiness is attained in
sincere, active and enduring interests in objects in which all
persons can share. This type of happiness does not come from
material accomplishments, but from the fulfillment of the self
which accompanies interest in others and in those things which
promote their development.[20] Happiness is not a reality which
can be pursued for itself as an object or goal to be achieved.
It is a by-product, an effect or an added recompense which
results when man acts virtuously. Teilhard speaks of a happiness of movement as opposed to either happiness of tranquility
or of pleasure. Then he qualifies this by recognizing within
it a happiness of growing, of loving and of adoring, each of

which corresponds to one of the three natural phases of personalization described above.[21]

It is evident from our analysis of personalization through union that there is a distinction between personality and individuality. Individuality is conceived in terms of more external or superficial traits or characteristics which set a person off from his fellow men. An excessive emphasis on individuality understood in this sense separates men and directs them backward toward plurality and matter. The fullness of man is not to be achieved in superficial diversity, but in what is interior and unique in each.

Emphasis on the superficial *separates;* union *differentiates.* Personal union based on love does not absorb the individual in the masses but enables him to be, that is, to find, develop and differentiate himself fully. This is as true of individual societies and nations as of individual persons. The excesses of individualism in modern society are counter-evolutionary as are isolationist, egoistic and racist doctrines. Modern man needs to develop a sense of totality, a sense of the whole world and of humanity as one. He must also organize human energy and social relations so as to develop the maximum of personality in each individual person at the same time as he strives to form a personal and personalizing society.[22]

II. *The Term of Evolution Perceived by Extrapolation*

The foregoing description of evolution through personal union has indicated that the whole cosmic process will culminate in a super-unity of mankind coiled in on itself and centered in an ultimate personal Center greater than the personal centers of particular individuals or groups. By means of extrapolating on the basis of what has happened in the past and what is happening at present Teilhard proposed the development of a super-humanity and described in minimal detail its shape and the structure of the critical point of ultra-reflexion which the evolutionary process will attain. Because he extrapolated from basic evolutionary laws he was able to point out the indications, which, taken as a whole, oblige man to regard the achievement of this super-humanity as certain and to affirm that it is neither a speculative nor a utopian ideal, but a reality with a scientific justification. Accepting it is the most logical and consistent conclusion based on the process of extrapolating the curve of anthropogenesis (the appearance and continued development of man). We must look at these indications and at his basic lines for this super-humanity now.

From the outset evolution was governed by the law of complexity-consciousness; its higher form in living beings is the law of cephalisation.[23] *The extreme example* of the law of cephalisation is, in fact, the appearance and continued evolution of man. Beginning with the first members of the human group up to *homo sapiens* it is possible to record a movement which drives the group from *slightly* to *higher* cerebralised and socialized states. Cerebralisation and socialization are the terms of human evolution. In fact, cerebralisation and socialization are basically the same thing. Individual cerebralization is the organization and development of the human brain, a process which appears to have reached a climax biologically. Socialization is merely the association and organization of the brains or reflective activities of men. There is, therefore, a fundamental biological identity between individual cerebralisation and collective cerebralisation or *socialization*. The appearance and further development of mankind in the past is an undeniable objective reality, and the acceptance of its continuation in the future is equally obligatory. We have also seen earlier that anthropogenesis and the laws governing it are continuations of the underlying laws governing the whole of atomic and biological evolution. Thus what happens in man cannot be regarded as exceptional or as a local accident. The only logical position, therefore, is to admit a further process of socialization resulting in a future super-humanity as the most consistent outcome of the extrapolation of the curve of anthropogenesis.[24]

As indicated above further development in the nervous system of individuals is unlikely; thus one cannot look for anatomically super-cerebralised individuals composing a super-humanity. Because socialization extends cerebralisation one must look in the direction of a super-socialized humanity, not a multi-centered humanity nor merely a collectivized humanity, but a humanity totalized under the attraction of one' supreme Center. This totalization of mankind will not occur automatically. Man remains the responsible agent of evolution who can foster or frustrate it. It will occur only if men freely and deliberately adhere to the proper conditions for true personal union. Totalization can lead and has led to the mechanization of society and human life, to the sub-human state of the ant-hill instead of to brotherhood. This has been due to the incorrect manner in which totalization has been conceived and applied, not to the *principle* of totalization itself. Only where men are united person-to-person by the internal attraction of love can super-personalization be achieved. As the process of planetization occurs conditions can be developed in which a new kind of love will emerge. If it pursues authentic personalization for all men, humanity can and will find its single heart and will develop the powers of sympathy and unanimity.[25]

Super-humanity, therefore, is neither a speculative nor utopian reality, but the higher *biological* state mankind must attain if it carries to the extreme the process from which it emerged historically and therefore becomes completely totalized upon itself. Super-humanity already represents at least the imminence of a reality of the *scientific order*.[26] What Teilhard says about both the fact of its existence and its form is simply the extrapolation of the curve of anthropogenesis.

The very structure of time as man understands it today and the structure of a converging universe force Teilhard to extrapolate toward a supreme *goal* toward which human energy is moving. This is not to imply, of course, that these structures of themselves will force man *to attain this goal.* The proposed point of ultra-reflexion will be attained neither because of the shape of the earth nor because of the underlying laws involved in the evolutionary process, but, once again, only on the condition that men commit themselves to achieving personal union.

Nevertheless, using the method of extrapolation (which gives Teilhard's thought its scientific foundation), the hypothesis of an indefinite progress, an endless process of growth for the universe, is contradicted by the convergent nature of the whole cosmic process itself. The evolutionary process is a converging process; some final goal must be envisaged because of the very nature of evolution. Teilhard can conceive of three possibilities for mankind: a) senescence, a mere exhaustion and withering away, b) a paroxysm or violent convulsion of forces causing extinction, or c) a paroxysm of transformation. He rejects the first two.[27]

The only scientifically conceivable goal of the process of evolution is a paroxysm of transformation, a critical point of ultra-reflexion on the scale of the whole world. At that point the converging movement will have attained such intensity that mankind will be obliged to reflect upon itself at a single point. This point will coincide with a *definitive* access to the irreversible, to Omega, and will involve mankind giving up its foothold on the planet so as to shift its center completely to the transcendent Center on which it has been increasingly concentrated. This shift will be the end of the world. Mankind will have reached a critical level of maturity, and in an act which externally will be akin to death, it will leave all that portion of the material universe which has not been spiritualized and incorporated into itself to lapse back into primordial energy while it performs this final act of metamorphosis and arrives at complete synthesis. This critical point is one of emergence from the universe and emersion in Omega, of psychic maturation and escape from the material.[28]

We have seen that the possibility of unending growth in a

converging evolutionary process is inconceivable for both the material universe and mankind. The whole process of evolution, because it is a process of spiritualization, must culminate in the release of that which has been spiritualized from that which has not at a final point in which mankind is totally centered on itself. In his description of this final paroxysm of transformation, Teilhard is not looking for an escape for man from the world. He has described an issue or way out not *from* the universe but *for* the universe as well as for man. That portion of matter which has been incorporated within mankind and centered in Omega will be transformed. This is the final spiritualization and fulfillment of matter. This transformation, therefore, ultimately adds meaning to the whole universe and to all man's activity in it now. The residue of the material will elapse back into nothingness, but there is consistency here with the whole evolutionary process, because every step forward in it has always entailed waste.

Finally, Teilhard's description of this final critical point as an escape from the material as we know it now must not be interpreted as a failure to ultimately overcome a dualism between matter and spirit. Even at this final point man does not reject matter. Any rejection of the material by man prior to or even at this final point would be a futile attempt to reject and escape from himself. But when that portion of matter incorporated into mankind has been spiritualized as much as is possible, and even the duality which exists now between matter and spirit has been minimized, man will have no other choice but to emerge from non-spiritualized matter if he is to move on to his ultimate stage of fulfillment.

Teilhard proposes two contradictory suppositions regarding the physical and psychic state of mankind as it approaches the final stage of maturation. The first hypothesis is that evil, disease, hunger and hatred will have disappeared under Omega's intense influence. The final convergence will occur in peace. The second hypothesis suggests that the enormous powers liberated by the increased cohesion of men will be divided. There will be conflict between those who seek to fulfill themselves collectively upon themselves alone and those who seek to fulfill themselves personally on a greater Center. This will be a conflict between choice or rejection of Omega, between "arrogant autonomy" or "loving excentration." In the second situation, at its critical point of ultra-reflexion, the noosphere will split and each faction of mankind will be attracted to the pole of adoration it has chosen. Only that portion of mankind which has chosen Omega will detach itself and find consummation in Omega. No matter which of these hypotheses will correspond with the future reality, Teilhard assures us that the excess of interior tension will bring about a final paroxysm.[29] And on the basis of all the available evidence he rejects the utopian climate in which perfect harmony will have been achieved. The second hypothesis which foresees polarization and tension is more realistic.

In one brief formula for the final goal toward which human energy is moving Teilhard sums up what we have already described, and emphasizes the supporting and unifying role of Omega without which the final paroxysm cannot occur. He describes the goal as

> . . . an organic plurality the elements of which find the consummation of their own personality in a paroxysm of mutual union and limpidity: the whole body being supported by the unifying influence of a *distinct centre* of super-personality.[30]

Although we have referred frequently to Omega we have not described it. The role and attributes of this distinct Center must now be examined.

III. *The Attributes and Role of Omega in this Process*

From the moment a person conceives of a convergence of the cosmic lines of evolution or of an evolution toward spirit on the basis of phenomenological observation and philosophical reflection, Teilhard insists that he must also recognize, *on the level of philosophical reflection,* the existence of a higher Center of consciousness or supreme Personality in which the process culminates. Teilhard arrived at an awareness of the need for a personal Center, which transcends the cosmic process and also acts within it, in terms of the requirements of an evolving universe itself. This personal Center called Omega, conceived of as prime mover, present active force and lure-from-beyond, is a philosophical concept. It is not a theological construct whose fundamental existence is made known first by revelation or religious faith and then imposed from without on the evolutionary process.

As Teilhard developed his phenomenological-philosophical thought to its limits he saw philosophically the need of a transcendent personal Center of convergence and described its role and attributes philosophically. Later, without confusing philosophical and theological data and method, he turned to revelation, and on the basis of what he learned from it recognized that the functions and attributes of Omega are identical with those of Christ. Thus ultimately he was able to show that his phenomenological-philosophical thought complemented theological thought, and that the functions he had attributed to Omega are, in fact, performed by God. We shall restrict our present discussion to the philosophical level.

As an ultimate Center of convergence, Omega is objective by nature, that is, it corresponds to a biological bringing together of men's personalities and not merely to their concepts and desires. It is a Center with an irreversible totalizing power capable of gathering together and consummating what is most incommunicable and personal in men in its own supreme Center. In order to unite these personal centers without destroying them, Omega must necessarily be an autonomous reality with its own personality, a Person distinct from all the persons it fulfills.

Omega cannot be merely a Center resulting from the con-

213

vergence of personal centers in it, but must be a Center of dominance with the capacity to effect union and synthesis. Therefore it must be a *present reality* capable of reaching and acting upon and in man *now* both indirectly and directly. In order to perform this activity, without doing violence to man's personality, Omega must be both supremely loving and lovable. It radiates love and also attracts this energy back to itself. Since ultimately all cosmic energy is love energy, Omega is the source and term of the energy of evolution.

The successful completion of noogenesis not only requires that Omega be present now, it also requires that it be transcendent. Since everything within the realm of time and space is perishable, a non-transcendent Center of convergence could not definitively eliminate death as it too would disintegrate. Omega is the last term of its series, but is also outside all series. As the conscious pole of the world it emerges from the rise of consciousness insofar as the movement of synthesis culminates in it, yet it has already emerged from this genesis. It is actual, autonomous, irreversible and transcendent.

As a consequence of becoming conscious of one's personal relations with this supreme personal Center, a process of unification begins in and among persons which extends ultimately to the totalization of each person and all his actions in collective humanity. Omega's present love energy is at the basis of the whole process of personal unification. The evolutionary process is no longer an impersonal matter; the presence of Omega both at the heart of reality and as its consummation personalizes the universe and its fulfillment. Once Omega's presence is experienced in even the least movement of evolution every action and thing which is in the line of progress becomes the object of man's total commitment. He can come to realize how totally he belongs to the world and how he can love it.[31]

Earlier we saw that men are the responsible agents of evolution; now we have also seen the need of a personal transcendent pole beyond men which promotes evolution by radiating love energy and attracting this energy back to itself. Thus the two complementary aspects of the evolutionary process have been revealed. Man remains the responsible agent of evolution, but within the framework in which Omega is both prime mover and lure-from-beyond. Apart from Omega the evolutionary process is neither self-sufficient nor self-motivating. It is totally dependent upon Omega for its primary source of energy, its daily motivating and activating power and its final consummation. Neither human energy nor human ideals of themselves are sufficient to keep the process evolving. Omega acts by the power of love interiorly within man so that he in turn acts freely, intelligently and responsibly. His activity is absolutely essential as a necessary, but in itself, insufficient condition of cosmic fulfillment.

Man's role as evolver is neither threatened nor diminished from what it is in the eyes of the naturalist. Omega's activity, in fact, increases man's responsibility because it gives him access to a power of love energy he would otherwise not have. It also reveals the personal depth dimension of every man and confronts him with possibilities of personal interaction and communion beyond those offered him in a purely naturalistic universe. The universe too is given a relationship and meaning it could not have apart from a transcendent term. Man co-operates with Omega (whom we shall see later is identical with God) in bringing the universe to fulfillment. Without His efforts on behalf of evolution the creative process could not continue.

IV. *Personhood and a Personalizing Universe*

In our affirmation that the cosmic process will culminate in a critical moment of transformation which will enable mankind to transcend the limits of the material world, we have radically diverged from a naturalistic world view in which no such transcendence is possible. As indicated earlier, the ultimate or most comprehensive meaning of a thing or event is determined in relation to its end. Therefore, the ends proposed for the cosmic process by different world views are of major significance in determining the ultimate value of the different views themselves. The meaning or value of the end reflects back on every facet and stage of the whole process and either adds or detracts from its meaning.

No world view can be regarded as adequate if it does not incorporate within itself an adequate theory of personhood (of what it is and means to be a person), and if it does not succeed in describing an evolutionary process which can guarantee the greatest possible opportunity for developing persons to their utmost. Both the end set forth in our world view and that proposed by a naturalistic world view have inherent consequences which affect their respective theories of the human person. The differences in the ends proposed by the two world views also have inherent consequences which make the very process of evolution more or less personal and personalizing. At this point, therefore, it will be enlightening to discuss these ends and their respective consequences.

Throughout his naturalistic world view, Dewey shows a great deal of respect for man and his ability to evolve and realize himself. He finds the worth and dignity of man to reside in human nature itself, in the connections persons sustain to one another in their natural environment. The foundation of human dignity is firm because it is in man and nature and not in something existing outside the constitution of man in nature. Living for Dewey is equated with evolution or growth, and Dewey has great confidence in man's capacity to go on evolving. He is also convinced that science has presented man with an open universe, one infinite in space and time and without limit at either end.[32] Man no longer exists in a closed universe which lacks the infinite complexity capable of continuously challenging his intelligence. The movement of humanity, therefore, is one which remains within nature but evolves by a continual transformation of the physical and animal toward an ever-increasing participation by all men in the increasingly complex social and technical interactions of persons living in community.

It is evident, therefore, that there is, at least up to a certain point on the natural level, a close similarity between the term of the naturalistic evolutionary process and the process we are proposing. Both are, in fact, processes of totalization directed toward the full self-realization of individual persons in a unified, universal or world community.

The radical difference in the terms of the two processes lies in the fact that in our vision this process of totalization continues to a point where mankind can evolve no further. Thus it undergoes a radical transformation and continues on a transcendent level. In the naturalistic process there is no totally consummatory term which either the individual person or humanity as a whole can ever achieve. The goal is an imaginatively projected ideal and as such is always beyond the present realization of mankind at any stage of evolution. The open-endedness of the universe is found in the continuous possibility of further self-realization for individuals and for mankind, in spite of the fact that the naturalist cannot guarantee that the world as we experience it now will not come to an end.

To understand this term we are forced to examine Dewey's concepts of God and "experience that is religious." (He does not develop a concept on the philosophical level comparable to Omega.) Although not all Dewey scholars agree, there appears to be little question that Dewey regards "experience that is religious" as capable of effecting the most inclusive unifications, the deepest consummations and the most universal community possible among men.[33] Thus the comparison we wish to draw regarding the ends of these processes and their consequences for personhood cannot be accomplished without some understanding of his concept of God and religious experience and the consequences these have on personhood.

Dewey denies that there is a specific religious experience separate from experience as esthetic, moral and political. The quality "religious" can belong to all these experiences. The religious quality of an experience does not concern its manner or cause, but is the effect produced, namely, the fuller adjustment in life and the conditions of living. This adjustment involves adapting conditions to man's purposes, commitment to causes and very inclusive, deep-seated changes within persons. These changes pertain to one's whole being; the modification they effect is enduring, a composing and harmonizing of the elements of the person's being. This deep-seated adjusment results in a religious attitude, a change of will involving one's whole person. Religion does not bring about this change of will according to Dewey; rather when it occurs a religious attitude is present.[34]

Any idea of a whole, whether that of the self or of the universe, is an imaginative idea. The whole self is an imaginative projection, an ideal; and the idea of a thorough harmonizing of the self with the universe is also the product of imagination. Man cannot unify his own self in what he does and undergoes in terms of himself alone. The self is always directed to something beyond itself; thus its unification depends upon the imaginative whole called the universe which Dewey defines in terms of all the conditions with which the self is connected.[35]

Ideal elements in experience are intimately connected with imagination. Faith is also connected with the imaginative and the ideal. The power of an ideal is the unseen power which controls man's destiny. Possibilities, as such, are ideal in character. Every attempt to attain something better is motivated by believing in what is possible not by adhering to the actual. *Such faith is not even motivated by any guarantee that the good sought will necessarily prevail.* It is the intrinsic nature of the ideal itself, not its outcome when executed, that gives it its authority and claim to man's allegiance.[36] The religious attitude is that which identifies what is ideally good with the possibilities of existence which one must commit oneself to realize. It promotes endeavor which looks to the future and never attains certainty.[37]

Dewey describes faith that is religious as

> . . . the unification of the self through allegiance to
> inclusive ideal ends, which imagination presents to
> us and to which the human will responds as worthy
> of controlling our desires and choices.[38]

The ideal means really having a sense of the infinite connections between man and nature and among men. Even in times of conflict a consciousness of the comprehensive whole is possible. Whenever a person, out of conviction, pursues an ideal end of general, lasting value, in the face of the possibility of personal loss, his action is religious in quality.[39]

The passages which express Dewey's final thoughts on religious experience and the elements of a common faith of mankind stress that religious experience involves a self-sacrificing effort on behalf of all men and that it brings the agent into communion with all men both past and future in a community of causes and consequences which is the most extensive symbol of that whole the imagination calls the universe. This symbol embodies the all-encompassing scope of existence and is the context in which all aspirations and ideals are formed. The continuing life of this vast community of persons includes all men's achievements in communication, friendship, art and science.[40]

The ideal ends to which men attach their faith take very concrete form in man's understanding of his relations with his fellow man and in the values of these relations. Each individual is part of a universal community of persons extending into the past. In its constant interaction with nature and through its actions and sufferings the continuous human community has developed those things in civilization which men prize today. As members of this community the responsibility of the present generation is to expand the values it has received and make them accessible to its successors. These principles, according to Dewey, are the basic tenets of a common religious faith of mankind. This faith must be made more explicit and militant if it is to act as the motivating force in accelerating evolution.[41]

Dewey rejects a God conceived of as an eternally existing Being; prior existence is equated with non-ideal existence. Such a God is also unacceptable to him because He transcends nature and any ideal must have its roots in natural conditions; that is, an ideal emerges when imagination idealizes existence by using the possibilities offered to thought and action.[42] For Dewey, "God" means the unity of all the ideal ends that arouse man to desire and action — those ideal ends that at a particular time have authority over a person's will and emotions, the values to which he is supremely devoted insofar as these ends take on unity through imagination.[43]

The idea of "God" or of the divine is the sum total of all the possible ideals projected by the imagination and attainable by the co-operative work of all men. This idea of "God" is connected with all the natural forces and conditions which promote the growth of the ideal and foster its realization. These natural forces and conditions include man himself and such things as human association, friendship and scientific inquiry.[44]

Dewey emphasizes the fact that the ideals under discussion are neither ideals which are completely embodied in existence nor illusions. There are forces in nature and society that generate and support these ideals, and they are further unified by the action that gives them coherence and solidity. To illustrate this he points out that the ideals or values of art, knowledge, friendship, love and education exist concretely and yet not as fully as is possible. A clear, intense conception of the union of these ideal ends with actual conditions can be nourished by every experience regardless of its subject matter. Such a conception in turn is capable of arousing intense and enduring emotion. It is to this active relation between the ideal and the actual that Dewey gives the name "God," and he insists that the need for such an idea is urgent today. It can unify the interests and energies of men, direct action and generate emotion and intelligence. He speaks of this working union in terms of *a presence* – it is *operative* in thought and action, indicating that its function is identical with the force attributed to God in religions with a spritual content.[45]

In this analysis of the lofty ideals Dewey claims man can achieve through "experience that is religious," he shows great respect not only for humanity as a whole but for individual persons. Persons are never to be used as mere means to an end. No community can be significant if it is not composed of individuals who are significant. There ought not to be a problem as to whether the individual is subordinate to the society or not. Society is the *process* of associating in such a way that experiences, ideas and values are communicated and made common. Both the individual and the whole (the institutionally organized) are subordinate to this process. The individual is subordinate because *he is* in and through relations with others. The society or state is also subordinate because it remains vital through its service in facilitating and enriching the personal communication among its members. The interaction between individual and society is organic and the balance between them must also be organic.[46]

Even what Dewey says regarding the organic relationship between the individual and the society is sensitive to the dignity and worth of each person, but when we scrutinize this relationship carefully are not both the individual person and the whole of humanity subordinate to the on-going evolutionary *process* itself? There is no goal in the sense of a comprehensive, enduring consummation attainable by either the individual or mankind as a whole. *Growth is the only absolute,* and in such a context a greater dignity and worth is ultimately attributed to the *process* by which evolution occurs than to the persons who are the agents of the process.

In this naturalistic world view an eternal dignity is attributed to art and labour in that they bring about a permanent reshaping of the environment which is the foundation for future security and progress. Individuals flourish and wither away but their works endure. The best man can accomplish for posterity is to transmit with some added meaning an environment which makes a refined life possible. Man's individual habits are links in the endless chain of humanity and their significance is established in terms of their contribution to this continuum.[47] Man must commit himself wholeheartedly to fostering the evolution of humanity and remain confident that good will come to him because of this commitment.

> When we have used our thought to its utmost and have thrown into the moving unbalanced balance of things our puny strength, we know that though the universe slay us still we trust, for our lot is one with whatever is good in existence.[48]

There are serious limitations placed upon the concept of man due to the inherent logic of the naturalistic perspective. Humanity itself

> . . . is but a slight and feeble thing, perhaps an episodic one, in the vast stretch of the universe.[49]

And the individual person, just as all other things in nature, is subject to the process of birth, growth and death, by which he gives place to subsequent individuals.[50] This total end for the individual person is accepted as natural and unproblematic. There is no explanation or justification for it. There is no way in which man, and possibly humanity as well, can transcend physical and *total death*. The only intimation of transcendence Dewey offers the individual person is very limited.

> Within the flickering inconsequential acts of separate selves dwells a sense of the whole which claims and dignifies them. In its presence we put off mortality and live in the universal.[51]

There is no question, therefore, that the only transcendence open to man in this naturalistic perspective is a very fleeting experience or sense of the whole which enables him to "put off mortality" momentarily and live in the universal. We maintain that this is psychologically inadequate for man. The end for thought can only consist in not having a limit. In order to be consistent with this philosophical principle the naturalist maintains that man can never conceive of the universe as a whole (further, more inclusive concepts are always possible). This concept of the whole as the projection of the sum total of all man's attainable ideals is inadequate because it is a projection which is always in process of being revised. It is ethereal and evasive. Although man's intellect is oriented toward and capable of grasping the fullness of truth no person nor group of persons can ever attain this goal; it always exceeds their grasp.

Man is also capable of loving and uniting himself with infinite goodness. The end for love can also only consist in not having a limit, and yet this process is definitively terminated by death in the naturalist's perspective. These restrictions imposed by the inherent limitations of naturalism frustrate man, reduce his dignity and impersonalize the whole process of evolution for him. Reflective, loving persons must know that the process of evolution of which they are a part is irreversible; this requires immortality and transcendence. No positive element must be excluded from the all-inclusive end toward which evolution is moving. The universe of the naturalist is ultimately not open-ended; the total death from which there is no escape closes it in and stifles man. Denying man any possibility of transcending death deprives him of the motivation required to maintain the continued and very demanding sacrifices and efforts entailed in committing himself wholeheartedly to fostering evolution. Even the possibility of continued survival and growth on a level of fulfillment beneath that which he has imagined to be possible of attainment (an unending experience of the fullness of truth and goodness) limits man's motivation to act because its ultimate meaning is diminished.

Throughout Dewey's very insightful analysis of the dynamism inherent in experience, we see the need to balance activity and passivity (being acted upon or dying to oneself). Suffering and partial death are never seen as ends in themselves; they become meaningful because they are an inherent part of experiences which lead to fulfillment and life. To be consistent, therefore, the final act of physical death also ought to be part of a final experience which also leads to life. To give physical death a different meaning, namely, that of a mere stoppage of life, reflects back on the meaning attributed to the partial, daily deaths to self that man must undergo in order to live more fully and detracts from their ultimate significance. Dewey's naturalistic concept of religious experience does not treat the problem of physical death adequately. The consequences of this limitation reflect back on the meaning of being a person now.

Dewey erroneously identifies the supernatural and the transcendent and rejects: a transcendent spirit in man, life after death, and a personal God, on the grounds that they withdraw man from nature and distract him from commitment to the evolutionary process. He speaks of the evolutionary process as one of spiritualization. In our view man's unique interiority is never completely absorbed in or by nature but transcends it. Nevertheless, this does not diminish man's intimate relationship with nature.

Evolution is a movement toward spirit but not away from nature; it is nature which is being spiritualized and brought to fulfillment. Nature is not a type of matter or even a milieu in which spirit is inserted as paint is put in a can. Spirit can be said to triumph over the physical and carnal insofar as it orients them, integrates them into the whole and brings them to their fulfillment. The emphasis is on neither sublimating nor cancelling out nature. Even at the final critical point evolution occurs through a transformation and spiritualization of nature. In brief, the process of spiritualization we are proposing upholds all the natural, terrestrial values cherished by naturalists, but extends beyond them in a fulfillment the naturalist must reject.

One final major difference which has consequences that pertain to the whole process of evolution and to personalization concerns the acceptance or rejection of a final *personal* goal in which the whole is consummated. Our vision maintains that the capacity to love all men and to achieve universal community can only be maintained with the assistance of and as a direct response to a super-personal Center who stands in a personal relationship to each member of the world community. Naturalism, as proposed by Dewey, places no great emphasis on love either as a means of self-realization, as a cosmic evolutionary force or as a necessity for developing universal community.

One must ask whether the naturalistic view really faces the problem of what force is strong enough to unite people in a universal community in such a way as to respect their personalities. Dewey's thought reveals an excessive faith in science and an unbounded confidence in its capacity to constantly challenge men to commit themselves to fostering evolution in spite of the grave hardships involved. This is all the more amazing because he explicitly speaks of man's tendency to isolate himself from his fellow man.

The realist must recognize that there is nothing particularly lovable about the masses and that *loving all men* is extremely difficult for most, if not all, persons. We have proposed a cosmic evolution activated primarily by love and a theory of personal development achieved through love. This requires the presence of a super-human love radiated to man from a personal Being who is the beginning, the sustaining foundation and the end of the cosmic process. Humanity can only achieve a universal communion in love indirectly by being united with such a Being who loves all men and gives them a share in that love which enables them to respond to each other and to Him with an intense activating force beyond their own natural capacity to love.

The "God" proposed by Dewey is incapable of exercising this function. There is no doubt that man creates natural symbols, and that these symbols act as generators and catalysts motivating man to aspire toward and achieve ideal ends. Dewey developed a naturalized religious faith; his symbol "God" is a human symbol, a mental construct, with no divine Being or power of love behind it. It can act as a strong motivating force which will release a power of human energy to accomplish good; but it is an inadequate substitute for a personal God. Its power is a finite, human power, and the ultimate consummation it offers man is also finite and inadequate. The power of love required to personalize men and to make the universe a personal and personalizing one must be an infinite, personal power of love who is both transcendent and immanent. Thus we find the end proposed by Dewey's naturalistic concepts of God and "experience that is religious" to be extremely inadequate to assure the fullest degree of personal self-realization possible to man.

FOOTNOTES

1. *PH*, pp. 293-94 [Eng. trans. pp. 264-65]; "L'Esprit de la terre," *ÉH*, pp. 40-41 [Eng. trans. p. 33]; "La Centrologie," *AÉ*, pp. 122, 125 [Eng. trans. pp. 115-16, 118-19].
2. "La Montée de l'autre," *AÉ*, p. 77 [Eng. trans. pp. 70-71].
3. Pierre Teilhard de Chardin, "Réflexions sur le bonheur," *Réflexions sur le bonheur*, inédits et témoignages, Cahier II (Paris: Éditions du Seuil, 1960), pp. 60-61, hereafter cited *RB*; "Esquisse d'un univers personnel," *ÉH*, pp. 80-81 [Eng. trans. p. 63].
4. *PH*, p. 287 [Eng. trans. p. 259].
5. "L'Union créatrice," *ÉTG*, pp. 192-93 [Eng. trans. pp. 170-71].
6. *PH*, pp. 293-96 [Eng. trans. pp. 264-66]; "L Esprit de la terre," *ÉH*, pp. 51-52 [Eng. trans. pp. 42-43]; "La Grande Option," *AH*, pp. 74-75 [Eng. trans. pp. 52-55]; "Les Singularités de l'espèce humaine, . . .," *AppH*, pp. 367-69 [Eng. trans. pp. 268-70]; "Esquisse d'un univers personnel," *ÉH*, pp. 80-85 [Eng. trans. pp. 63-67]; "La Centrologie," *AÉ*, pp. 122-26 [Eng. trans. pp. 115-20].
7. "Esquisse d'un univers personnel," *ÉH*, p. 82 [Eng. trans. pp. 64-65]; "La Vie cosmique," *ÉTG*, pp. 6-7 [Eng. trans. p. 16].
8. In note 1, appended to the title "Super-humanité, Super-Christ, super-charité," *SC*, p. 193 [Eng. trans. p. 151], Teilhard explains that the prefix "super" does not refer to a change or difference in nature but to a more advanced *degree* of realization of the reality involved. This interpretation is also valid for its use in other texts as well.
9. "Esquisse d'un univers personnel," *ÉH*, pp. 103-05 [Eng. trans. pp. 83-84]; "Réflexions sur le bonheur," *RB*, pp. 60-63.
10. *Experience and Nature*, pp. 242-47.
11. *Human Nature and Conduct*, pp. 138-39.
12. *Theory of the Moral Life*, pp. 158-62.
13. *Theory of the Moral Life*, p. 164.
14. *Theory of the Moral Life*, pp. 164-65.
15. "Esquisse d'un univers personnel," *ÉH*, pp. 105-09 [Eng. trans. pp. 84-88].
16. *Theory of the Moral Life*, pp. 128-30.
17. "Intelligence and Morals," *The Influence of Darwin on Philosophy*, p. 69.
18. *Theory of the Moral Life*, p. 98.
19. *Theory of the Moral Life*, p. 167.
20. *Theory of the Moral Life*, pp. 167-68.
21. "Réflexions sur le bonheur," *RB*, pp. 57-60, 64. For further discussion of happiness and its relation to self-realization or personalization see: *The Public and its Problems*, pp. 213-14; *Reconstruction in Philosophy*, pp. 179-80; *Human Nature and Conduct*, pp. 293-94; *Theory of the Moral Life*, pp. 43-47.

22. *PH*, pp. 270-72, 292-93 [Eng. trans. pp. 243-45, 263-64]; "Les Fondements et le fond de l'idée d'évolution," *VP*, pp. 194-96 [Eng. trans. pp. 140-41]; "L'Heure de choisir," *AÉ*, pp. 24-25 [Eng. trans. pp. 17-19]; "L'Énergie humaine," *ÉH*, p. 164 [Eng. trans. p. 131].

23. This law indicates that in all animal groups the nervous system increases in volume and organization and concentrates in the cephalic region of the body. Considered from the point of view of the cerebral ganglia, all of life moves in the direction of the largest brains. See: "Super-humanité, super-Christ, super-charité," *SC*, p. 199 [Eng. trans. p. 155].

24. "Super-humanité, super-Christ, super-charité," *SC*, pp. 197-201, including the important editor's note, p. 198 [Eng. trans. pp. 153-56].

25. "Super-humanité, super-Christ, super-charité," *SC*, pp. 201-05 [Eng. trans. pp. 156-60]; "Vie et planètes," *AH*, pp. 151-52 [Eng. trans. pp. 118-19]; "La Formation de la noosphère," *AH*, pp. 224-25 [Eng. trans. pp. 177-78]; "L'Atomisme de l'esprit," *AÉ*, p. 53 [Eng. trans. p. 46]; *PH*, pp. 284-86 [Eng. trans. pp. 256-57].

26. "Super-humanité, super-Christ, super-charité," *SC*, pp. 196-97 [Eng. trans. pp. 152-53].

27. "La Structure phylétique du groupe humain," *AppH*, pp. 229-33 [Eng. trans. pp. 167-70]; "Du Pré-humain à l'ultra-humain," *AH*, pp. 383-85 [Eng. trans. pp. 295-97].

28. *PH*, pp. 302-05, 319-20, 341 [Eng. trans. pp. 271-73, 287-88, 307]; "Du Pré-humain à l'ultra-humain," *AH*, p. 385 [Eng. trans. pp. 296-97]; "Vie et planètes," *AH*, pp. 155-56 [Eng. trans. pp. 122-23]; "La Structure phylétique du groupe humain," *AppH*, pp. 233-34 [Eng. trans. pp. 170-71]; "Un Sommaire de ma perspective 'phénoménologique' du monde," *Les Études Philosophiques*, 10 (1955), pp. 570-71.

29. *PH*, pp. 320-21 [Eng. trans. pp. 288-89]; "Note sur le progrès," *AH*, pp. 30-31 [Eng. trans. pp 18-19].

30. "L'Énergie humaine," *ÉH*, p. 180 [Eng. trans. p. 145].

31. For discussion of the attributes and function of Omega see: *PH*, pp. 289-302 [Eng. trans. pp. 260-72]; "La Grande Option," *AH*, pp. 76-77 [Eng. trans. pp. 55-56]; "L'Esprit nouveau," *AH*, pp. 121-22 [Eng. trans. p. 92]; "Remarques complémentaires sur la nature du Point Omega . . . ," *AppH*, pp. 371-74 [Eng. trans. pp. 271-73]; "Mon Univers," *SC*, pp. 75-76 [Eng. trans. pp. 47-48]; "La Centrologie," *AÉ*, pp. 117-19, 127-29 [Eng. trans. pp. 111-13, 120-22]; "Construire la terre," *CT*, pp. 33-36 [Eng. trans. pp. 67-70]; "L'Énergie humaine," *ÉH*, pp. 182-83 [Eng. trans. p. 147]; "Comment je crois," *CJC*, pp. 134-38 [Eng. trans. pp. 113-18].

32. John Dewey, "Antinaturalism in Extremis," *Naturalism and the Human Spirit*, ed. by Yervant H. Krikorian (New York: Columbia University Press, 1944), p. 9; *Reconstruction in Philosophy*, pp. 60-61.

33. Robert J. Roth, *John Dewey and Self-Realization*, pp. 101-04.

34. John Dewey, *A Common Faith*, (New Haven: Yale University Press, 1934), pp. 10-11, 13-14, 16-17.

35. *A Common Faith*, pp. 18-19.

36. *A Common Faith*, pp. 19, 23.

37. *The Quest for Certainty*, pp. 303, 307.
38. *A Common Faith*, p. 33.
39. *Human Nature and Conduct*, p. 330; *A Common Faith*, pp. 27-28.
40. *A Common Faith*, p. 85.
41. *A Common Faith*, p. 87.
42. *A Common Faith*, pp. 42, 48.
43. *A Common Faith*, p. 42.
44. *A Common Faith*, p. 50.
45. *A Common Faith*, pp. 50-52.
46. *Reconstruction in Philosophy*, p. 207; *Art as Experience*, p. 204; *Individualism, Old and New*, p. 50.
47. *Human Nature and Conduct*, pp. 20-21.
48. *Experience and Nature*, p. 420.
49. *The Public and its Problems*, p. 176.
50. "Time and Individuality," *On Experience, Nature, and Freedom*, p. 236.
51. *Human Nature and Conduct*, pp. 331-32.

CHAPTER 9

EVOLUTION EXTENDED THROUGH ENCOUNTER WITH A TRASCENDENT GOD

I. *The Biological Foundation of Religion in Cosmic Evolution*

We have already established the need of a transcendent, personal Absolute to attract and motivate the elements of the universe so that they will converge in the direction of spirit. A converging evolution cannot continue independently of its influence. The personal Absolute necessary to the whole cosmic process is divine and identifiable with traditional concepts of God. In its broadest sense "religion" encompasses both God's historical self-revelation to man and man's response to God. In this context religion is born because the *earth* needs a God who acts on its behalf and reveals the presence of this activity so that man can respond in a free, personal manner.[1]

Before the appearance of man the attractive activity of God was received vitally but blindly by the earth. In man, the attractive power of God is at least partially conscious in the form of reflective freedom. Thus it gave rise to and continues to sustain religion. In itself religion is not a purely individual matter of personal choice or intuition, but an organically-founded and universal reality. It represents the long disclosure of God's being as it has been experienced collectively throughout the history of mankind. God has manifested Himself personally to men in order to orient and guide them. His laws are meant

230

to direct and channel men's energies and activities toward a successful fufillment in Himself.[2]

The appearance of man released free reflective energy into the world, an indeterminate energy capable of getting out of control. The organic function of *morality* is to be the expression of the energetics of thought, to control and co-ordinate this free energy. *Religion* provides a foundation for morality by introducing a dominating principle of order and an axis of movement for reflective beings. Biologically, then, religion is the counterpart to the release of the spiritual energy of the earth. It is an energy which sustains and propels the progress of life and at the same time provides a structure for progress. Its laws, especially that of love, lead persons to know and center themselves on God whom they cannot attain unless they strive to achieve unity in and among themselves.[3]

Precisely because religion is the necessary counterpart to the release of the earth's spiritual energy, the religious function must increase proportionally with human evolution in both direction and speed. The notion that the concepts of divinity and religious response characterized man's primitive attempt to cope with natural phenomena about which he lacked scientific knowledge is, therefore, inadequate. Because it fails to recognize the organic and universal foundation of religion, it reduces religion to an accidental response of some men to particular situations. It also implies that as man's scientific knowledge increases religion will necessarily decrease. In fact, the opposite is true. The more man develops his humanity the more he needs to worship. Certainly as man evolves religion must take on new forms. True religion has an origin and development as extensive as man's history and must share in the nature of a phylum whose origins can be traced to the beginning of time. This means that at any moment in history all the religious currents are not equally developed or of equal relevance to cosmic evolution. One specific current of religious thought must represent in a fairly distinct form the most advanced, living element of the faith in which the future will develop. At any historical point one religion or group of religions must represent the place at which persons can most effectively experience and forward the progress of bringing the world to convergence in God.[4]

It is also evident that a religion must fulfill certain conditions relative to each particular age if it is to fulfill its biological function of *giving form* to the world's free psychic energy. The only form acceptable to mankind is a process of development which leads to *a supreme unification of the universe of which man is an integral part*. Any form which attempts to dominate the psychic energy of the world by an ideal, established order to be accepted and preserved is unacceptable to modern man. Religion, like the entire social order, must be *dynamic* if it is to be *salvific*. Modern man does not seek salvation in a religion which stifles or limits his development, but in one which initiates research and motivates him to develop the world and fulfill it and himself. When Eastern and Western religions and secular moral systems are tested by these criteria Teilhard affirms that Christianity alone is capable of measuring up to them and fulfilling the needs of a religion for the future.[5] An analysis of the christian religion and the church as the axis of evolution must be made, but it cannot be fully intelligible until some understanding of Christ in His Incarnation and in His functions as Omega and head of both mankind and the cosmos has been achieved.

II. *Christ and His Function in an Evolving Universe*

The historical Jesus is the fullness of the revelation of God to men; He is the divine-human point of contact between them. Jesus was not only *a* man, but man, the total man who summed up in His consciousness the consciousness of all men; thus His experience extended to the universal. Our vision emphasizes the historical reality of Jesus and His universality as well as the fact that there is an identity between the historical Jesus and the risen Christ. The New Testament reveals the spiritual or mystical union which exists now between men and the glorified, risen Body of Christ. It also reveals that the risen Christ is head of and spiritually united to the whole universe.[6]

In the Incarnation the Word became flesh; the divine penetrated into man's nature and a new life was born. This new life is an unexpected, unmerited enlargement and prolongation of man's natural capacities. It is grace, a single and identical life shared by all men so that they become identified with the super-human reality of Christ. Grace super-humanizes men so that their union with God exceeds a juridic justification; it represents a physical[7] enrichment which amounts to a new creation. The effect of grace is not restricted to man alone, but includes a renewal and restoration of the whole universe. Christ became the instrument, center and end of all of creation. Through Him all things have been created and sanctified.[8] The law of the Incarnation is "to plunge into in order then to emerge and raise up. To share in order to sublimate."[9]

The cosmic dimensions of Christ's death and resurrection must also be emphasized. Through His death Christ conquered death and physically gave it the value of a metamorphosis. Thus the whole world entered along with Christ's physical body into God. His resurrection marked the effective assumption of His position as universal Center from which He radiates His transforming life.[10] This elevation or transformation by grace is completely gratuitous. Neither man nor natural reality can attain or even aspire to have Christ as their Center or point of fulfillment; nevertheless, as Teilhard states:

. . . it remains true that the Incarnation so completely *recast* the universe in the supernatural[11] that, in *concrete fact*, we no longer ask, or imagine, towards what Centre the elements of this world, had they not been raised up by grace, would have gravitated. Physically speaking, there is only one dynamism in the present world, that which gathers all things to Christ.[12]

Through the Incarnation, therefore, Christ entered into the whole universe as a directing principle by uniting it organically with Himself. He works from within, animating without disturbing the processes of the world. Nature and man retain all their most specific attributes; in fact, union with God involves prolonging and expanding these characteristics *beyond their ordinary capacities*. Union with God, as all union, causes differentiation.[13]

In one sense, the *specific* goal of grace is the building up of the "Mystical Body" of Christ, that is, the continued extension and deepening of the spiritual or mystical union of persons with the resurrected Body of Christ. Nevertheless, the Mystical Body does not exhaust the fullness of the incarnate Word. Christ also has a "Cosmic Body;" He is also the Center of the entire universe having entered into union with it in the Incarnation. Thus Teilhard speaks of the "Mystical Christ," the "Cosmic Christ" and the "Universal Christ." By these titles he refers to the risen Body of Christ spiritually united to mankind, the world, and indeed the whole of created reality. Therefore, these titles refer to the same risen Christ spoken of in the Gospels and presented to us specifically by John and Paul. Christ is the organic Center of the entire universe; His unifying activity extends to the whole. Neither the Mystical nor Cosmic Christ have as yet attained their fullness because neither all men nor the whole universe are as yet brought to consummation in Him. Thus the Cosmic Christ *is* and yet *is becoming*. In this becoming there is the motive force of love which animates all creative activity.[14]

At the term of this process of becoming, that is, when God's work of establishing the Kingdom has reached maturity and all the chosen persons and forces of the universe have been united to Christ and transformed, Christ will close in upon Himself and all that He has sanctified. In doing so He will rejoin the trinitarian Center from which He emanated but has never been separated. In this union in God through Christ all persons will be super-personalized. The *pleroma,* or fullness of which Paul speaks will be achieved; Christ in the fullness of His individual Body and His Mystical and Cosmic Body will be the New Jerusalem. At this point, as Paul says, God will be all in all.[15]

We have seen, therefore, that there are two lines of convergence in the cosmic process. The first is the natural line of convergence, which, quite apart from any religious consideration, but by reason of experience and philosophical reflection, led us to see the need of Omega, a personal, transcendent point of convergence. The second is the christic or supernatural line of convergence culminating in Christ as universal Center.

In order to demonstrate that Christ and Omega are identical Teilhard turns to John and especially Paul. He quotes Col. 1:17 "He holds all things in unity" and Col. 2:10 "in Him you too find your own fulfillment." From these texts it follows that "Christ is everything and is in everything" (Col. 3:11) which is equivalent to the very definition of Omega. One can only deny the identification of Christ and Omega by claiming that the cosmic qualities of Christ in Paul's writings belong to the Godhead alone or by weakening the texts by reducing the ties subjecting all reality to Christ to juridical or moral bonds. Teilhard rejects these claims.[16]

The natural and supernatural lines of convergence must meet in Christ. However supernatural the operation of Christ may be, it cannot proceed in a direction diverging from the natural convergence of the world. The christic Center and the cosmic Center must coincide. Christ could not be the sole mover and term of the universe if it could integrate itself apart from Him. He would also be physically incapable of centering the universe upon Himself supernaturally if the universe had not provided Him with a favourable point at which its various strands are structured to converge by nature. Christ, therefore, fills the place and role of Omega. He is the head in whom the whole process of cephalisation is completed in a super-natural depth achieved in harmony with the whole "natural" process. He is a Super-Christ on the scale of the super-human-ity to be attained.[17]

Within a static concept of the cosmos Christ's function as Saviour on whom both man and the universe depend was re-cognized but difficult to defend rationally. It was more de-fensible in juridic and moral terms than in the organic sense which alone expresses its fullness. Little attempt was made by theologians in the past to incorporate His function into any precise cosmic order, and His domination was even reduced at times to an extrinsic super-imposed power.[18]

In an evolutionary, convergent cosmos Christ retains His primacy as beginning and end of salvation and He also becomes Christ-the-Evolver. He is given a position at the apex of the cosmic movement from which His Spirit can radiate. The genetic links between all the elements in such a cosmos en-able His love to penetrate the whole mass of nature in evolu-tion. In such a universe Christ cannot sanctify the spirit with-out elevating and saving *all matter*. The gulf between faith in God and faith in the world is diminished. Biological evolu-tion is not left indeterminate, but is given a specific person-alizing term which personalizes the whole evolutionary process. At the same time Christ is made truly universal, capable of answering *all* the needs of christians and of supplying their deepest aspirations for progress with the cross which, in this milieu, becomes the symbol, way and very act of progress.[19]

Christ's passion-death-resurrection not only enables man to attain the fullness of life, but extends the possibility of fulfill-ment to the whole universe. The power and love of His death are not restricted to a part of reality but vivify the whole process of cosmic evolution. Man's share in the cross, which is a symbol of attaining life through accepting hardship and death, extends to all the endeavours, sufferings and sweat he must undergo in the pursuit of progress. There is no inherent conflict, therefore, between the cross and human progress; in fact, they are inseparable. Ultimately scientific and social developments occur only as a result of human effort and suffering which has been redeemed and made redemptive by Christ.

In conformity with his principle of regarding all reality in terms of genesis, Teilhard refers to the building up of the Mystical and Universal Christ as a Christogenesis. In a convergent universe in which Christ is the Center, Christogenesis (which is gratuitous) is the extension of noogenesis. When Christ is seen as Evolver He is both the beginning and end of evolution, and the entire cosmic process can be summarized in a series of equated terms:

cosmos = cosmogenesis→biogenesis→noogenesis →Christogenesis.

In such a universe man can discover and experience God *in the whole of evolving creation.* He can also love God not only with his own person but also with every fibre of the universe.[20]

Once we have recognized the extent of Christ's activity as Evolver and Lord of the entire universe, the extent and depths of the Incarnation become evident and we are forced to come to grips with the problem of pantheism. Our vision outrightly rejects a pantheistic doctrine which maintains that the universe conceived as a whole is God and one which affirms that there is no God other than the combined forces and laws that are manifested in the universe.

In its broadest sense pantheism is a religious preoccupation with the whole. Such a preoccupation is essentially religious because the whole, with its attributes of unity and universality, cannot reveal itself to man without man recognizing the presence of or at least the shadow of God. It is also questionable whether God can possibly reveal Himself to man without in some way being present to, animating or passing through the whole.[21] Certainly there have been serious errors made by christians in their attempts to comprehend and explain the relationship of God to the material universe and the ways in which His presence in it is experienced. Nevertheless some qualified form of "pantheistic" tendency is not only justified but necessary in our world view.

Teilhard recognized two basic forms of pantheism: a pantheism of identification in which the individual centers disappear and all being is identified with God. We have already rejected this approach. And secondly, a pantheism of unification in which the individual centers remain distinct and reinforce each other in their union with God who also remains distinct. God is all in all, in Paul's terminology, and yet neither man nor God is absorbed or dissolved in the other.[22]

In Teilhard's thought we find developed what he describes as a christian transposition of the fundamental pantheistic tendency. It is a pantheism of unification in which the love of God attracts all the personal centers and impersonal elements of the universe to unite in and through Christ. Since love differentiates the personal centers, there is no question of their being dissolved or fused into God. And in and through His spiritual presence and activity in created reality God can be encountered by man in his daily experiences with nature, and yet nature and God are not identical. Finally, in the *pleroma* or fullness, as Paul describes it, God will not remain alone but will be all in everyone. Only this transposition of pantheism is able to prolong the movement of evolution beyond the limits of nature, and it alone is able to fulfill man's deepest aspiration to be united to all things, purified and concentrated in the innermost self of God.[23]

III. *Esthetic and Mystical Experience as Modes of Personal Fulfillment*

By concluding our discussion of the functions of Christ in an evolving universe with a brief analysis of His spiritual presence to man in and through creation we have prepared the way for a few observations regarding mystical experience. This mode of experience is of paramount importance in our world view because through it man transcends himself by encountering God in and through nature. Because esthetic experience is intimately related to religious and mystical experience, we shall begin with an analysis of esthetic experience. Since we regard both esthetic experience and mystical vision to be essential for personal self-realization, they deserve a place in our world view. And since Teilhard made only a few passing comments on the esthetic, this is another area in which the thought of Dewey can enrich our world view.

The roots of the esthetic are to be found in all interactions within nature which culminate in increased harmony, greater integrity or wholeness and deeper adjustment of man with the conditions of existence. Art is a mode of interaction of the living creature with his environment characterized by successful integration; it is prefigured in the very process of living.[24] The *esthetic*, therefore, can be a *part of every experience;*

> . . . any practical activity will, provided that it is integrated and moves by its own urge to fulfillment, have esthetic quality.[25]

There are no sharp dividing lines marking off esthetic experience from the other modes of experience, because every form of experience, in order to be such, must culminate in a consummation or satisfaction which is enjoyed or had. In esthetic experience the different elements of man's being, which are emphasized and realized *separately in other experiences*, are *merged*. They are so completely united in the immediate wholeness of esthetic experience that each is submerged in the larger whole.[26] The felt integration or experience of wholeness characteristic of esthetic experience is present in varying degrees of intensity and is possible at least to some degree in all experience. The continuity of esthetic experience with daily experience is of primary importance concerning man's self-realization. Once man actually experiences the esthetic quality of his daily activities there will be an accelerated unification among the elements of his own self and an increased adjustment of his person with his environment. It is not surprising, therefore, to hear Dewey speak of esthetic experience as experience in its integrity. It is unique — experience freed from the factors which subordinate an experience as it is directly had to things beyond it.[27]

Dewey analyzes esthetic experience a) in terms of the esthetic quality of thought and scientific inquiry, b) in terms of "art as an experience," and c) in terms of the esthetic experience involved in being human. Since we have already discussed the fact that every complete intellectual and scientific experience culminates in a consummation which is esthetic in quality, we shall not analyze the esthetic element in thought and research further.

In discussing esthetic experience in terms of "art as an experience" Dewey affirms that art is the concrete proof that man uses materials and energies of nature deliberately to expand his life in accord with the structure of his being. It is living proof that man can consciously restore, on the level of meaning, the union of sense, need, impulse and action.[28] Restoring unity on the level of meaning marks a fulfillment for man as does the production of objects which can be perceived as immediate goods and directly enjoyed. Such activities are the work of the fine arts which must not be too narrowly restricted, but ought to include a great variety of acts which provide esthetic experience and lead to further activities capable of enriching human life.[29]

Integration is the dominant quality of esthetic experience described in terms of "art as an experience." There is an intimate combination of the instrumental and consummatory, and of activity and undergoing. Its unique, pervasive quality unites all its elements. Elements which are distinguished in reflection and between which men have often established dualisms are experienced intuitively as integrated within the one experience. "Art as an experience" provides added possibilities for unity among experiences and extends the context in which experiences are had. Dewey sums up its capacity to overcome apparent dualisms and to effect integration when he says:

> In art as an experience, actuality and possibility or ideality, the new and the old, objective material and personal response, the individual and the universal, surface and depth, sense and meaning, are integrated in an experience in which they are all transfigured from the significance that belongs to them when isolated in reflection. "Nature," said Goethe, "has neither kernel nor shell." Only in esthetic experience is this statement completely true. Of art as experience it is also true that nature has neither subjective nor objective being; is neither individual nor universal, sensuous nor rational.[30]

In another penetrating passage Dewey analyzes the capacity of a work of art to elicit and accentuate the quality of being a whole and of belonging to the all-inclusive whole which is the universe. The presence of this capacity provides an explanation for the feeling of intelligibility and clarity man has in the presence of an object experienced with esthetic intensity and for the religious feeling which accompanies intense esthetic perceptions. In esthetic experience man is introduced, as it were, into a *world beyond this world*, which is, in fact, the *deeper reality of this world* in which he lives in his ordinary experiences. He is carried beyond himself to find himself. The only psychological ground for such properties of an experience is that the work of art operates to deepen and raise to a greater clarity the sense of an enveloping, undefined whole that accompanies every normal experience. This whole is then felt as an expansion of the self. Wherever egoism is not the measure of reality and value, men become citizens of the world beyond themselves, and any intense realization of its presence with and in them brings a very satisfying sense of unity in itself and with themselves.[31] Esthetic experience, therefore, is more efficacious than either scientific or moral experience in expanding the scope of man's relations and establishing him as a social or relational being in the personal universe of men where he must find himself.

It is not surprising, therefore, that there is an esthetic quality or experience in being human. The material of this experience is all the material which constitutes man's social relations. Dewey insists on the need for esthetic appreciation without which men will become economic monsters constantly driving hard bargains with nature and with each other and incapable of using leisure effectively. He also claims that esthetic experience is a manifestation, record and celebration of the life of a civilization, a means of promoting it and the ultimate judge of its quality.[32] There is no question, therefore, of its central role in promoting the self-realization of individual persons and the evolutionary process of mankind and the whole universe.

The capacity of esthetic experience to effect wholeness and unification in ever-increasing spheres of activity is the basis for its intimate connection with mystical experience. Esthetic experience forces man to transcend himself and to find himself in union with the whole. Teilhard also recognizes that the pursuit of personal fulfillment can turn us in on ourselves and force us into the limitations and isolation of individuation, yet

> . . . each one of our emotions, *the more it is aesthetic*, the more it tends to break up our autonomy. The Real incessantly reawakens us to an impassioned awareness of a wider expansion and an all embracing unity. It is in the arousing of this restless yearning that the hallowed function of sense-perception finds its consummation.[33]

In this passage Teilhard is not primarily concerned with esthetic experience, but with mystical vision. The point he is stressing is that the real, which on the surface is nature alone, presents itself to man in order to enable him to build up his own integrity. The deeper truth of the matter is that in revealing itself to man the world draws him into itself and causes him to flow outwards into something belonging to it, something that is everywhere present in nature and more perfect than it. If man remains solely bound up with the outward appearance of things he does not advance to this second stage of perception and never becomes aware of what Teilhard describes poetically as "that aureole," that "indefinite fringe of reality surrounding the totality of all created things."[34] By this language he is referring to the divine presence at the heart of reality, a presence which can be experienced in our encounters with nature.

The mystic, that is, the man animated by the Spirit of God who has really learned how to see and to allow reality to reveal itself as it is, is led by the beauty of nature to its very depths where it reveals to him a presence which exists equally everywhere and grows in clarity and depth so that through this presence the unique essence of the universe is disclosed at every point of contact. It is in contact with this presence, the presence of God at the very depths of nature, that man begins to appease his mysterious need for fullness of being. Man must not reject the world once he has attained this communication with the divine presence through it, but realize that through the goadings of sense beauty he is led to ever deeper insight and communication with God revealing Himself as Universal Being behind the sounds and colours of nature. The whole of nature becomes for man a mystical or divine milieu.[35]

Teilhard's emphasis in the passage quoted above is on sense perception leading to mystical vision; the esthetic dimension is introduced as an addition. Nevertheless the importance of the esthetic dimension is brought out by the fact that he deliberately italicizes those words which introduce the esthetic. Mystical vision is not a matter of intellectual vision alone but vision accompanied and enriched by emotion. And only to the degree that man's emotion is esthetic does it break up his autonomy and allow reality to reveal itself in such a way as to awaken in him an impassioned awareness of the whole. The esthetic in its intimate relation to intellectual vision and emotional drive enlightens and moves man to integration and fulfillment in union with the whole which includes God. Here we get a glimpse of the intimate connection between sense perception, esthetic appreciation and mystical vision.

One final point must be made regarding our understanding of the esthetic as a means of opening men to experience the transcendent God through the natural universe. It is not esthetic experience *in itself* which has the capacity to lead men to encounter God although it is an *instrument* in this activity. Ultimately it is God Himself spiritually present in both man and nature who awakens man and reveals Himself through the beauty of His creation.

In bringing together the thought of Dewey and Teilhard concerning the esthetic we must not overlook the fact that there are differences between them. Teilhard speaks of the esthetic quality of *nature* as instrumental in opening man and leading him to experience wholeness, whereas Dewey speaks of the capacity of a *work of art* to elicit this experience. Since art is nature brought to its fulfillment, there is no real discrepancy in their thought on this point. However, when Dewey maintains that esthetic experience introduces man into a world beyond this world which is the depth dimension of this world he intends to contain his thought within the strict limits of his naturalism. There is no possibility of encountering a personal God in, through or beyond nature.

Nevertheless, we maintain that *neither* the expansive movement in man towards unification with even an imaginatively projected whole *nor* the concept of becoming a citizen of the world community and realizing oneself in this integration need to stop at the naturalistic limits Dewey imposes on them. His thought at this point is particularly open to the transcendent. Besides denying the validity of his naturalistic limitations one does not have to do violence to any of his other insights into esthetic experience to open it to the possibility of acting as an instrument by means of which man can experience the divine at the depths of the natural. In fact, this extension of Dewey's thought enriches it.

IV. *The Role of Christianity and the Virtues in Evolution*

Christianity must be regarded as a specific phenomenon situated within the larger human phenomenon. Historically the origin of this reality is the person of Jesus in whom is to be found the maximum intensity of all creative power. He is the personal meeting point between God and man, the person through whom God chose to channel all creative power. The christian movement is a response by men to the inspiration and revelation of God. It can be regarded phenomenologically as a phylum because it is a reality which is rooted in the past and subject to constant development.

Although its source, inner life and power transcend that of the other social phyla, Christianity remains an observable phenomenon the evolutionary influence of which can be seen and at least to some extent evaluated. In an evolutionary cosmos ascending toward greater consciousness the christian phylum is observable as a phylum of *love*. It tends toward a synthesis or unity based on love. As a movement of thought and love it has initiated and influenced many evolutionary developments. Christianity cannot be regarded as an accessory shoot or an alien proliferation in the human social organism. It has roots in the phenomenon of man, and constitutes *the* main axis of socialization.

We have already seen that evolution involves the genesis of a super-organism achieved by the converging effect of co-reflexion and that a supernatural organism is also achieved through the organic unification of all men in God. In chris-

245

tian thought these super-realities harmonize; the former is the physical condition and experimental aspect of the *parousia*, the second coming of Christ. There is a coherent subordination between the genesis of mankind in the world and the genesis of Christ in mankind through the church. The second process requires the first as the reality which it superanimates, and the first is personalized by having Christ as its clearly defined and personal term. Christ takes to Himself the whole universe and the universe is animated by the light and immortality of Christ. The christian current of thought is the only movement of thought in the noosphere that can engender the energy of love which alone is capable of motivating *all* the human forces of evolution to function *to their full capacity*. It is the only spiritual current which can develop in persons the sense of the absolute and the universal *conceived of as personal*. It is *the* religion of personality, and therefore is the very core around which the human social organism grows.[36] It can perform these functions because it participates in the power of divine love itself.

Christianity is the only form of belief which is also a religion of universal progress. In the context of an evolving cosmos and converging space-time it receives new support and should be able to develop its fundamental tenets and achieve added coherence and clarity. Nevertheless, because of the inadequate way in which it is so frequently understood, presented and practised it is not as vital as it should be. More emphasis should be placed on the Universal Christ and on Christ as Evolver, Saviour of the world and its hopes. As well, Christianity must open itself to encompass all the new religious energy generated by humanistic ideals so as to refine it. It must become a religion which fills men with the spirit of criticism, enthusiasm, inquiry and conquest.[37]

The church is the visibility of God's living presence among men; in it man finds the extension of the Incarnation (the Body of Christ) and the love that can guarantee the success of cosmogenesis and its prolongation in Christogenesis. God has sent His own Spirit to dwell in the minds and hearts of His people. Thus the christian community is, and should always be visible as, an inner core of divine love which impregnates and sustains the whole movement of evolution toward spirit. Because the fullness of divine revelation was manifested in Christ, Christianity should also be recognizable as the current of consciousness in which the idea of God and the activity of worship have reached their highest level of coherence and quality.

Christianity is based on the physical primacy of Christ and the moral primacy of charity. Enough has been said about the former, but charity and some of the other virtues must be examined in order to understand more fully why Christianity actually can be the main axis of socialization. It has been shown that *love* in the noosphere *led to union and that union forced man to center himself, to move beyond himself to establish his center in mankind,* and finally *to center himself in Omega.* If noogenesis involved a degree of detachment from self and renunciation, it is not surprising to find that detachment and renunciation play a vital role in Christogenesis. First we shall examine these virtues (related as they are to charity) and then examine the expanded roles of purity and charity in an evolutionary context showing how they too are related respectively to centering and de-centering man.

A radical renunciation and detachment are inherent in the very structure of a universe which finds its ultimate fulfillment in a transcendent God. The term toward which the universe is moving is *beyond the sum total of things* and *not* some supreme reality brought forth *from within itself;* therefore, man can never be united to the vital core of the universe by living for himself nor by spending himself through commitment to any earthly cause no matter how exalted it be. There is need of a radical reversal of ex-centration which involves detachment from *all* human achievement and progress if the world is to be definitively united to Christ. In order to give oneself totally to Christ one must die to both one's own ego and the world.[38]

247

In a letter to Auguste Valensin concerning his correspondence with Maurice Blondel, Teilhard wrote:

> I am in fundamental agreement with him that the completion of the world is only consummated through a death, a "night," a reversal, an excentration, and a quasi-depersonalization of the monads. A monad's integration into Christ presupposes that it has effected a kind of internal disintegration, that is, a modification of its entire being, a requisite to its recreation and entry into the Pleroma. In essence, union with Christ presupposes that we transpose the ultimate center of our existence into Him — which implies the radical sacrifice of egoism.[39]

But this detachment must not be set off in opposition and contrast to the attachment and committed activity necessary for the christian. Attachment and detachment are the two phases of one natural process, phases which are fused together in one effort whenever a person strives to develop his own person and take possession of the world for Christ.[40]

The doctrine of the cross can no longer be regarded as making mortification primary and an end in itself. The self-denial and suffering inherent in both the cross and in furthering evolution are necessary means to be accepted if personal growth is to be achieved and cosmic evolution furthered. The cross is quite in harmony, therefore, with both the dynamic balance between activity and passivity found in human experience and with the fundamental laws of evolution. These laws reveal that growth requires self-denial and that life must move in a specific direction if it is to continue to evolve. Every increase in life is a movement toward the highest spiritualization; this can be attained only by expending the greatest possible effort. Mortification and detachment are not ends in themselves, but necessary means to perfecting human effort. Christ's life grows in men not only through their suffering and mortification, but also through their positive efforts and through the development of human nature. The cross symbolizes *all* the efforts of mankind to bring created reality to fulfillment in Christ. Renunciation involves *liberating all* the spiritual power in one's body and in the whole cosmos. It compels man to develop the world with a passionate zeal, yet enables him to be and to pass beyond everything in the world. Teilhard sums up the twofold nature of renunciation by the phrase "passionate indifference."[41]

The supernatural, while awaiting and supporting the development of the natural, ultimately purifies and perfects this development *only in an annihilation.* There is an intimate union of human progress and renunciation in God up to a final point of transformation where the latter takes the ascendency.[42] Once this is recognized it is not difficult to see why Teilhard, in spite of his utmost respect for the material, attributes no definitive or absolute value to natural human constructions because these will disappear or be recast in a totally new plane of existence.[43] Nor is it inconceivable to understand why a man who passionately loves the earth and commits himself wholeheartedly to research and progress can at the same time recognize their limitations and say that nature itself makes him accept death because death is the only complete organic transformation or metamorphosis which can enable him to comprehend nature's inner core.[44]

Many other virtues play a role in enabling persons to center or unify themselves and to move out beyond themselves to others. In this way virtues are dynamic and instrumental in the evolutionary process. We shall limit our further discussion to purity and charity. Purity is a basic condition of self-renunciation. The person who surrenders to his passions is torn asunder; his spirit is dispersed. The man who strives for purity attempts to overcome plurality within himself and in so doing masters his materiality. In its struggle against the powers which disintegrate, purity achieves, maintains and furthers the unity of the spirit. It unites the inner powers of the person's soul and unifies him in his own self. Its goal is not mortification, but the fundamental cohesion of the person *within himself* which is essential if he is to practice charity which will bring about union *among all persons.*[45]

Modern man objects to the negative, static and "detached" quality of christian charity as it is frequently practised. So often charity is reduced to not injuring one's neighbour, and the supernatural gift of self to God and neighbour appears to be opposed to and even destructive of the natural bonds of feeling uniting men to each other and to earthly realities.[46] This ought not to be so. The *natural love* which unites and mutually spiritualizes the lovers does not unite them directly as much as it causes them to converge together on Christ. This love, which begins on the sensible level through confrontation and mutual knowledge, can never dispense with matter.[47] In discussing *the love of God* Teilhard says that God has not given man a distinct center of affection by which to love Him. He maintains that

> In accordance with the particular ordering of our world, in which *everything is made by the transformation of a pre-existing analogue*, it seems evident that, initially, divine Charity exists in us simply as the flame, supernaturalized and purified, that is kindled at the prospect of the Earth's promises. It could never possibly persist in a heart that had ceased to be fired by the quickening contact of tangible realities. Great love of God normally presupposes the maintenance of a strong natural passion.[48]

Once charity is transposed within the structure of a convergent universe it is only able to draw two elements closer together by causing their whole layer of the world to move toward the apex. In such circumstances a man cannot love his neighbour without drawing nearer to God nor can he love either God or neighbour without assisting the entire physical progress of the synthesis of spirit. *Because* men love and *in order to love* they must participate in all the aspirations, efforts, tensions and affections of the earth insofar as these are directed toward ascension and synthesis.[49]

Once Christ is recognized as the motive force and end of evolution He becomes attainable in and through that entire process. The commandments to love God and to love one's neighbour for the love of God are synthesized; the christian loves God in and through the genesis of the universe and of humanity. Charity is universalized, synthesized and made dynamic. To sum up the difference between this extended range and function of charity and its narrower, static dimensions, Teilhard states that in the latter the christian sought to be able to love *at the same time as he was acting*, but now he sees that he can love *by his activity*, that is, he can be directly united to Christ by his every action.[50] Charity enables man to develop a sense of what human relations require, and man can love God and achieve union with Him in and through his actions on behalf of humanity and cosmic evolution.

Throughout our analysis of the foundation of religion, the person and functions of Christ, mystical experience, Christianity and the virtues, we have striven to attain a balance between the transcendent and immanent. We have avoided an extreme transcendentalism in which God remains detached from the current of evolution. On the other extreme we have also avoided a radical immanentism which cuts itself off from the transcendent and so is reduced to a naturalism.

We have not taken an either/or approach but a both/and position which stresses neither transcendence nor immanence at the expense of the other. We have shown the depths and extent of the Incarnation and revealed Christ's role as Mediator. Christ is God Incarnate, the meeting point of the transcendent and the terrestrial and the Mediator between the trinitarian God and men. The whole of natural reality is ultimately to be united to the Trinity through the mediation of Christ. In Teilhard's terms, Omega, the final Center of convergence, is one super-center in which the cosmic and christic are united in the trinitarian Center through the mediating activity of the Incarnate Christ.

Even if Dewey's contention that prior existence is always non-ideal existence were universally true, our concept of the Cosmic Christ overcomes this problem. God is not merely a transcendent Other who is complete in Himself. Without rejecting the *primacy of being* over becoming, our understanding of the biblical texts concerning the Body of Christ and the *pleroma* enable God not only to be conceived as complete existent Being, but also in another sense as an ideal and very personal reality in process of becoming. Through the Incarnation of the Son in the man Jesus, God has also taken roots in the natural. In the extension of the Incarnation, that is, not only in the church or Mystical Body but also in the Cosmic Body which Christ is bringing to completion through the co-operative activity of men, God in His Incarnation is being brought to completion. The fulfillment of the Mystical and Cosmic Body of Christ is an ideal attainable by man's co-operative efforts in Christ. And this ideal is also an effective motive force because it is far more than a mere projection of the imagination.

At the same time as God remains a transcendent lure-from-beyond He is also present to men now in His indwelling Spirit. He is active and present as an *interior* transforming principle of life and love moving men to fulfill the universe and themselves in Christ. The relationship between the actual and ideal spoken of by Dewey is enriched in christian thought in terms of "the already" and the "not yet." The actual or "the already" is a present participation in divine life won for man through the passion-death-resurrection of Jesus Christ. This present share in the divine life is to be lived and fostered in order that the ideal, the "not yet," which is a total participation in the divine life not yet attained, may be achieved.

It is impossible to see how Dewey's ideal projection which he refers to as "God" can ultimately fulfill the concrete, personal needs of men. Certainly the thrust of a great deal of the writing of Robert O. Johann, a dedicated promoter of much of Dewey's philosophy, is that his thought on the inclusive ideal can only be taken seriously if it is completed and understood in the sense of a personal relationship. Thus there is need of a universal Other, a Transcendent, with whom men relate personally. Johann treats of religion in terms of the celebration of this relationship and shows how men love each other in relation to this transcendent Other.[51]

In our world view Christ retains His traditional role of being the beginning and end of salvation, but is also revealed as the beginning and end of the whole cosmic movement. The Christology presented here starts from traditional doctrines and titles and in the process of demonstrating the compatibility of Christ with evolution further develops and re-expresses Christological truths. The new titles given to Christ draw attention to the inexhaustible quality of the mysteries involved in Christianity and point to the fact that christians show respect for their doctrines by not absolutizing their inadequate expressions of them.

Throughout this chapter we have set forth many fundamental principles regarding the relationship between the christian religion and the evolutionary process. It is only with all these principles as a broad foundation that the conflict between faith in God and faith in man can be approached and adequately comprehended. It is time now to turn to the multifaceted conflict between these two faiths. First the problem itself must be interpreted, and then the numerous elements, each of which sheds light on and contributes in some way to a solution, must be examined. The solution will involve such things as the christian's responsibility to commit himself to earthly activity, the relationship between science and religion, the added significance of research for the christian and how the christian can attain eternal salvation through fulfillment of the earth.

FOOTNOTES

1. "Le Christianisme dans le monde," *SC*, p. 131 [Eng. trans. p. 98]; "Comment je crois," *CJC*, p. 139 [Eng. trans. pp. 118-19].
2. "L'Esprit de la terre," *ÉH*, pp. 56-57 [Eng. trans. pp. 46-47].
3. "Le Christianisme dans le monde," *SC*, pp. 132-33 [Eng. trans. pp. 99-100]; "Le Phénomène humain," *VP*, p. 242 [Eng. trans. p. 173]; "Réflexions sur le progrès," *AH*, pp. 99-100 [Eng. trans. pp. 75-76]; "Construire la terre," *CT*, p. 28 [Eng. trans. p. 62].
4. "Le Christianisme dans le monde," *SC*, pp. 131, 133, 135, 143-44 [Eng. trans. pp. 98, 100, 102, 110-11]; "Comment je crois," *CJC*, n. 1, p. 139 [Eng. trans. n. 6, p. 119].
5. "Le Christianisme dans le monde," *SC*, pp. 135-39 [Eng. trans. pp. 102-06].
6. Pierre Teilhard de Chardin, *Nouvelles Lettres de voyage, 1939-1955* (Paris: Bernard Grasset, 1957), Letter, November 8, 1953, p. 171 and editor's note 2, p. 171 [Eng. trans. p. 347], hereafter cited *NLV*; *MD*, pp. 140-41 [Eng. trans. pp. 116-17]; "Mon Univers," *SC*, pp. 90-91 [Eng. trans. pp. 61-62].
7. The word "physical" is used in a similar manner by Teilhard in numerous places. "He [Christ] is consecrated for a cosmic function. And since the function is not only moral but also (in the most real sense of the word) physical, it presupposes *a physical basis* in its humano-divine subject.

"If things are to find their coherence *in Christo*, we must ultimately admit that there is *in natura Christi*, besides the specifically individual elements of man — and in virtue of God's choice — some *universal physical reality*, a certain cosmic extension of his Body and Soul." "Forma Christi," *ÉTG*, p. 338 [Eng. trans. p. 252]. The French editor's note states that "physical" is used here in opposition to "juridical." The corresponding note in the English text refers the reader to Christopher F. Mooney, *Teilhard de Chardin and the Mystery of Christ* (New York: Harper and Row, 1966), p. 85. Mooney agrees that "physical" is opposed to what is juridical, abstract or extrinsic to reality. He also suggests that its closest equivalent is "ontological" which is applied to anything having existence in the present concrete order. This interpretation is amply supported elsewhere by Teilhard where he deplores the excessive emphasis placed on logical, moral and juridical relationships by philosophers. He says: "It is simpler, safer (totius), more convenient (as Our Lord's example shows), to express the relations between God and man as family or domestic relationships. Such analogies are true, in as much as union in Christ is effected between persons, but they are incomplete. If we are to express the whole truth we must correct them by analogies drawn from realities that are specifically *natural and physical.*" "Note sur le Christ universal," *SC*, p. 43 [Eng. trans. pp. 18-19].

8. "La Vie cosmique," *ÉTG*, pp. 40, 48 [Eng. trans. pp. 50, 58]; "Introduction à la vie chrétienne," *CJC*, pp. 180-81 [Eng. trans. pp. 152-53].

9. "Réflexions sur la conversion du monde," *SC*, p. 166 [Eng. trans. p. 127].

10. "Mon Univers," *SC*, p. 92 [Eng. trans. pp. 63-64].

11. Fuller consideration must be given later to the relation of the natural and supernatural; for the moment you are referred to a note by Teilhard accompanying "Comment je crois." He avoids defining the positive content of the supernatural, but states that whatever it might mean "supernatural" cannot mean anything but "supremely real" or "supremely in conformity" with the conditions of reality which nature imposes on beings. "Comment je crois," *CJC*, n. 1, p. 147 [Eng. trans. n. 10, p. 127].

12. "L'Union créatrice," *ÉTG*, pp. 195-196 [Eng. trans. p. 174].

13. *MD*, p. 142 [Eng. trans. p. 118]; "Mon Univers," *SC*, p. 87 [Eng. trans. pp. 58-59]; "Forma Christi," *ÉTG*, pp. 350-51 [Eng. trans. p. 266].

14. "La Vie cosmique," *ÉTG*, pp. 47-49 [Eng. trans. pp. 57-59]; "Note sur le Christ universel," *SC*, pp. 39-42 [Eng. trans. pp. 14-17].

15. "L'Union créatrice," *ÉTG*, pp. 196-97 [Eng. trans. pp. 175-76]; *PH*, pp. 327-28 [Eng. trans. p. 294].

16. "Mon Univers," *SC*, pp. 82-84 [Eng. trans. pp. 54-56].

17. "Super-humanité, super-Christ, super-charité" *SC*, pp. 209-12 [Eng. trans. pp. 165-67]. See also: "Du Cosmos à la cosmogénèse," *AÉ*, pp. 270-73 [Eng. trans. pp. 262-64].

18. *PH*, p. 330 [Eng. trans. pp. 296-97]; "L'Esprit nouveau," *AH*, pp. 123-24 [Eng. trans. pp. 94-95].

19. "Christianisme et évolution," *CJC*, pp. 210-11 [Eng. trans. pp. 180-81]; "L'Esprit nouveau," *AH*, pp. 123-24 [Eng. trans. pp. 94-95].

20. *PH*, pp. 330-31 [Eng. trans. p. 297]; "Conclusion, dernière page du journal," *AH*, pp. 404-05 [Eng. trans. p. 309].

21. "Panthéisme et christianisme," *CJC*, pp. 74-77 [Eng. trans. pp. 56-57, 60].

22. Pierre Teilhard de Chardin, "Le Christ dans la matière," *Hymne de l'univers* (Paris: Éditions du Seuil, 1961), pp. 56-57, n. 1, p. 56 [Eng. trans. pp. 53-54], hereafter cited *HU*; "Pour y voir clair: Réflexions sur deux formes inverses d'esprit," *Les Études Philosophiques*, 10 (1955), p. 576; *NLV*, Letter, August 7, 1950, p. 99, editor's note 1, p. 99 [Eng. trans. p. 302].

23. "Panthéisme et christianisme," *CJC*, pp. 83-91 [Eng. trans. pp. 66-75]; *GP*, Letter, February 2, 1916, p. 117, Letter, July 14, 1916, pp. 142-43 [Eng. trans. pp. 93, 112]; *MD*, p. 139 [Eng. trans. p. 116]; "Réflexions sur la conversion du monde," *SC*, p. 163 [Eng. trans. p. 124]; *PH, Résumé*, p. 344 [Eng. trans. pp. 309-10]; "Esquisse d'un univers personnel," *ÉH*, pp. 85-87, 103-04 [Eng. trans. pp. 67-69, 83-84]; "Introduction à la vie chrétienne," *CJC*, pp. 199-200 [Eng. trans. pp. 171-72].

24. *Art as Experience,* pp. 13-19, 24-25.
25. *Art as Experience,* p. 39.
26. *Art as Experience,* p. 274.
27. *Art as Experience,* p. 274.
28. *Art as Experience,* p. 25.
29. *Experience and Nature,* p. 365.
30. *Art as Experience,* p. 297. See also: *Art as Experience,* pp. 37, 41-43, 48, 192, 194; *Experience and Nature,* pp. 392-93 for further discussion of the unifying, pervasive quality of art as an experience and its ability to resolve dualisms.
31. *Art as Experience,* p. 195.
32. *Reconstruction in Philosophy,* p. 127; *Art as Experience,* p. 326.
33. "Le Milieu mystique," *ÉTG,* p. 138 [Eng. trans. p. 118].
34. "Le Milieu mystique," *ÉTG,* pp. 138-39 [Eng. trans. p. 119].
35. "Le Milieu mystique," *ÉTG,* pp. 138-40 [Eng. trans. pp. 118-20].
36. *PH,* pp. 324-32 [Eng. trans. pp. 219-99]; "Agitation ou genèse?" *AH,* pp. 285-87 [Eng. trans. pp. 223-25]; "Hérédité sociale et progrès," *AH,* pp. 50-51 [Eng. trans. p. 34]; LV, Letter, May 4, 1931, p. 149 [Eng. trans. pp. 177-78]; "Esquisse d'un univers personnel," *ÉH,* pp. 110-13 [Eng. trans. pp. 89-91].
37. "Le Christianisme dans le monde," *SC,* pp. 139-43 [Eng. trans. pp. 106-10]; "Réflexions sur la conversion du monde," *SC,* pp. 164-65 [Eng. trans. pp. 125-26]; "L'Esprit nouveau," *AH,* p. 122 [Eng. trans. p. 93]; "Christianisme et évolution," *CJC,* p. 206 [Eng. trans. p. 176].
38. "La Messe sur le monde," *HU,* pp. 30-31 [Eng. trans. pp. 30-31].
39. "Teilhard de Chardin's First Paper to Auguste Valensin," *Correspondence* [Eng. trans. p. 31]. In this text Teilhard refers to ex-centration of the monad as a quasi-depersonalization. Elsewhere in this letter [Eng. trans. p. 36], he speaks of man's "supernatural depersonalization *in Christo.*" In spite of the use of the word "depersonalization" in a few of his earlier works, it is a constant theme throughout his writings that ex-centration and union in Christ *super-personalize* man. For a treatment of this matter see Henri de Lubac's footnotes n. 4, p. 75 and n. 32, pp. 89-90 in the English translation of the *Correspondence.*
40. "Forma Christi," *ÉTG,* pp. 344-49 [Eng. trans. pp. 259-64]; *MD,* p. 106 [Eng. trans. pp. 95-96].
41. *MD,* pp. 107-09, 116-19, 144-46 [Eng. trans. pp. 96-97, 102-04, 119-21]; "Teilhard de Chardin's First Paper to Auguste Valensin," *Correspondence* [Eng. trans. p. 33]; "Introduction à la vie chrétienne," *CJC,* pp. 197-99 [Eng. trans. pp. 168-70].
42. *MD,* pp. 114-15 [Eng. trans. p. 101].
43. "Teilhard de Chardin's First Paper to Auguste Valensin," *Correspondence* [Eng. trans. p. 34].
44. *GP,* Letter, July 12, 1918, pp. 277-78 [Eng. trans. pp. 213-14].
45. "La Lutte contre la multitude," *ÉTG,* pp. 125-31 [Eng. trans. pp. 107-13]; "L'Union créatrice," *ÉTG,* p. 194 [Eng. trans. p. 172].
46. "L'Esprit nouveau," *AH,* p. 124 [Eng. trans. p. 95].
47. "L'Union créatrice," *ÉTG,* pp. 192-93 [Eng. trans. p. 171].

48. "La Maîtrise du monde et le règne de Dieu," *ÉTG*, pp. 75-76 [Eng. trans. p. 83]. To explain Teilhard's statement that everything comes about by way of a transformation of a pre-existing analogue the editor quotes a later essay of Teilhard: "Le Phénomène humain," *SC*, p. 122 [Eng. trans. p. 91], where he speaks of "the essential correction that must always be applied to our views each time we try to follow any line of reality through a new circle of the universe. The world is completely transformed from one circle to another. It undergoes an interior enrichment and recasting. On every occasion, in consequence, it presents itself to us in a new state, in which the sum of its earlier properties is partly retained and partly given a new form." Natural love and supernatural charity remain distinct in Teilhard's thought but their intimate relationship is of vital importance.

49. "L'Esprit nouveau," *AH*, pp. 124-25 [Eng. trans. pp. 95-96].

50. "Super-humanité," super-Christ, super-charité," *SC*, pp. 212-18 [Eng. trans. pp. 167-73]; "Christianisme et évolution," *CJC*, pp. 214-15 [Eng. trans. pp. 183-85].

51. Robert O. Johann, *The Pragmatic Meaning of God* (Milwaukee: Marquette University Press, 1966), pp. 1-66.

CHAPTER 10

EVOLUTION FULFILLED IN THE DYNAMISM OF THE INCARNATION

I. *The Conflict between Faith in God and Faith in Man and Science*

A. *A Statement of the Problem*

The fact that modern man experiences an apparent conflict between faith in God and faith in mankind, science and the world is not new. To outline the rise of this conflict and show its historical development is beyond the scope of this work. Therefore, only a few historical comments will be made so as to situate the problem. Practically until the Renaissance there was no clear distinction made between the current of life coming from God and the church and the evolutionary current of life. When the autonomous pressure of natural aspirations increased to the point where the identification of human development and religious perfection was recognized as inadequate, a rupture between the church and world occurred. Each reacted against the other, and both have consequently suffered because of their isolation and fragmented approach to reality.

The earth turned away from the church and sought to develop independently of it. After a period of denying the need of the infinite (presupposed by the search for truth and its practise) and a period of relaxing in its own sufficiency, the world saw its internal need for an absolute and attempted to establish such things as science and mankind as absolutes. It also found difficulty in establishing a natural basis for morality so that its imperatives were left absolutely unqualified or based on economic necessity.

Religion was also left impotent and defenceless, appearing to reject nature which continued, nevertheless, to influence its members. It appeared to sanctify and guard man for itself alone apart from the earth which gave him life. A conflict arose in christians between their religious faith and their natural inclinations and aspirations; this conflict rent their spiritual life in two. The church lacked the strength to assimilate the natural forces around it and could not convert a world it did not love. Thus it tended to anathematize the world, to be fearful of change and defensive in an evolutionary world it had to follow instead of lead.[1]

It is not adequate to characterize the modern world either by unbelief or by lack of religion. Knowledge of evolution and of the immensity of time and space has introduced into man's outlook the concepts of futurism and universalism. The universalism and futurism of an evolving world not only cause a new psychological outlook, but by their very nature they define a religion, and Christianity is cut off from this natural human religious current. Man has been converted to a new religion of the world which has little dogma but clear moral directives which include a) recognition of the primacy of the whole over the individual, b) passionate faith in the value of human effort, and c) deep appreciation of the value of all research and progress. God is recognizable only in the continuation of some type of universal progress or maturation. The new human religious ideal does not appear to correspond with the christian religious ideal in spite of the fact that the latter is *also futuristic* and *universalistic*. The conflict is not, therefore, between believers and non-believers, but between those who believe in and hope for *a personal consummation beyond and outside of the world* and those who believe in and commit themselves to achieving *a perfection of the world which culminates in some form of immanent reality within the universe itself.*[2]

Some persons adhere to a doctrine of salvation by science. Others adhere to an operative naturalist faith which strives for a transformation of the experiential universe through the instrumentality of the human mind alone. Man's intelligence is the agent of betterment, the dynamic center extending to all things and exerting a direct influence on them which will reanimate and vitalize the cosmos.[3] Man is the sole maker of history and agent of evolution.

Increasing numbers of men of good will have cut themselves off from Christianity and Christ *out of love* because they no longer find Christianity fine enough to satisfy their aspirations. They do not find its dogmas and moral principles too demanding; rather they seek something better because Christianity gives the impression that Christ is hostile to the need to attain earthly fulfillment for themselves and the world, a need which they experience as an absolute. "Christian" and "human" no longer appear to coincide. Christianity appears to withdraw men from the common task of building up the earth and to diminish them by making them be false to their nature. Because they are already saved through Christ's redemptive activity on their behalf, their faith in God appears to make them lazy and concerned with self-interests rather than with the common task. On the other hand, the man who does not believe in anything beyond death is spurred on to fulfill himself on earth in disinterested work and more direct compassion for his neighbour, activities which constitute the moral ideal of our era.[4]

In brief, this problem is a conflict between two faiths: the first being a faith in God which soars upward unaware or even indifferent to both human progress and the super-humanity to be achieved through evolution, and the second, a faith in the world which has its own "God" and formally denies a transcendent God.[5] There is no doubt about the complexity of this problem and its apparent irreconcilability. Before we develop Teilhard's multi-faceted solution which will shed light on how the gap between faith in God and faith in man can be bridged, we shall examine the problems of evil and sin. They add to the problem because large numbers of persons find it increasingly difficult to reconcile the presence of a loving God whose saving action is supposedly operative now with the presence of widespread physical evil and the atrocities of men who claim to believe in Him.

B. *The Problems of Evil and Sin*

There is no doubt that the problem of evil is an immense intellectual problem and a cause of scandal for modern man. Insight into this problem must be sought by situating it within the context of an evolving universe. God chose to create an imperfect universe, one in which individual beings do not appear in a fully developed or perfect form. He has created a universe in which there are physical laws which are allowed to work on their own terms, a universe in which beings appear in a very incomplete form and must develop themselves according to their own natures and their possibilities to interact with each other. In a universe in which there are some deterministic laws inherent within nature, but also room for the play of chance, interaction and freedom, there are bound to be interferences, inaccurate connections and missing links. In brief, in this type of universe in process of evolution, there is bound to be an element of physical, biological and mental deformity and disability quite apart from the moral evil men introduce. For it to be otherwise the capacity of nature to develop within a rather wide range of possibilities would have to be taken away.

It is physically impossible on all levels — the pre-living, the living and the human — to have beings in process of developing from states of multiplicity and lack of arrangement toward increased arrangement, centration and unity without disorders, deformities, failures, decomposition and death. In a universe groping toward fulfillment the interplay of large numbers makes it inevitable that advances in unity be paid for or be accompanied by physical evils. Evil is structurally a part of a universe in evolution; it is a secondary effect or inevitable by-product of advance in such a universe.[6]

To understand this more clearly we must recognize that evil is a lack of due good, a privation of a good which should be present in a thing or action. On the sub-human level of reality there is *physical* evil in things, a physical lack of arrangement, derangement, disorder and failure. These affect the inanimate and animate beings in which they are found; but they also affect other beings that interact with them. In this way physical evil apart from man also affects man himself. There is also *physical* evil *in man* himself. Corporeal suffering on the sensible level, pain, illness and decomposition are examples of physical evil *in man* quite *apart from the moral evil* which he introduces into the universe. Decomposition takes its ultimate form in death; it is a form of evil of disorder and failure. The evils of isolation and anxiety are peculiar to man because his consciousness awakens to the meaning and demands of the universe and of life itself with effort and time.[7]

As man becomes more aware of the cosmos in evolution and of his place in nature he can distinguish more clearly those evils of decomposition, etc. which are necessary for maintaining and developing life from those failures and disorders which are excessive and unnecessary. He can see more clearly that evil on the sub-human level is increased and becomes a catastrophe when it affects himself. He can also see that the lack of due good and the limitations of beings are the foundation or the basis on which the *possibility* of disorders and failures arise as well as being the basis on which they actually *occur*.

When we examine the problem of evil from the point of view of growth and man's struggle to develop a personal universe we can see its necessity. A personalizing evolution has to be painful because its starting point is plurality and its advances are achieved by differentiation and metamorphosis. As we have seen earlier, every experience which accomplishes growth involves suffering, being acted upon and dying to one-self. This inherent relationship between suffering and growing governs all transformations of spirit-matter.[8]

The greatest of all the physical evils in man we have discussed so far is death. It is the consummation of all man's diminishments, a purely physical evil insofar as it results organically in the complex structure of physical nature itself. But death is more than merely physical evil. It is also a moral evil insofar as both in ourselves and our society the abuse of our freedom spreads disorder and by so doing converts the manifold complexity of our nature into the source of all evil and corruption.[9] Man cannot commit himself wholeheartedly to life and work if total death is inevitable; however, a meaning or a positive value for death as a physical evil is found in the fact that the human spirit is immortal. Physical death for man is ultimately an act of transition or metamorphosis between two different stages of personal development. Through it man can enter directly into the sphere of a higher personal Center, God.[10]

Ultimately man's psychological need to find some positive value that can transfigure pain and evil is answered on the level of divine revelation. Through His activity on behalf of mankind Christ struggled against evil. In His providence God also converts it into good. Frequently the obstacles and sufferings men undergo divert their activities to more spiritual goals. Loss often moves men to seek more comprehensive, enduring goals and to find their satisfactions in less materialistic pursuits. Suffering can concentrate and develop men's inner lives. It can become a means of transformation enabling a man to find himself in unity with other people and God. Death itself provides the entrance into one's inmost self by making man undergo an extreme dissociation with himself through which he can come to know himself fully in Christ the Center. God does not spare man the partial deaths nor the final death which form an essential part of their lives, but transfigures these by integrating them into a deeper, more comprehensive plan for life provided men love and trust Him. Even moral evils, provided man repents of them, can be transformed by God. Through His power everything is capable of being used to produce good.[11]

Man too must struggle with God against evil through effort and prayer in order to reduce it; however, when suffering is inevitable, it can be made an expression of love and a principle of action. After striving to his utmost to resist evil and reduce it, the believer can accept and resign himself to that which remains. In doing so he unites himself to God on a level deeper than evil. When humbly accepted physical evil can assist man in conquering moral evil. Suffering can act in a sacramental way uniting the believer and the suffering Christ, and it can lead the sufferer to sympathy with all forms of suffering, to a universal, cosmic compassion.[12]

Within the Body of Christ persons perform many functions which complement one another and build up the whole. The sufferer, along with the contemplative and the man of prayer, has been given a special calling to raise the world above immediate enjoyment. He must put all his confidence in the grace of God. In speaking of suffering men Teilhard says:

> It is for them to bring aid to their brothers who are working like miners in the bowels of matter. Thus it is those who bear in their weakened bodies the weight of the world in motion that, by providential compensation prove the most active agents in the very progress that seems to be sacrificing and breaking them.[13]

In our world view, therefore, suffering, which is a form of physical evil, not only expiates for sin, but is a consequence of our efforts to evolve. And the cross is a symbol of both expiation and progress.

We have not as yet discussed moral evil, that form of evil which is not merely *in* man but arises *from* man as free person and determines to a great extent whether he will develop his potential as a person. In our discussion of moral experience we saw that man is free, and that his free will is the basis of morality. The moral level is the level of conscious, free self-realization. Man experiences the presence of an inner natural law, the law of his own personal development experienced as a real possibility to be achieved and a task to be accomplished. Man's conscience is his deepest self-awareness or self-consciousness acting as a capacity to determine in all his choices what will or will not promote his self-realization. There is moral evil and guilt whenever man freely chooses to be unfaithful to this inner law of self-realization by rejecting what is authentically good and choosing a pseudo-value.

Teilhard maintains that in an evolving universe a certain amount of moral evil is inevitable; it will necessarily occur. Man is incomplete and immature, groping to realize himself in situations which have new and confusing elements. Not only his awareness is limited, but his freedom too is limited by many physiological, emotional, economic and social influences. Frequently external, material acts, which are objectively sinful, are not the result of free inner decisions.

To be virtuous an action must be objectively good and subjectively willed as such. Thus moral failures and sins are inevitable in the type of world in which we live. This fact is recognized in both the Scripture and in tradition where we are told that it is impossible to remain free of sin without the grace of God. Nevertheless, recognizing the facts that a certain amount of moral evil is inevitable and that men commit material actions which have detrimental consequences in spite of the fact that they are not fully guilty for these actions, is not to deny that man is sinful and commits sinful actions in the full sense of that word.

Teilhard makes it very clear that if we observe carefully we see an abundance of evil and malice in the world, a quantity and intensity of sinfulness which is well in excess of that which is inevitable as a normal effect of evolution. This fact is explainable only in terms of a primordial deviation or catastrophe, an original sin which disoriented man and caused him to seek his self-realization according to his own plan rather than in accord with the will of his Creator. Thus the evolutionary process is not merely one in which a world is striving for fulfillment, but one in which a fallen world led by sinful men is rising again toward re-union and fulfillment in its God.[14]

Moral evil or sin cannot be understood apart from the role that human freedom and love play in furthering evolution. Man is free, and individually and collectively responsible for organizing and developing the whole of cosmic energy. Tangential energy necessarily continues its inevitable progress, but the forces of love (radial) energy are not subject to inevitable progress. Their development depends upon man's free, deliberate choices and "the more subtle and complex man becomes, the more numerous the chances of disorder and the greater their gravity."[15] Every new stage of growth, therefore, increases man's responsibility, but at the same time acts as a lure which tempts him to be complacent in his accomplishments and to give in to the forces of hatred and repulsion which surround him.

Love energy is *the* energy of evolution. The essence of moral evil or sin, therefore, is the free rejection of love, the refusal of the very energy of life which promotes evolution and personal union. Love is the physico-moral energy which builds up and spiritually transforms our universe through the moral activity of men. When men limit love, they sin.[16] Because increases in consciousness increase both man's capacity to love and the possibility of abusing this capacity by not using it, it is not surprising to find increases in both virtue and vice in modern man.

Since God, who is infinitely loving and lovable, is both the source and goal of love energy, He alone enables man to love, to reject evil and to commit himself wholeheartedly to fostering evolution. To reject God and His love is to sin. Man is imperfect, immature, in process and open to failure; but he is not sinful simply on account of this. Sin is a willed or chosen immaturity, a rejection and a refusal to accept and to grow in love. It involves not merely weakness and failure, but resistance. Sinful man not only needs completion, he needs conversion.

Sin involves not only a rejection of God and His love but an *inordinate* turning toward created reality in such a way as to set it apart from God and absolutize and idolize it. The sinful man attempts to achieve unity and synthesis by turning to and uniting himself with the material, the individual and the multiple. All forms of concupiscence attract men by offering them a superficial and degrading form of unity which ultimately fetters them to materiality. The proud man flatters himself by attempting to overcome the lack of integrity and unity in reality by reducing it to his own individual unity. In doing so he establishes himself at the center of the universe. The final result is a descent of the matter-spirit slope toward plurality. The multiple is re-established in forms beyond which the person had evolved or new forms of plurality arise which are dangerous and pernicious.[17] Moral evil not only arises, therefore, in the process of attaining a good (which may not involve fault), but also in the corruption of attained good, that is, in the turning back toward multiplicity. When this is voluntary it is always culpable.[18]

For the christian the natural law of self-realization remains intact and operative, but the moral order is elevated or assumed into a supramoral order, the moral-religious order. This occurs through the gift of divine life or grace which extends man's capacity to achieve self-realization beyond itself by enveloping it in a new interior relationship of sonship with God. Moral duty is in no way suppressed in this gratuitous relationship with God, but given a new "ought." The norm of ethical conduct in the moral-religious order is this intimate relationship of love between God and man. Man's conscience, moved by divine love, determines what will promote or destroy love. In this order moral evil is constituted not merely by that which hinders human self-realization, and especially not by simple transgression of external, positive laws; but primarily by a refusal or a violation of divine love.

Sin is not merely an opposition to law, but an opposition to divine grace, a rejection of God and His love. It is a deep-seated inner rebellion, a hardening of the heart and a refusal to open oneself in love to God and creation which He has assumed into His covenant relationship with man. It is a deep inner rebellious attitude from which sinful actions or transgressions flow. Teilhard recognizes this fact when he states that

> the powers of evil, in the universe, are not only an attraction, a deviation, a minus sign, an annihilating return to plurality. In the course of the spiritual evolution of the world, certain conscious elements in it, certain monads, deliberately detached themselves from the mass that is stimulated by your attraction. Evil has become incarnate in them, has been 'substantialized' in them.[19]

Sinfulness, therefore, is a lasting disposition in the heart of man. It is not merely external acts injurious to his fellow man and creation which cut man off from God, but his inner sinfulness. External acts are visible manifestations of a person's inner dialogue with God. And since the whole of man and all his activities have been assumed into this dialogue, not only acts directly related to man's supernatural relationship with God, but also those opposed to the natural order of creation are sinful.

In a processive world view sin is not a static reality nor is it peripheral or insignificant. It is anti-evolutionary, opposed to the very current of evolution itself. Teilhard does not propose a type of evolutionism in which progress is inevitable, a process in which sin merely slows down or temporarily frustrates the evolutionary process. Sin is not merely a disgression, but a free, deliberate movement opposed to and destructive of spiritualization. It fragments and destroys men and prevents them from attaining self-realization. As we have seen earlier, Teilhard does not accept the hypothesis that the quantity and intensity of sin will diminish as evolution continues. On the contrary, he recognizes that evil will go on growing alongside good so that at the final point of convergence it too will attain its fullness. Those who have rejected God and sought to fulfill themselves in themselves alone will cut themselves off definitively from the love of God and destroy themselves in isolation rather than fulfill themselves in love.[20]

Our analysis of the problems of sin and evil has shed light on the apparent conflict between faith in God and faith in man and science. It has shown that the presence of physical evil in the world is natural to a universe in evolution. In doing so it has reduced the scandal caused by such evil. If God were to eliminate physical evil from the universe He would have to handicap nature by restricting its capacity to interact and develop itself within a wide range of possibilities. Physical evil only remains a catastrophe insofar as it injures man, and man has been given the ability to develop science and overcome this type of evil as much as possible. We have also shown that the physical evil which cannot be overcome can have some positive value or meaning in relation to the over-all process of growth of which it is a part. Its deepest significance is to be found in revelation where even death itself becomes a means of transition to fuller life. Thus it ought not to be a scandal causing man to reject faith in God.

So too the presence of moral evil, the constant scandal of man's inhumanity to his fellow man, is not attributable to God and ought not to turn man from Him. God acts in all beings according to their natures. He has not only revealed Himself, He has given us His Spirit to act as an interior source of healing and love. But He will not force us to accept Him or His love. To do so would be to destroy man's inner freedom and to take away his relative autonomy. Man must love and respect himself and his achievements if he is to evolve. He must retain faith in himself and science.

The problem of sin does not stand in opposition to faith in God, but remains as a warning cautioning man against absoluting his faith in himself and science. Science can and does educate, liberate and even heal man, but it cannot convert him. By itself science is incapable of leading men to mutual love and service. It needs to be motivated by the love given us by God if it is going to promote authentic personhood and community. Faith in science, therefore, needs to be complemented by faith in God.

II. Elements Involved in Overcoming the Apparent Conflict in these Faiths

A. The Special Significance of Work and Leisure for the Christian

We have already seen that man is in evolution and is responsible for forwarding it. Christianity must not dichotomize man or make him inhuman. In some way his commitment to the world and his work[21] must be integrated with his religious experience. The very depths to which Christ became incarnate require that His followers strive to become not only authentically christian but also fully human. Thus we shall show that man's natural obligation to foster evolution not only remains intact, but also takes on a *specifically new dimension* for the christian. The world is not only to be fulfilled in its natural dimensions but also in its higher potentiality of becoming part of the Body of Christ.

It has not always been evident how this dual task is to be worked out concretely. That is, it is not immediately evident how the christian can commit himself wholeheartedly to secular responsibilities in the name of everything that is most christian in him and at the same time direct all his energies toward God. There is a great temptation to dichotomize one's life by attempting to serve two masters independent of each other. Many christians attempt to solve this apparent conflict by a) repressing their taste for the earthly and confining themselves to purely religious objects whenever possible, b) dismissing the evangelical counsels and choosing to lead what they regard to be a full human life, or c) attempting a compromise involving wholehearted commitment to neither God nor temporal achievements. None of these solutions are adequate.[22]

Because Christ is the personal Center toward which the universe is evolving, everything which is directed toward some type of *unification* contributes to the physical building up of His Universal Body. In a converging evolutionary process every process of material growth and every effort of human work which is directed toward unification is directed toward spirit, and all spiritual growth is directed toward Christ. The world, both in all its natural dimensions and in its higher potentiality of becoming part of the Cosmic Christ, is presented to man in an incomplete form to be brought to fulfillment by him. Besides its temporal value work completes in man the subject of his union with God. God is attainable to man through his temporal work, and yet this more spiritual achievement does not in any way detract from or disturb the *human endeavour* as such. In and through his work man attains union with Christ and at the same time builds up the Universal Christ who is and yet is becoming. With all its great natural richness the universe will be fulfilled only in Christ and Christ will be attained by man only through the universe developed to the limit of its capacities. If God is to establish His Kingdom on earth, man must develop the world.[23]

Christ condemned the world of *selfish* enjoyment and pleasure-seeking, not the world of constructive, disinterested effort. In fact, the will of God for man is made incarnate by time and the activities time situates and at least partially determines for him. Sanctity is adhering to God with one's full strength, that is, fulfilling, in the world organized around Christ, the exact function to which the person is destined according to his natural potentialities and supernatural gifts.[24] A christian does not have to renounce being a man in the fullest human sense. If at present Christianity needs rejuvenation it is, in part, because it has slackened in its true human compassion and passionate admiration of the universe. At the same time and as a consequence of this, its capacity for detachment has been impaired because wholehearted commitment to developing oneself and the universe in a christian manner has às a consequence the effect of increasing the person's detachment.[25] Teilhard ties all these ideas together when he states that

> . . . one of the surest marks of the truth of religion, in itself and in an individual soul, is to note to what extent it brings into action, that is, causes to rise up from sources deep within each one of us, a certain maximum of energy and effort. Action and sanctification go hand in hand, each supporting the other.[26]

Human action can be related to and assist in building up the Cosmic Christ not only in the *intention* of the work but also by the actual *material content* of the work accomplished. All progress can be directed toward Christ even in its object because, in itself, all progress is organically integral with spirit and spirit depends on Christ. This realization destroys the theoretical barrier between human and christian effort. Human effort becomes divinisable in the work itself as well as in the intention so that for the christian the world becomes a divine milieu in its entirety.[27] Teilhard states clearly that

> . . . through the *work* accomplished, we are working towards the completion of Christ, by preparing the material, more or less close at hand, of the Pleroma.[28]

Henri de Lubac supports Teilhard's position on this matter, maintaining that insistence on the value of the work done does not impose a fundamentally naturalistic vision upon Christianity. Rather a balance is achieved when the necessity of a good motive is not underestimated and the objective work itself is regarded as a contribution toward fulfilling one of the *natural conditions* of completing the world in Christ. The work itself plays an indispensable but indirect role in fulfilling the Body of Christ.[29]

When sufficient emphasis is placed on the value of the work itself, it becomes clear why the christian must not be indifferent toward its success. He must succeed if he is to remain in existence and be motivated to continue his efforts. As well, the spiritual success of the whole universe is associated with the continued release of the energy of its parts. Since it is a matter of vital importance, therefore, for the christian that temporal enterprises succeed, he must commit himself to them and combine the spirit of commitment to progress with that of detachment or abandonment.[30] Detachment is not understood in this more integral context as a leaving behind or a cutting off, but as that which leads on and raises; it is a way through, an act of emerging.[31]

We can see the special significance of work for the christian even more clearly if we examine Sebastian Moore's definition of work and relate it to the dynamism Dewey found in all experience and that to be found in the passion-death-resurrection of Christ. Moore defines work as "patient action bearing fruit."[32] This definition of work highlights the ˜same inherent dynamic in the activity of working that Dewey found in all experience which is consummatory. The positive activity of trying or doing is balanced by patience, suffering or being acted upon by the laws of the matter upon which the agent is acting. And the fruit or result of the over-all activity is in direct proportion to the balance between acting and being acted upon achieved by the agent.

When we examine the redemptive work of Christ's passion and death we see once again the same inherent dynamic operative in that work. Christ was passive; He allowed Himself to be acted upon and suffered being seized and put to death although, being the incarnate Son of God, He did not have to undergo this suffering. He had come to redeem sinful mankind and He suffered all the consequences involved in that mission. His passion and death also involved positive activity on His part. Although He never chose death, He willed to accept suffering and death out of obedience to the Father and love for mankind in order to attain total life for His own humanity and for men. It was the perfect balance between the activity-passivity of His work of redemption which made it perfect and enabled it to bear the fruit of eternal life for all men.

Thus we see that the passion and death of Christ, *the* work of redemption *par excellence,* has an inherent dynamic involving a balance of trying or doing and suffering. This act provides the model for all redemptive activity. And since we have already seen that all authentic experience and work which culminate in increased unification possess this same dynamic, we can be assured that they have a natural redemptive quality. They are not only productive of life insofar as they achieve their own temporal goals, they also possess the capacity of being open to man's task of uniting all things in Christ. All such activity is open to the possibility of being redemptive as well as evolutionary if the agent performing it is united to Chirst, or at least open to the fullness of goodness and truth as he has experienced them. Thus for the christian work retains its full temporal meaning, but has an added significance as well.

We have placed a great deal of emphasis on the value and dignity of work for the christian, but man is more than a functionary or worker. If work is to be properly understood it must be seen in relation to leisure. Unfortunately our modern secular work ethic has given an absolute value to work. The personal identity, self-respect, dignity and success of a person are all defined today in terms of the work the person does. We have lost sight of the real meaning of leisure and its significance in the christian's life. In fact we go so far as to define leisure in terms of work. Leisure is time off from work, a rest, reward or even an escape from work. It is frequently reduced to a time to recreate (re-create) oneself so as to prepare to return to work.

In this context there is a reversal of values. Traditionally leisure conferred meaning on work; today work justifies leisure. We have succumbed to a materialism in which the goods achieved through work are directed primarily toward financial gain and the multiplication of services and products to be consumed. Leisure is also caught up in this endless spiral in which man works to acquire more products which he can either use or consume in the pursuit of pleasure during his time off from work. We continue to pursue this policy in spite of abundant evidence that it de-humanizes persons and is destructive of family life and many other aspects of our culture.

Certainly man is more than a mere functionary, and he must be educated to search for a personal identity and a view of reality as a whole which exceeds the narrow boundaries of his workaday world. In childhood work and play are undifferentiated; as we mature they are distinguished, but remain complementary. The latter is an end in itself and must not be artificially compartmentalized and reduced to an instrument and mere support of the former. Leisure is a condition of the spirit. It is a mental and spiritual attitude which is not simply achieved as a result of certain external factors. Although man cannot achieve this attitude if he is constantly fettered to work, he will not necessarily acquire it if he is given free time.

Compared to the ideal of work as utility, function and activity, leisure is an attitude of non-activity, inner calm and silence. It is a receptive attitude of mind, a contemplative attitude of the man who is open to the whole of reality, at peace with himself and free from the temptation to cling to the present moment as if its material goods were absolute and to be possessed forever. Leisure is an absence of constraint, and therefore it is an attitude of freedom. It frees man's mind from immediate, habitual concerns for self-discovery and the contemplation of ultimate concerns. Thus it is an occasion for discovering the meaning and purpose of life in its broadest and deepest perspectives.[33]

Leisure is an active, creative attitude possible only when man is at one with himself as a person who is not only intimately connected with nature, caught up in time and present activities, but also aware that he is not totally circumscribed by these. The attitude of leisure ought to permeate not only man's free time, but also his work. It is a sense of grace and freedom which enables man to disengage himself from the pressures of his daily routine and experience a sense of transcendence and of eternity while he is still committed to the temporal.[34]

Leisure is contemplative celebration; man celebrates the end of his work and contemplates the goodness of the whole of creation. In celebration all the elements of leisure are focussed — its relaxation, effortlessness and active creativity, which is superior to all functions man performs. And since the meaning of celebration is to be found in man's positive experience and affirmation of the whole of creation, celebration and leisure find their foundation and justification not in work but in divine worship. In praising the Creator of the universe, man experiences and expresses his most intense affirmation of the world, and in liturgical celebration he acknowledges the goodness of the entire cosmic process and his oneness with it.[35]

In liturgical celebration man affirms and honours the whole of life and all the activities that make cosmic evolution possible. He acknowledges the creative, evolutionary activity of God and expresses gratitude for the share he has been given in it. Liturgy is a consummation, an emminent source of the joy and peace which must permeate man's work if it is to integrate and personalize man. Worship also prevents the christian from allowing his work to become an idol, and is a source of the grace and freedom which enable him to balance his commitment to work with the spirit of detachment from it.

276

B. *The Relation between Science and Religion*

Throughout our discussion of work we emphasized its terrestrial value while at the same time showing its limitations and its openness to a further end known by faith. In doing so we narrowed the gap between faith in the world and faith in God. In a somewhat similar manner we shall relate science and religion by pointing out the necessity for the christian to draw from the universe all the truth it can reveal and by showing how faith in God can complement and assist this process.

Man has a fundamental duty to act as though there were no limit to his power to extract from himself and the earth all the riches and truth they can yield. The fact that man has been given divine revelation and saved by Christ does not in any way release him from this duty. Rather, man must assist God with all his strength in furthering creation and delving into research as if his salvation depended entirely on his own efforts. Research is a sacred duty, one of man's most ennobling functions, combining the spirit of progress and adventure with the openness and confidence of religious faith. Research keeps a constant pressure on the surface of reality. And extending the boundaries of consciousness is a supreme gesture of faith in Being itself and therefore also a genuine act of adoration.[36]

God's creative power, in which man shares, is hidden and operative in research. The new consciousness brought into being by means of research would remain incomplete if it were not deliberately drawn by christians into the scope of the Incarnation and Redemption. Knowledge of evolution has enabled man to recognize the broad dimensions of research, and forced him to ask questions he did not have to face in the same way when he conceived reality to be static. The research worker no longer works in order that man may merely continue to exist in the best possible conditions. He can and must concern himself not only with *well*-being, but with *fuller*-being, *more*-being or *super-life*.[37]

Teilhard recognizes three major lines of scientific and evolutionary advance: a) the further organization of research, b) the concentration of research on man (the development of a science of spiritual or human energetics which will bring man face to face with religion), and c) the conjunction of science and religion. The zeal of the research worker will be extinguished if he is not guaranteed that the results of his efforts are limitless and that moral perfection and social improvement have a definite term to which they are directed. Evolution can tentatively imply that such an ideal term exists and suggest the direction in which it can be attained, but it cannot name or define it. Religion complements evolution by providing this term.[38]

> Religion and evolution should neither be confused nor divorced. They are destined to form one single continuous organism, in which their respective lives prolong, are dependent on, and complete one another, without being identified or lost: the one offering an infinite ideal and immutable laws, and the other providing a focus of activity and a stuff that is essential to the transformation of beings in process of growth.[39]

Thus religion can be described as the soul biologically necessary for the future of science. In its early analytic phase scientific study of the world leads man toward the multiple. But because this very analytic knowledge of things indicates to man the synthetic structure of the world, science must reverse its direction and naturally culminate in the realization of a unique center of things. When man is oriented toward the future and the *whole* of reality, he cannot help but engage in religion. Mankind is unthinkable now without science and science is impossible without some religion to animate it. Science and religion, therefore, are the two complementary phases of the one complete act of knowledge.[40]

Although many scientists still claim that mankind can fulfill himself by himself, without the "christic" vision of the world, two elements are missing which are necessary to guarantee man's progress to the very end. There is no divine guarantee that in spite of death the fruit of human progress is irreversible and indestructible. There is no attractive super-personal power capable of engendering the forces of love energy in man, energy without which evolution cannot succeed. Nevertheless, even after it has become abundantly clear that religious faith is not hostile to faith in progress, but aids it, the conflict between these two faiths will not end. Mankind will continue to be divided between these faiths even up to the Parousia, a time characterized in revelation by acute moral crisis and a strong naturalistic atmosphere.[41]

When Teilhard considers the possibilities of success of the whole process of cosmogenesis, he affirms that the whole extrapolation which led him to anticipate a super-humanity is extremely vulnerable and hypothetical. Man hopes for the success of the universe, and in order to support that hope, Teilhard provides a number of scientific arguments or rational invitations to an act of natural faith in the success of the whole process.[42] But on the scientific level there is *no infallible guarantee* of the success of the universe; faith in science cannot be absolute nor totally adequate for man. It is only with a knowledge of Christ and the recognition by christian faith that the whole consummation of mankind on earth is a necessary (but not in itself a sufficient) precondition of the Parousia that a *certain knowledge* of the success of cosmogenesis can be attained. Because this certainty is supernatural it does not do away with the necessity to forward the process and the tension and anxieties this involves.[43]

Once again, therefore, the complementary character of science and religion is manifested and one more step has been taken in overcoming the conflict between faith in God and faith in the world. The final solution to this problem is summed up in the phrase "to heaven, through fulfillment of the earth."

C. *To Heaven through Fulfillment of the Earth*

The *principle* which unites faith in God and faith in the world and thus produces *one* ascending movement is the general principle that there is a continual heightening of consciousness in the universe in and around man.[44] Here, of course, we have the underlying principle of the entire evolutionary process as we have described it. This principle has already been developed, and many of its implications have been applied to the problem of the two faiths. Yet there are a number of facets of the problem which require further discussion, facets which are clarified when seen in the light of this principle.

We have maintained that Christ and the world are related to each other in such a way that a person cannot be truly christian without being fully human. That is to say that the life of Christ mingles with the life-blood of evolution. But in order that this may be more clearly understood and achieved in practice certain trends of theological thought must be developed and certain requirements must be fulfilled.

First, the church must recognize that the context of the conflict between faiths has shifted from a two dimensional situation (the human soul and God) to a triangular one in which a third reality, the *future of the earth,* must be given its rightful place. It must also recognize that faith in the future of the world, to the extent that it really is *a faith* and therefore demands sacrifice and the abandonment of oneself to something greater than oneself, *necessarily implies something divine.* Once this is acknowledged a great barrier is overcome, and it will be easier for the church to incorporate this natural faith in the world within its supernatural faith. In doing so it will assert that the evolving universe cannot eclipse God, but rather awaits Him to be transfigured and consummated. Acknowledgment that the modern religion of the earth is an unconscious impulse toward heaven and not a threat to Christianity will enable chrisians to practice their supernatural charity more boldly in word and deed as men dedicated to *spiritual earthly* things precisely because they are christians. In assuming the religious spirit of the modern world and living it fully on the christian plane, christians would consummate it, and to consummate any reality is to christianize it.[45]

Many christians experience serious inadequacies in traditional theology. Some feel that the image of God offered to them is not worthy of the new dimensions of the universe. Besides stressing the divine and human attributes of Christ, His universal and cosmic attributes must be emphasized. Therefore a theology of the Universal and Cosmic Christ, Christ the Evolver and Saviour of the idea and reality of evolution must be elaborated. The religious aspirations of humanitarianism are vague; theology must show that Christ alone can concretize them. Many avowed atheists do not reject the notion of a God absolutely, but reject Him because He has been presented to them as extrinsic to the cosmic process or as man's problem solver. These concepts of God weaken man's incentive to work, and Christianity must rid itself of such unworthy elements.[46]

When christians recognize that there is only *one evolution* they will recognize more clearly the need to revise the very notion of christian perfection and the role of *all* the virtues. They will also recognize a greater similarity between the axes of christian faith (futurism, universalism and personalism) and the axes of humanism. The universalism of Christianity has not embraced modern cosmology nor extended its views of the Incarnation to these new dimensions.

Christianity, although futuristic in the extreme, has allowed itself to appear *extra*-terrestrial whereas its dogma demands that it be *supra*-terrestrial and therefore a motive force of human effort. It has even allowed its personalism to be obscured through emphasis on juridical and moral rather than organic and cosmic bonds. What is needed is a re-incarnation to bring Christianity into line with the human front and make it a fully human and progressive religion without destroying its supernatural reality or confusing the perfecting of mankind with naturalism.[47]

The christian achievement realized through faith in God must be distinguished from a naturalistic fulfillment. First, supernatural faith integrates natural events into a larger whole without destroying their individual qualities in any way. Second, the christian achievement occurs both on the level of natural human events and on the level of supernatural holiness. Third, God is the ultimate agent, source and medium of the development of all this activity achieved in faith, not merely man alone. In spite of these distinctions between the naturalistic and the supernatural and between the modes of operation of natural and supernatural faith, the latter is a very concrete and comprehensive *cosmic energy*. As a form of cosmic energy christian faith does not restrict itself to the realm of the supernatural but enters into, molds and enlarges the phenomenal world in which supernatural being is rooted and from which it is nourished.[48]

The problem of relating the two faiths, therefore, is ultimately one of developing a precise theological description of the relationship between the natural and supernatural. To do this we shall outline the development of Teilhard's thought on this matter chronologically, rather than merely setting forth his most mature reflections. Over the years he accepted and later rejected a number of different positions on the topic. His final statement is the most adequate, but presenting his earlier ideas will afford an opportunity to set forth alternative positions, point out their weaknesses, and in the light of these see why his final description is preferable.

As early as 1916 Teilhard was strongly motivated to achieve *unity* and the *reconciliation of mankind's natural and supernatural evolution*. He saw that neither a too detached Christianity nor an exclusively secular worship of the world is capable of nourishing the heart of man nor of existing in isolation, yet both are suited to complement each other.[49]

In essays such as "L'Ame du monde" and "Mon Univers," written in 1918, he saw natural evolution moving toward a point of convergence, an Omega Point, but also recognized that the principle of this movement (Christ) as well as the supernatural point of convergence (the *pleroma*) were also Omega. To clarify the duality between the natural and supernatural terms of evolution he referred to the former as Omicron and the latter as Omega. Then, of course, he had to examine the various possible ways of relating these terms and select the most compatible. In making his choice he sought: a) to overcome *dualisms*, b) to maintain the possibility of experiencing God in natural energy, and c) to find a universal, absolute value in all human action.

At this point in his thought development he recognized Omicron and Omega as hierarchized terms. Natural human effort and grace concur in the development of spirit which is formed in its natural substance at the same time as God elevates it to the supernatural level. His theory here was one of conjoined ends, and he constantly repeated that the *real problem* at stake was one of achieving a *unified interior vision*. The supernaturalization of the world is not merely an abstract theological problem, but one which can introduce a dualistic tendency in the practical christian life. So frequently the christian encounters a dualism in action between reconciling renunciation of the world (necessary for life in Christ) and love of the earth (necessary for motivating human effort). This first dualism is prolonged in a second one on the religious level where the person is torn between two absolutes: experience (the universe) and revelation (a transcendent God). Teilhard insisted on establishing a union between these poles which is both *organic* and *rational*.[50]

In "L'Ame du monde," 1918,[51] he spoke of a "soul of the world" which was similar to Omicron; later the "soul of the world" concept as well as that of Omicron disappeared from his writings. In a preliminary note to "L'Ame du monde," the French editor suggests that Teilhard affirmed Omicron and the soul of the world in the first place because of a theology in which the supernatural end was presented as a *superaddition to a natural end which is more or less supplanted*. Gradually Teilhard rejected this theological approach.[52] This rejection and his subsequent understanding of the relation of the natural and supernatural are of major significance for his ultimate solution of the conflict between faith in God and faith in man.

In his later thought Teilhard strongly rejected "a certain intransigent supernaturalism" which offers man a *choice* between *two consummations* of the world, one natural, the other supernatural. There is only one Center and term to which evolution is moving, Omega or Jesus Christ. Concretely the christian can no longer even imagine toward what Center the universe would move had it not been elevated by grace. This shows the extent to which the whole universe has been recast in the supernatural. It is even erroneous to distinguish two different attractions in man influencing him toward an hypothetical natural end of the cosmos and toward the anticipated supernatural end. The one Center in the universe is at once natural and supernatural moving all of creation *along the one line*, toward the fullest development of consciousness and toward the highest degree of holiness, that is, toward self-fulfillment and toward association in Christ. The supernatural end completes the world naturally at the same time as the whole is brought to Christ.[53] Thus we see that the two extremes, the either/or positions of naturalism and extreme supernaturalism are rejected as well as the two-term concept. A reconciliation between the natural and supernatural is worked out in terms of one end and one Center of evolution — Christ in His *pleroma*.

As has been indicated earlier, "supernatural" means "supremely real," or "supremely in conformity with the conditions of reality which nature imposes on beings."[54] The supernatural *pleroma* grows out of the natural universe according to the law of transformation and not by a complete rupture. There is a real *transformation* involved: a) the supernatural rearranges the elements of the world making them more and other than they were, and b) the natural elements are necessary to the work of salvation in that they provide it with a suitable material to be transformed. The supernatural is constantly being formed by the super-creation of man's nature. There is not a complete break or rupture between the natural and supernatural, but there is a radical transformation of the natural. The notions of transformation and critical points, applied analogously, are as important in connecting the natural and supernatural as they were in the movement from non-living to living beings and in the appearance of man. The critical points that occur at the reception of grace enable nature and supernature to be linked in a manner similar to the union between matter and spirit.[55]

Continuity is maintained, but the transformation occurring in the supernaturalization of reality is radical. Grace does not introduce man into another universe but moves him into a prolongation of the universe in which nothing of what he is remains *as such* but every element is utilized and transformed. Everything in the supernaturalized universe *maintains its form and natural appearance but is inwardly animated by God.* God acts on individual natures and on the movement of the whole in such a way that His immanent activity acts through the natures of things while allowing their determinisms to remain untouched. It is not difficult, therefore, to see why Teilhard does not attribute any absolute or definitive value to earthly constructions; they are or will be recast in a new plane of existence. He speaks of their instability in Christ and of their being on a forward tilt, inclined toward the *present* center of the *pleroma*. It is also evident why he dissociates the process of sanctification from naturalism and humanism. Grace respects and preserves all the values cherished by naturalists and humanists but by extending nature transforms and enriches them.[56]

The ultimate, summary solution to the conflict of faiths, namely, *to heaven through fulfillment of the earth,* is merely a recapitulation of every element of the problem discussed above. It rejects both a faith in God which is indifferent to the super-evolution of mankind (a strictly "vertical" faith ascending toward God) and a faith in the world which denies the existence of a transcendent God (a strictly "horizontal" faith driving forward to the super-human). The solution is to be found in a christian faith which reconciles the upward and forward movements of faith in the person of Christ who is Mover and Saviour of the whole cosmic process. This solution is neither a destruction nor a reduction of christian faith. It is not a compromise faith, but a *resultant, enriched christian* faith which combines and strengthens all the commitments and sacrifices inherent in faith in God and in the future of mankind.[57]

Christian faith cannot be complete in its ascending movement unless it reaches out to embrace all man's spiritual dynamism nor can faith in the world be psychologically possible if the evolutionary future of the world does not encounter a transcendent personal term. In a comprehensive christian faith God is made cosmic and evolution is personalized. All man's powers of activity and research as well as his capacity for adoration are brought to their fulfillment.[58] Teilhard is so convinced of this that he can envisage the coming development of faith on earth

> In the form, . . . , of a slow concentration of man's power of worship around a Christianity that has gradually reached the stage of being '*religion for the sake of research and effort.*'[59]

The christian ascends spiritually toward God, therefore, by way of his forward movement on earth. He not only finds and develops himself in the universe, but encounters God through experiencing the depths of created reality. He builds up the Body of Christ by his temporal activities as well as by prayer and liturgical worship. And finally he achieves complete integration and satisfaction in nature only by going to its ultimate term who is its hidden, mysterious Creator.

A faith in God that is indifferent to mankind and earthly progress is not a genuine christian faith. The comprehensive christian faith we have described is an organic reconciliation of the natural and supernatural currents or energies of faith. It is not merely an intellectual assent but involves a commitment and response of the whole person to God and created reality; therefore it must be lived in practice. It is an operative faith with far reaching consequences in all areas of life. Christians must develop a true humanism which complements their religious beliefs. Once christians recognize that evolution is fulfilled in the dynamism of the Incarnation and Redemption they can also develop

> the sense of the earth opening and exploding upwards into God; and the sense of God taking root and finding nourishment downwards into Earth. A personal, transcendent God and an evolving Universe no longer forming two hostile centres of attraction, but entering into hierarchic conjunction to raise the human mass on a single tide.[60]

Action flows from vision. The consequences of not acting in the light of a unified, comprehensive vision of reality encompassing both the terrestrial and the divine are devastating. When man's vision of the whole is fragmented or dualistic it does not furnish sufficient direction and meaning to enable him to co-ordinate his experiences and find ultimate meaning in life. Recognizing a specific personal consummation to life, a personal goal toward which man can orient all his activities, reflects back on every facet of living, augments its meaning and enables men to know and love themselves and to make decisions and set policies in the light of the whole, whereas pragmatic decisions arising out of an inadequate view of reality are always limited in scope. Their consequences operate at cross purposes causing waste of resources, energy and love.

As christians adopt a truly cosmic vision of reality the apparent *dualisms* which have caused so much fragmentation in their lives can be eliminated, and they will be better equipped to cope effectively with the *dualities* at the core of reality and the *tensions* inherent in the christian life. Their common faith and hope in the cosmic-christic process will provide a firm foundation for a truly ecumenical dialogue out of which all men can strive to develop an authentic world community.

FOOTNOTES

1. "La Maîtrise du monde et le règne de Dieu," *ÉTG*, pp. 77-79 [Eng. trans. 84-87]; "Réflexions sur la conversion du monde," *SC*, p. 166 [Eng. trans. p. 127].

2. Pierre Teilhard de Chardin, "Note pour servir à l'évangélisation des temps nouveau," *La Parole attendue*, inédits, témoignages et travaux de l'association, Cahier II (Paris: Éditions du Seuil, 1963), pp. 12-13, hereafter cited *PA*; "La Parole attendue," *PA*, pp. 24-25; "Réflexions sur la conversion du monde," *SC*, pp. 157-59 [Eng. trans. pp. 118-20]; "L'Incroyance moderne," *SC*, pp. 149-51 [Eng. trans. pp. 113-15]; "Réflexions sur le progrès," *AH*, pp. 101-02 [Eng. trans. pp. 76-77]; *MD*, Advertissement, p. 17 [Eng. trans. p. 43]; "L'Ame du monde," *ÉTG*, pp. 224-26 [Eng. trans. pp. 182-84].

3. "La Foi qui opère," *ÉTG*, pp. 315-16, 318 [Eng. trans. pp. 233, 236].

4. *MD*, pp. 59-61 [Eng. trans. pp. 68-69]; "L'Incroyance moderne," *SC*, pp. 151-52 [Eng. trans. p. 115]; "L'Ame du monde," *ÉTG*, pp. 221-22, 226 [Eng. trans. pp. 179-80, 184]; *GP*, Letter, July 30, 1918, pp. 290-91 [Eng. trans. pp. 223-24]; "Note pour servir à l'évangélisation des temps nouveau," *PA*, pp. 13-14.

5. "Le Coeur du problème," *AH*, pp. 343-44 [Eng. trans. pp. 263-64].

6. "Un Seuil mental sous nos pas: du cosmos à la cosmogénèse," *AÉ*, pp. 267-68 [Eng. trans. pp. 259-60]; "L'Esprit nouveau," *AH*, p. 119 [Eng. trans. p. 90]; "La Signification et la valeur constructrice de la souffrance," *ÉH*, pp. 62-63 [Eng. trans. pp. 50-51].

7. *PH*, pp. 345-48 [Eng. trans. pp. 311-13].

8. "Esquisse d'un univers personnel," *ÉH*, pp. 105-08 [Eng. trans. pp. 85-87].

9. *MD*, p. 84 [Eng. trans. p. 82].

10. "L'Union créatrice," *ÉTG*, pp. 178-79 [Eng. trans. pp. 156-57]; *PM*, pp. 302-03 [Eng. trans. p. 272].

11. *MD*, pp. 89-94 [Eng. trans. pp. 86-89].

12. *MD*, pp. 80-87, 99-100 [Eng. trans. pp. 80-84, 92-93]; "La Vie cosmique," *ÉTG*, p. 57 [Eng. trans. p. 68].

13. "La Signification et la valeur constructrice de la souffrance," *ÉH*, p. 64 [Eng. trans. pp. 50-51].

14. *PH*, p. 347 [Eng. trans. p. 313]; *MD*, p. 89 [Eng. trans. p. 86].

15. "La Vie cosmique," *ÉTG*, p. 56 [Eng. trans. p. 67].

16. "Le Phénomène spirituel," *ÉH*, p. 134 [Eng. trans. p. 108].

17. "La Lutte contre la multitude," *ÉTG*, pp. 120-21 [Eng. trans. pp. 102-03].

18. Bruno de Solages, *Teilhard de Chardin*, p. 288, n. 84, quotes Teilhard's Cahier VIII, May 9, 1920.

19. *MD*, p. 188 [Eng. trans. p. 147].

20. *MD*, p. 187 [Eng. trans. pp. 146-47].

A PROCESSIVE WORLD VIEW FOR PRAGMATIC CHRISTIANS

21. In the discussion which follows the term "work" is not restricted to any particular type of labour, but also includes any form of experience or activity which attains some positive completion.

22. *MD*, pp. 33-36 [Eng. trans. pp. 51-53].

23. *MD*, pp. 41-50, 52-54 [Eng. trans. pp. 56-62, 63-65]; "La Vie cosmique," *ÉTG*, pp. 42, 51-52 [Eng. trans. pp. 52-53, 62-63]; "Le Prêtre," *ÉTG*, pp. 298-99 [Eng. trans. pp. 219-20]; *GP*, Letter, November 6, 1916, pp. 181-82 [Eng. trans. pp. 141-42]; *GP*, Letter, February 5, 1917, p. 235 [Eng. trans. pp. 181-82]; "Mon Univers," *SC*, p. 96 [Eng. trans. pp. 67-68].

24. "La Vie cosmique," *ÉTG*, pp. 44-45 [Eng. trans. pp. 55-56]; *MD*, pp. 56-57 [Eng. trans. p. 66]; *GP*, Letter, June 19, 1916, p. 130 [Eng. trans. p. 103].

25. *MD*, pp. 57-58, 63-67 [Eng. trans. pp. 67, 70-73]; "La Vie cosmique," *ÉTG*, pp. 7-8 [Eng. trans. p. 17]; "Forma Christi," *ÉTG*, p. 347 [Eng. trans. p. 262]; *GP*, Letter, July 28, 1918, p. 288 [Eng. trans. pp. 221-22]; "Mon Univers," *SC*, pp. 96-97 [Eng. trans. pp. 68-69].

26. *GP*, Letter, July 4, 1915, p. 71 [Eng. trans. p. 58].

27. "Note sur le Christ universel," *SC*, pp. 41-42 [Eng. trans. pp. 16-17]. See also: "Le Prêtre," *ÉTG*, p. 296 [Eng. trans. p. 217]; *MD*, pp. 39-41 [Eng. trans. pp. 54-56; "Teilhard de Chardin's First Paper to Auguste Valensin," *Correspondence*, [Eng. trans. pp. 32-33, 35].

28. "Teilhard de Chardin's First Paper to Auguste Valensin," *Correspondence*, [Eng. trans. p. 35].

29. Henri de Lubac, "Notes to Teilhard de Chardin's First Paper to Auguste Valensin," *Correspondence* [Eng. trans. n. 13, pp. 79-80, n. 27, p. 86].

30. "La Vie cosmique," *ÉTG*, pp. 42-46, 54 [Eng. trans. pp. 53-57, 65]; *LV*, Letter, April 8, 1930, pp. 129-30 [Eng. trans. pp. 163-64].

31. "L'Esprit nouveau," *AH*, p. 125 [Eng. trans. p. 96].

32. Sebastian Moore, "The Work of the Intellect," *Work: Christian Thought and Practice*, ed. by John M. Todd (London: Darton, Longman and Todd, Ltd., 1960), p. 182.

33. Josef Pieper, *Leisure the Basis of Culture*, trans. by Alexander Dru (New York: Pantheon Books, 1964), pp. 27-28; Robert Lee, *Religion and Leisure in America* (New York: Abingdon Press, 1964), pp. 34-35.

34. Josef Pieper, *Leisure the Basis of Culture*, pp. 27, 29; Gordon J. Dahl, "Time, Work and Leisure Today," *Christian Century*, 88 (February 10, 1971), pp. 187-89.

35. Josef Pieper, *Leisure the Basis of Culture*, pp. 30, 44-45.

36. "Le Prêtre," *ÉTG*, p. 299 [Eng. trans. p. 220]; *GP*, Letter, August 4, 1916, p. 148 [Eng. trans. p. 116]; *GP*, Letter, September 8, 1916, pp. 161-62 [Eng. trans. pp. 126-27]; "Construire la terre," *CT*, pp. 26-27 [Eng. trans. pp. 60-61]; "Science et Christ," *SC*, pp. 58-59 [Eng. trans. pp. 32-33].

37. "Sur la Valeur religieuse de la recherche," *SC*, pp. 259-60 [Eng. trans. pp. 201-02]; "Recherche, travail et adoration," *SC*, pp. 284-85 [Eng. trans. pp. 215-16]; *MD*, pp. 61-62 [Eng. trans. pp. 69-70].

38. *PH*, pp. 309-10, 312-15 [Eng. trans. p. 278, 280-83]; "Construire la terre," *CT*, p. 21 [Eng. trans. p. 55]; "La Maîtrise du monde et le règne de Dieu," *ÉTG*, pp. 72-73 [Eng. trans. p. 80].

39. "La Maîtrise du monde et le règne de Dieu," *ÉTG*, p. 80 [Eng. trans. p. 87].

40. *PH*, pp. 315-17 [Eng. trans. pp. 283-85]; "La Mystique de la science," *ÉH*, pp. 222-23 [Eng. trans. pp. 180-81]; "Science et Christ," *SC*, pp. 47-48, 59-62 [Eng. trans. pp. 21-22, 33-36]; "En regardant un cyclotron," *AÉ*, pp. 376-77 [Eng. trans. p. 357].

41. "Catholicisme et science," *SC*, pp. 239-41 [Eng. trans. pp 189-91]; "La Maîtrise du monde et le règne de Dieu," *ÉTG*, pp. 83-84 [Eng. trans. p. 91].

42. *PH*, pp. 258-59, 307-08 [Eng. trans. pp. 323-24, 376]; *PH*, Résumé, pp. 342-43 [Eng. trans. pp. 307-08]; *PHN*, pp. 167-73 [Eng. trans. pp. 117-21].

43. "L'Union créatrice," *ÉTG*, p. 196 [Eng. trans. p. 174]; "Note sur le progrès," *AH*, pp. 34-35 [Eng. trans. p. 22]; "Les Directions et les conditions de l'avenir," *AH*, pp. 304-05, n. 1, p. 305 [Eng. trans. p. 237].

44. "Réflexions sur le progrès," *AH*, p. 103 [Eng. trans. pp. 77-78].

45. "La Parole attendue," *PA*, pp. 25-26; "Réflexions sur la conversion du monde," *SC*, p. 160 [Eng. trans. p. 121]; "L'Incroyance moderne," *SC*, pp. 152-53 [Eng. trans. pp. 115-17]; "Sur la Valeur religieuse de la recherche," *SC*, pp. 261-62 [Eng. trans. pp. 203-04]; "Le Coeur du problème," *AH*, pp. 344-46 [Eng. trans. pp. 265-66].

46. "Réflexions sur le progrès," *AH*, pp. 104-05 [Eng. trans. p. 79]; "Le Coeur du problème," *AH*, pp. 339, 346 [Eng. trans. pp. 260, 266-67]; *MD*, pp. 24-25 [Eng. trans. p. 46]; "L'Element universal," *ÉTG*, pp. 410-14 [Eng. trans. pp. 299-302]; "Réflexions sur la conversion du monde," *SC*, p. 160 [Eng. trans. pp. 121-22]; "La Parole attendue," *PA*, pp. 26-29; "Christologie et évolution," *CJC*, p. 97 [Eng. trans. pp. 78-79]; "Le Christ évoluteur," *CJC*, pp. 169-73 [Eng. trans. pp. 144-48].

47. "Sauvons l'humanité," *SC*, pp. 188-91 [Eng. trans. pp. 147-50]; "Recherche, travail et adoration," *SC*, p. 289 [Eng. trans. p. 220]; "Note pour servir à l'évangélisation des temps nouveaux," *PA*, pp. 17-21; *LV*, Letter, August 7, 1927, p. 107 [Eng. trans. pp. 142-43]; "Réflexions sur le progrès," *AH*, pp. 104-05 [Eng. trans. p. 79].

48. "La Foi qui opère," *ÉTG*, pp. 324-26 [Eng. trans. pp. 343-45].

49. "La Maîtrise du monde et le règne de Dieu," *ÉTG*, pp. 67-68 [Eng. trans. pp. 75-76].

50. "Mon Univers," *ÉTG*, pp. 273-79.

51. "L'Ame du monde," *ÉTG*, pp. 221-32 [Eng. trans. pp. 179-90].

52. "L'Ame du monde," *ÉTG*, editor's introduction, pp. 217-19 [Eng. trans. pp. 177-78].

53. "Réflexions sur la probabilité scientifique et les conséquences religieuses d'un ultra-human," *AÉ*, pp. 288-89 [Eng. trans. pp. 277-79]; "L'Union créatrice," *ÉTG*, pp. 195-96 [Eng. trans. p. 174]; "Forma Christi," *ÉTG*, n. 5, p. 340, pp. 341-42, n. 8, p. 342 [Eng. trans. n. 6, p. 255, p. 256, n. 9, p. 256]; "Teilhard de Chardin's Second Paper to Auguste Valensin," *Correspondence* [Eng. trans. p. 49].

54. "Comment je crois," *CJC*, n. 1, p. 147 [Eng. trans. n. 10, p. 127].

55. "Pierre Teilhard de Chardin to Auguste Valensin," December 8, 1919, *Correspondence* [Eng. trans. p. 29]; "Teilhard de Chardin's First Paper to Auguste Valensin," *Correspondence* [Eng. trans. p. 33]; "Le Prêtre," *ÉTG*, p. 298 [Eng. trans. p. 219]; "L'Atomisme de l'esprit," *AÉ*, p. 63 [Eng. trans. pp. 56-57].

56. "Teilhard de Chardin's First Paper to Auguste Valensin," *Correspondence* [Eng. trans. pp. 34, 36]; "Teilhard de Chardin's Second Paper to Auguste Valensin," *Correspondence* [Eng. trans. pp. 47-48, 50 and Henri de Lubac's footnote n. 16, pp. 114-16]; "Note sur les modes de l'action divine dans l'univers," *CJC*, pp. 37-38 [Eng. trans. pp. 27-28].

57. "Le Coeur du problème," *AH*, pp. 343-49 [Eng. trans. pp. 263-69].

58. "Sur la Valeur religieuse de la recherche," *SC*, p. 261 [Eng. trans. pp. 202-03]; "Christologie et évolution," *CJC*, p. 111 [Eng. trans. p. 93]; "L'Étoffe de l'univers," *AÉ*, p. 404 [Eng. trans. p. 381].

59. "Le Christianisme dans le monde," SC, pp. 144 [Eng. trans. p. 111].

60. "Réflexions sur le progrès," *AH*, p. 105 [Eng. trans. p. 80].

CONCLUDING REMARKS

Man has always experienced a need to know himself and to find meaning for himself and his activities in his entire cosmic context. There is little doubt that the relatively modern realization that all of reality is processive or evolutionary has had numerous consequences with regard to man's self-understanding. The rather sudden recognition of the vast, unfathomable extent of both space and time has placed man in what appears to be a new, impersonal and very frightening context.

For the past few centuries modern man regarded himself rather complacently as the relatively static and absolute center of the universe, that toward whom and for whom everything else in the universe exists and is developing. He saw himself situated more vis-à-vis nature than as an integral part of it. He was aware that he and his actions were in time, but time appeared to be accidental to personhood itself. Man's real dignity as a person was not seen as being inextricably bound up with time and space. In this context he felt relatively self-sufficient, made secure by his observable successes, by rates of change which he felt he could control and by definable or at least imaginable boundaries of space and time. He was not forced to face the long-term consequences of many of his attitudes and actions nor to observe the limited scope of his activity in the light of the whole cosmic process.

The realization that the whole of reality is one interdependent process has forced man to recognize that he was preceded and prepared for by an immense work of material and biological development and is thus a relative newcomer on earth. This fact makes it more difficult for him to regard himself as the center of this process and to absolutize himself. Confronted with the immensity of time and space and made more aware of his own contingency, individual man (whose life can be snuffed out by a falling icicle) and humanity as a whole (which can be totally destroyed by nuclear weapons) must re-appraise both their limitations and their dignity as persons.

Situating individual and even collective actions within the immense context of time and space has been a major factor in impersonalizing human actions and making it increasingly difficult for men to see how they can make the cosmic process for which they are responsible a personal and personalizing one. Even man's most consequential acts can appear so small and so inconsequential that they seem to lose their meaning. Both the immensity of time conceived of in terms of minutes, hours, years and millions of years, and the speed at which time moves, impersonalize human actions and therefore reduce man's capacity to commit himself wholeheartedly to those acts which foster personal life and community. Working for long-term, inclusive aims and goals appears uninviting. Thus man must find a new way to understand time. In a universe that is evolutionary or processive *time must be personalized*. A new way of understanding the intimate connection between time and human personality must be found. The concluding remarks to our cosmic vision will shed light on how this can be done, not only because this endeavour will add something new to our vision, but also because it will knit together many of the themes already developed.

In a processive world view for pragmatic christians it is not adequate to look at time and the present moment simply in terms of fleeting minutes. The present moment means more to a person than merely time; it is filled with the density of personal encounters, the presence of persons to each other. *The present means presence,* the presence of God to men and of men to each other. The present moment is the presence of me to you and you to me, a spiritual presence bodied forth in and through the material and corporeal, a presence which is grounded in the infinite presence of God. Thus it is something to which man can commit himself wholeheartedly.

Certainly the present moment regarded in terms of personal presence is fleeting; it gives way to successive moments and to changes in the degree and manner in which persons are mutually present to each other. Nevertheless, it is never really lost because personal presence is a dialogue through which persons build the *future*. Mere physical juxtaposition of persons is not personal presence. In order to be present to each other men must be open to and aware of each other as persons. They must accept each other's differences in personality, background and present situation, and be willing to enter into at least a minimal form of dialogue with each other.

Even very superficial exchanges between persons promote personhood because they are an initial opening or giving of oneself to the other. As such they are an invitation to a response which leaves the door open for a further reply which can be more personal and will therefore increase the degree 'of personal presence among the parties involved. Wholehearted commitment to the present moment conceived as a personal dialogue is made easier and more meaningful because man can commit himself to persons far more completely and consistently than to ideas, systems or institutions.

When time is conceived in terms of personal presence one can resolve the perennial philosophical and theological conflicts concerning whether man should concentrate his full attention on the present moment or on the future (the end), on the existential or the eschatological. Responsibility, as we have seen, is using one's whole ability to respond; and one responds to the present situation, to the presence of persons and their needs here and now. The christian must commit himself completely to the present moment rather than to the future. That is, he must commit himself to the presence of his fellow men in such a way that he deliberately respects them as persons and sets out to interact with them in a manner which will build out of that interaction a future in which all parties can develop themselves and live in peace and harmony. In this way man is committing himself to the present and future at one and the same time. He takes responsibility for the future at the same time as he acts responsibly in the present. And in acting responsibily to his neighbour man is accepting responsibility before God; what we do for our brothers we do for Christ.

Irresponsibility is not merely wasting the present moment. Man acts irresponsibly when he does not make himself present to others in such a way as to invite a response from them and when he does not open himself to receive their response. Only when persons are present and open to each other can they work together to transform present environing conditions into future or consequent conditions which are desirable and satisfying for all. To be responsible an action must be made in the light of its consequences for building a personal future for all, a future to which all men can commit themselves completely, and therefore, one for which they are motivated to work. If men are going to commit themselves to the arduous task of building a satisfactory present and a desirable future they cannot treat each other impersonally and their actions must have personal significance. Time itself, therefore, must be personal and personalizing.

When time is regarded in terms of personal presence, the *past* also assumes its full significance for man. In such a context it is easy to see that the past is never entirely lost to mankind because past experiences become a part of man. Man *is* his past history. Man's personal relationships and interactions with God and his fellow men not only constitute his past, they constitute him. They make him precisely what he is today. Every man brings his past to his present relationships in a very real and dynamic way, and out of that present he must build his future with other men. Men can never deny or ignore their past, but must acknowledge it and build on it. It is just as foolish to attempt to reject the past as it is to attempt to return to it.

This same approach to time as personal presence sheds new light on and gives added relevance to the concept of *eternity*. In doing so it is extremely beneficial because few concepts, integral to christian thought, cause as much confusion in the minds of christians today as do eternity and eternal life. When time is regarded exclusively in terms of a succession of minutes, hours, years, etc., the concept of eternity is conceived as endless time regardless of theologians' most ardent efforts to conceptualize it as entirely outside of and not measurable by time. Eternity is something quite different from an endless succession of fragmented or fleeting moments of finite personal encounters. It cannot be measured in terms of time at all because it is an experience of a *total* encounter with the infinite person of God as He is in Himself.

God is certainly present to man now, but our experience of His presence is through the created participation He gives us in His life, a presence that is limited and sequential in spite of the fact that it is both open to and to be consummated in His infinite, direct, personal presence. God's presence to man now is mediated to us through time. The experience of being in the direct presence of infinite personhood, however, will be neither temporal, sequential nor fragmented. It will be a direct, total encounter with God in His infinite Person; nothing will be lacking or left to be experienced at a latter moment. Therefore, it cannot be a mediated encounter nor fragmented into successive moments so that it must be outside of time.

Eternal life is an experience of total self-awareness, but not a self-awareness apart from God and other men. In knowing and loving God to the fullness of his capacity, each person will achieve a complete awareness of himself and at the same time he will know other persons as they are in themselves. But once again, this total communion or personal presence of men to one another will be possible because they will be united to each other in and through their communion with God.

When time is regarded in terms of personal presence the *complementary relationship between time and eternity* becomes more evident. Eternity in the presence of God is not an *unrelated* prize promised on the condition that one performs certain acts on earth. God's promise of an eternal resurrected life in communion with Him cannot be compared to the promise of a parent who tells her child he can have a reward tomorrow if he completes the task for which he is responsible today. In that case there is no *inherent connection* between the reward and the *process* of completing the work. The meaning of heaven or eternal life is drastically reduced if it is seen primarily in terms of a reward. Eternal life is the *culmination* of the whole process of living on earth, of everything we are and do when all of these are seen in terms of our mutual, personal presence to God and to our fellow men. In fact, eternal life is the *necessary culmination* of the *process* of life if what we are and what we do are to have any *ultimate* and *comprehensive* meaning and value here and now.

Any final culmination of life which would be a mere stoppage or cessation of men's mutual relationships and presence to one another would reflect back on the meaning and value of these relationships now. Human action is not limited to the immediate moment of time in which it occurs; it is transcendent. This fact is most evident when our actions and time itself are seen in their most personal aspect, that of personal presence. To affirm that one's personal relationships and acts are so limited that they can be totally terminated by death is to reduce their inherent quality of transcendence and drastically limit their meaning and value. As we saw earlier, man has both conceived of and experienced the need to enter into personal relationships and to perform works which can come to a final consummation and not be prematurely frustrated by ending in mere stoppages. The value of the concept of eternal life, therefore, is not to be found in recognizing it as a reward. It is psychologically beneficial to men now because it enables all their personal encounters to remain open-ended, capable of achieving a total consummation.

Perhaps the most effective way to recapitulate what I have said about the whole problem of commitment through regarding time and eternity in terms of personal presence is to examine the problem in terms of the means-ends relationship within any process. As we have seen, the means within a process find their deepest meaning not in themselves but in the end of the process. This is a fact of reality which cannot be denied, but its full truth is appreciated only when we realize that there is no radical separation between the means and end. At each step within the process the end is to some extent concretely realized in the means, and when the process is culminated, the means remain on in the end. The end, therefore, is the culmination of the process, and is not in any way separate from the whole.

What we have been saying about time and life regarded in terms of personal presence is further clarified in terms of this philosophical analysis of means-ends. The *ultimate* meaning of the process of living, and all the personal relationships and activities it involves, is to be found in the end of the process, that is, in the total personal communication between God and men in eternity. The christian approach to reality is certainly eschatological. This is not to say, however, that the christian is left uncommitted to the present moment and reduced to yearning for eternity. In fact, the opposite is true.

The final end of the process of living, which is achieved in eternity, is already being partially realized now a) through men's efforts in time to foster God's presence in themselves, b) through their commitment to the presence and needs of their neighbours, and c) through their efforts to develop the whole universe. In fact, that future end can only be achieved by wholehearted commitment to the present out of which it must be built. In brief, personal relationships which develop in time find their ultimate fulfillment in eternity, and the easiest way to realize this concretely and to increase one's commitment to fostering these relationships is by regarding both time and eternity in terms of the mutual personal presence of God and men to each other.

Although we speak and write a great deal today about personhood and personal relations, impersonalism is fostered by our failure to re-adjust our priorities so that the love energy that cultivates authentic evolution can radiate among us effectively. We live without experiencing the presence of God among us to the extent that many christians today proclaim His death. God is not dead; something in man is dead or lacking so that he cannot plumb the depths of reality and experience God's presence in himself and in his relations with his fellow man. The same impersonality in our living that makes it increasingly difficult for us to live consistently in the presence of each other makes it even more difficult for us to experience God's hidden presence in our midst. We must root out the obstacles to authentic, personal living, and create positive conditions which promote it. As we do so the love energy that unites, personalizes and promotes authentic evolution will begin to radiate freely, and we shall "have life, and have it to the full."

KEY TO ABBREVIATIONS OF
TEILHARD'S WORKS

AE

L'Activation de l'Énergie, Paris: Éditions du Seuil, 1963
[Activation of Energy, trans. by René Hague, New York:
Harcourt Brace Jovanovich, Inc., 1971].

AppH

L'Apparition de l'homme, Paris: Éditions du Seuil, 1956
[The Appearance of Man, trans. by J. M. Cohen, New
York: Harper and Row, 1965].

AH

L'Avenir de l'homme, Paris: Éditions du Seuil, 1959 [The
Future of Man, trans. by Norman Denny, New York:
Harper and Row, 1964].

CJC

Comment je crois, Paris: Éditions du Seuil, 1969 [Chris-
tianity and Evolution, trans. by René Hague, New York:
Harcourt Brace Jovanovich, Inc., 1971].

*Correspon-
dence*

Pierre Teilhard de Chardin Maurice Blondel Correspondence, Notes and commentary by Henri de Lubac, trans.
by William Whitman, New York: Herder and Herder,
1967.

CT

"Construire la terre," Construire la terre, Cahier I, extraits d'oeuvres inédits, Paris: Éditions du Seuil, 1958
["Building the Earth," Construire la Terre, Cahier I, trans.
by Nöel Lindsay, Paris: Éditions du Seuil, 1958, pp.
47-78].

ÉTG

Écrits du temps de la guerre, Paris: Bernard Grasset,
1965 [Writings in Time of War, trans. by René Hague,
New York: Harper and Row, 1968].

ÉH

L'Énergie humaine, Paris: Éditions du Seuil, 1962 [Human
Energy, trans. by J. M. Cohen, London: William Collins
Sons and Co., 1969].

GP

Genèse d'une pensée, lettres 1914-1919, Paris: Bernard
Grasset, 1961 [The Making of a Mind: Letters from a
Soldier-Priest 1914-1919, trans. by René Hague, New York:
Harper and Row, 1965].

HU

Hymne de l'univers, Paris: Éditions du Seuil, 1961 [Hymn
of the Universe, trans. by Simon Bartholomew, New York:
Harper and Row, 1965].

LV   *Lettres de voyage (1923-1939),* Paris: Bernard Grasset, 1956 [*Letters from a Traveller,* trans. by René Hague, Violet Hammersley, Barbara Wall and Nöel Lindsay, New York: Harper and Row, (Harper Torchbooks), 1968].

MD   *Le Milieu divin: Essai de vie interieure,* Paris: Éditions du Seuil, 1957 [*Le Milieu Divin: An Essay on the Interior Life,* trans. by Alick Dru, Nöel Lindsay and D. M. MacKinnon, London: William Collins Sons and Co., (Fontana Books), 1964].

NLV   *Nouvelles lettres de voyage (1939-1955),* Paris: Bernard Grasset, 1957 [*Letters from a Traveller,* trans. by René Hague, Violet Hammersley, Barbara Wall and Nöel Lindsay, New York: Harper and Row, (Harper Torchbooks), 1968].

PA   *La Parole attendue,* Cahier IV, Inédits, témoignages et travaux de l'association, Paris: Éditions du Seuil, 1963.

PH   *Le Phénomène humain,* Paris: Éditions du Seuil, 1955 [*The Phenomenon of Man,* trans. by Bernard Wall, New York: Harper and Row, (2nd ed. Harper Torchbooks, 1965].

PHN   *La Place de l'homme dans la nature,* Paris: Éditions du Seuil, 1956 [*Man's Place in Nature: The Human Zoological Group,* trans. by René Hague, New York: Harper and Row, 1966].

RB   *Réflexions sur le bonheur,* Cahier II, Inédits et témoignages, Paris: Éditions du Seuil, 1960.

SC   *Science et Christ,* Paris: Éditions du Seuil, 1965 [*Science and Christ,* trans. by René Hague, New York: Harper and Row, 1968].

VP   *La Vision du passé,* Paris: Éditions du Seuil, 1957 [*The Vision of the Past,* trans. by J. M. Cohen, New York: Harper and Row, 1966].